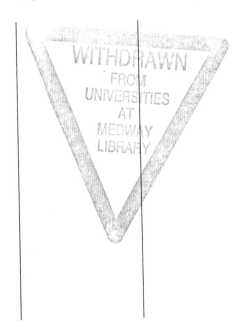

Moving Histories of Class and Community

Identity Studies in the Social Sciences
Series Standing Order ISBN 978–0–230–20500–0 Hardback
978–0–230–20501–7 Paperback
(*outside North America only*)

You can receive future titles in this series as they are published by placing a standing order. Please contact your bookseller or, in case of difficulty, write to us at the address below with your name and address, the title of the series and the ISBN quoted above.

Customer Services Department, Macmillan Distribution Ltd, Houndmills, Basingstoke, Hampshire RG21 6XS, England

Moving Histories of Class and Community

Identity, Place and Belonging in Contemporary England

Ben Rogaly
University of Sussex, UK

and

Becky Taylor
Birkbeck College, University of London, UK

First published 2009 by
PALGRAVE MACMILLAN

Palgrave Macmillan in the UK is an imprint of Macmillan Publishers Limited, registered in England, company number 785998, of Houndmills, Basingstoke, Hampshire RG21 6XS.

Palgrave Macmillan in the US is a division of St Martin's Press LLC, 175 Fifth Avenue, New York, NY 10010.

Palgrave Macmillan is the global academic imprint of the above companies and has companies and representatives throughout the world.

Palgrave® and Macmillan® are registered trademarks in the United States, the United Kingdom, Europe and other countries.

ISBN-13: 978–0–230–21993–9 hardback
ISBN-10: 0–230–21993–4 hardback

This book is printed on paper suitable for recycling and made from fully managed and sustained forest sources. Logging, pulping and manufacturing processes are expected to conform to the environmental regulations of the country of origin.

A catalogue record for this book is available from the British Library.

A catalog record for this book is available from the Library of Congress.

Printed and bound in Great Britain by
CPI Antony Rowe, Chippenham and Eastbourne

For Rosa Gill-Taylor
and
Susan and Joe Rogaly

Contents

Series Editors' Preface

The concept of identity has had a long and chequered history in the social sciences – many chafe at its ambiguity and frustrating complexity – yet it remains the pivotal site for exploring the relations between social life and subjectivity. Who we are is always complicated – a matter of social classifications, shifting social categorizations and group memberships, and a matter, too, of the ways in which social and cultural materials are organized as psychology and taken on as personal projects. Identity draws attention to 'names' and 'looks'. It is lived out in grand narratives and performances which construct sometimes passionately invested 'imagined' routes and destinies as well as in the more mundane arenas of everyday interaction, inter-subjective relations and in social institutions. Identity guides and predicts social action. It highlights positions and intelligibility defining what is possible and liveable and what is unthinkable and excessively troubled.

We suggest, in short, that identity is one of the most interesting points at which the trajectories of post-colonial societies, globalization and assumptions about 'liquid modernity' come into focus along with new formations of social class, gender relations and issues of inequality, rights and social justice. Identity is at the heart of some of the most intractable and troubling contemporary social problems – community conflict, racism, discrimination, xenophobia and marginalization.

It is the key laboratory, too, for any social psychologist focused on the interface of personal lives and social lives.

Identity Studies in the Social Sciences brings together psychologists, sociologists, anthropologists, geographers, social policy researchers, education researchers and political scientists to address this territory. The interdisciplinary reach of the series is matched by the degree of theoretical diversity. The books reflect on and take inspiration from the many 'theory wars' in the social sciences which have used identity as their hinge and also develop new theory and critique for current times, including new ontologies and new politics to do justice to contemporary amalgams of practices and subjectivities. The series includes empirical work, scholarly debate and research reviews on the core social categories and the intersections of these including 'race', ethnicity, social class, gender, generation, disability, nationality and sexuality along with less easily nameable social and institutional categorizations and affiliations. *Identity Studies in the Social Sciences* highlights the ways in which identities are formed, managed and mobilized in contexts and spaces such as schools, workplaces, clinics, homes, communities and streets. We welcome you to this rich collection of accounts from the various front lines of identity studies.

Margaret Wetherell,
Valerie Hey and
Stephen Reicher

Acknowledgements

This project has been entwined in both of our lives for a number of years, with the boundary between 'home' and 'work' no longer clear. Consequently, we are indebted to many people. Above all, we would like to thank everyone whose stories we have tried in some small part to convey in the following pages. We are particularly grateful to the members of the local history group and the staff of NELM New Deal for Communities Trust in Norwich, who opened many doors for us, and made so much of this project possible.

Special thanks also to Jo Chitty and Kiah Greenwood for opening your home and for your generous hospitality; to the three transcribers, Tamsin Browning, Joe Button and Tania Edwards; to Chris Clunn for his photographs; and to Lakshmi Holmström, Ed Simpson, Margie Wetherell and Sharon Wilkinson for reading and commenting on the draft manuscript. There are many others we sought and received help from in different ways, including Caroline Bardell, Tony Barnett, Bonnie Carpenter, Frances Channell, Val Clements, Tony Cooper, Jennifer Crook, Evelyn Dodds, Anne-Meike Fechter, Neil Forshaw, Paul Grant, Fred Hewitt, Emma Hiscock, Ruth Pearson, Nitya Rao, Janet Seeley, Dorothy Sheridan, Pat Thane, Al Thomson, Katie Walsh, Ann Whitehead, Martin Wingfield and Lucy Williams.

The research for this book was funded by a grant from the Economic and Social Research Council, reference RES-148-25-0047, as part of its Identities and Social Action programme. We would like to thank Margie Wetherell, Kerry Carter and all our fellow grant-holders on the programme, who have provided us with support, intellectual insights and perspectives we otherwise would have lacked.

Becky
I would like to thank Mell and Bec for support, friendship and child care; and Claire, for all those lifts. I would also like to thank Ben, whose patience and understanding over the last few years has done so much to smooth the rollercoaster that has so often been my life, and in the process has turned from a colleague to a friend. And thanks to Paul, Jack and Rosa, as ever, for everything else.

Ben

I am grateful to Richard Black, Anastasia Christou and Ceri Oeppen for taking on some of my duties while I worked on this book and to other Sussex Geography colleagues for being so supportive, especially Alan Lester, Simon Rycroft, Russell King and Brian Short. Becky has been the best collaborator and co-author I could have wished for. I will miss our almost-daily conversations about the research and life in general. I would like to thank both Becky and her partner Paul Gill.

No words can adequately express my thanks to Kirat Randhawa for literally making my part in this book happen, by doing more than her share of the housework and childcare in spite of a busy and stressful job, as well as always being there to offer moral support, ideas and incisive comments on draft sections. And as for Simran and Khem who have been growing up with it: thank you for your loving curiosity, and for willing it on, even though it sometimes ate up our time together.

List of Figures, Maps and Photographs

Figures

Maps

Photographs

Abbreviations

EDP	*Eastern Daily Press*
EEN	*Eastern Evening News*
MOH	Medical Office of Health
NDC	New Deal for Communities
NELM	NELM (North Earlham, Larkman and Marlpit) Development Trust
NHC	Norwich Housing Committee
NRO	Norfolk Record Office
UEA	University of East Anglia

1
Introduction: Moving Histories

Prelude

> I'm sorry in a way because I know that you're quite keen to
> break down the stereotypes...but I do feel, and again this
> is perhaps another source of my shame, that our family ful-
> filled absolutely every stereotype you can think of. So...my
> Mum had a drunken Irish Catholic father who everyone called
> Paddy...[her] mother died so the children were taken. My
> youngest aunt who was only a couple of years older than me
> was literally handed over the fence at the age of three to a
> neighbour who then brought her [up]...It was a mess...but
> I was obviously reasonably oblivious, or it was just ordi-
> nary to me then. All the family shipped around, stayed with
> various people on the estates...my granddad [sighs] went
> from...strength to strength in his drunkenness...living with
> various members of the family including us for a lot of years...I
> just remember his sitting on the corner of the bed with his false
> teeth out and nothing on his top half and he had this kind of
> breasts and chickeny skin, hacking his guts up and dipping his
> toast in his whisky...
>
> (Lorna Haley[1])

In her recollection of childhood in 1960s' and 1970s' England, Lorna
spoke of the shame she had felt because of where she came from. The
Larkman social housing estate in Norwich, where she grew up, and
the adjacent estates of Marlpit and North Earlham, which were often

1

associated with it, had a reputation in the rest of the city. Here is Lorna again:

> if someone says the Larkman, 'Oh, she lives over the Larkman, she comes from the Larkman', that engenders a very particular response from people in Norwich...even people who come from what I would consider other big council estates.

From at least the 1950s, the name of the Larkman estate was associated not only with the kind of family breakdown described by Lorna, but also with violence and criminality. As Harry Collins, another resident put it,

> the Larkman was classed as a very violent estate in the fifties...if anyone used to say 'oh are you going to the Larkman?', they'd [follow up by saying] 'Cor. What? You going up there? It's too rough'.

For Harry, this reputation carried forward into the present, based not on current reality but on past events:

> they only go on reputation. Years ago when that was a rough area, I mean in the teddy boy days there was always fighting up there, up the Larkman and things like that...when I was a young lad, I used to use the Larkman pub from the age of fourteen, until...they pulled it down. I had many a punch up in there when I was a youngster... The old Larkman pub was a lovely little haunt where all the crooks used to go in there and clerk this and buy...that.[2]

The descriptions of the estates given by both Lorna and Harry superficially reinforce what some commentators have referred to as a 'common sense' depiction of poverty and council estates in late twentieth-century Britain (see for example Damer, 1989; Jones and Novak, 1999). Such an outlook seems unproblematically to elide poverty, use of the welfare system, criminality, 'deviant' behaviour and family structures. Crucially, it sees both the causes and the outcomes of such patterns as being the responsibility of the individual or the area concerned. This 'common sense' depiction of the causes and results of poverty might best be summed up in former Prime Minister John Major's injunction that Britain should learn to 'condemn a little more and to understand a little less' about the poorest in society.

As we write, towards the end of the first decade of the twenty-first century, we find that mainstream media, with TV series such as Little Britain, seem to have taken Major's words to heart, with stereotypes of 'white trash' and 'chavs'[3] used as short-hand simultaneously to describe and write off vast sections of Britain's population – often white, often living on council estates and nearly always poor. Such phrases deploy universalizing stereotypes that link style of dress and speech with educational aspirations, involvement with welfare and social control agencies, and patterns of family behaviour. They also focus their spotlight solely on 'individuals', ridiculing or blaming them for their situation, and in so doing leave the context surrounding those individuals firmly out of the picture.

In this book, in contrast, we aim to turn this phenomenon on its head. Using the case study of a specific area and through exploring the lives of individuals within it, we argue instead for the importance of understanding how individual lives are closely entwined with changes at the local, national and international scales. The book is set in a rapidly changing England, covering a period from the 1930s' depression to Blair's New Labour regime in the twenty-first century. What became clear over the course of our research was, rather than being a bounded and isolated outpost of deprivation on the edge of a provincial city, the Norwich estates were intimately tied to the deep structural changes of the twentieth century. There was not a life revealed to us that had not been affected by the expansions and contractions of the state, by the shifts from the mid-1970s towards a neo-liberal deregulation of the labour market and consequent re-regulation of workplace relations, nor by profound changes in experiences of class, gender relations and cultural expectations.

Thus the context throughout is one of structural inequalities in English society – inequalities that shift over time, and have particular spatial characteristics. The area we study – the Larkman, North Earlham and Marlpit estates in Norwich – is neither metropolitan, nor rural. Such places have become associated with poverty and deprivation, with the kind of 'community' responses to individual and more collective problems of the kind outlined by Lorna Haley; and, in provincial cities like Norwich, with whiteness, stasis and isolation.

We set out, as Lorna pointed out, to question such stereotypes, which were in part about these specific estates, but were also more generally about class, as working class lives and social housing estates are often closely associated in public discourses on English society (Hanley, 2007). Our work is distinctive because, unlike many other studies, we insist that it is not possible to study the experience and identifications of any particular class in isolation from other classes. Moreover, discussions of working class lives in Britain are too often elided with discussions of whiteness, so that working class black and minority ethnic people in Britain are defined by their ethnic heritage alone. Indeed, white British-ness is often seen as being exclusively working class,[4] and, contrary to a long history of migration both within the UK and internationally, white working class people in Britain are portrayed as immobile, 'impacted on' by the immigration of foreign nationals.

From the outset we were interested in the ways in which in Jenkins' formulation (1996), people were categorized by others, and in how this influenced their own social identifications, whether individual or collective. Structural inequalities, produced and perpetuated in part through categorization, limited people's room for manoeuvre. But from the start of this work we were also interested in what people were able to do within changing structural contexts, within, for example, the kinds of jobs or housing or schooling that were available to them as estate residents, including through the instrumental use of social identity. To find out about this and other forms of individual agency, we wanted to record how people remembered their experiences in their own words.

It is precisely because structural inequalities have continued stubbornly and even worsened in the UK (and elsewhere) since the 1970s, that understanding the role of identification in people's responses is so pertinent. Class and community have been written about by many authors but this book breaks new ground through its simultaneous use of dynamic historical analysis and a spatial approach to identity, which brings out the importance of migration and transnationalism in relation to white working class people often constructed as entrenched and immobile, indeed, some would argue, 'fixed in place' by middle class social scientists (Skeggs, 2004). Life histories reveal the migratory patterns of individuals over the course of their lives and, crucially, when taken together, can show shifting patterns across generations.

Throughout the book we argue for the importance of grounding this understanding of individuals' lives within a wider material and structural context. From the 1940s to the 1960s, residents leaving school, male and female, could expect to be able to get work, most commonly a factory job in Norwich's boot and shoe, food processing, printing or engineering industries. Since the 1970s when these industries largely relocated and become more capital intensive, jobs for people with few formal qualifications became harder to get and more temporary. While the city's economy as a whole may have made a relatively successful transition away from manufacturing towards the service sector, pockets of the city where the population had relied heavily on the factories for employment – including the North Earlham, Larkman and Marlpit estates – experienced high and sustained levels of unemployment from the early 1980s.

Such a deep structural shift in the economy of the city was far more hidden than in towns of the industrial north, the Midlands or Wales, as the closures took place over three decades (the 1970s to the 1990s) and the economy was more diversified. As with the poorest households elsewhere in the country and through history (King and Tomkins, 2003), the residents of the Larkman, North Earlham and Marlpit estates continued disproportionately to engage in the casual agricultural and informal sectors of the economy (Taylor and Rogaly, 2007). They have also been at the frontline of changes in the welfare system, from an increased reliance on means-tested benefits, to the residualization of council house tenancies and the introduction of 'workfare' measures.

More generally in the area, the move towards a service economy was exemplified through the building of the University of East Anglia (UEA) in the 1960s, on parkland a stone's throw from the estates. Along with other large service employers in the city such as Norwich Union, the university acted as a magnet for white collar professional workers, the majority of whom were drawn from outside the region. People locally, including those from the estates, mostly found that any links to the institution have been as employees, with men having worked on the construction of the campus, or in security roles, and women working typically as cleaners. Our data revealed time and again how the schools local to the estates compounded rather than confounded class expectations, with children being prepared for 'working class jobs' and life in, rather than outside, the council estates. Working class lack of access to higher education and what can feel like the exclusive middle class culture of university students remain ongoing problems in Britain, and having UEA on the doorstep heightened the sense that this was 'not for the likes of us'.

However, understanding, for example, the worlds of cleaners in universities and in private homes, began to complicate categories such as 'working class' and 'middle class', because they involved class encounters. The stories we were told revealed diversity, ambivalence, contingency and sometimes silence in how people spoke of their own class identities, but above all they showed how much identification with or belonging to one class is often based on self-distancing from another. The relational understanding of class that emerges resonates with current approaches to the sociology of class (for example Devine and Savage, 2005; Strangleman, 2008). Indeed the book can be seen as taking a relational approach not only to class identities but also to identities based around gender and 'race', and the intersections between them (Valentine, 2007; McDowell, 2008).

Central to our analysis has been the concept of 'moving histories'. Our first intended meaning of this is to shift the way in which the history of a place is told by combining a social historian's skills with those of a contemporary geographer specializing in migration studies. While oral history is an important means of 'taking back' history to people and an area, it is equally a means by which that history can be 'taken out' into wider society, informing and 'moving' the writing of broader history (Thompson, 2000). McCall (2005) suggests starting with an individual, group, event or context, and working outwards in order to unravel how categories are lived and experienced. In taking the case study area of three estates, our intention then is to retell the history, not only of this area, but of the categorization of 'deprived' working class areas and people more generally.

In aiming to 'unfix' the telling and representation of a place we rejected the idea of the area and its inhabitants as bounded. Instead we started from the presumption that lines and divisions – social as well as spatial – are blurred, shifting and profoundly relational. Consequently we sought out and explored connections between places and between classes, and their changes over time. Similarly, we sought to write ourselves into our research, accepting that any boundary between the researcher and informant is equally 'highly dynamic and unstable' (Valentine, 2002: 119). As a result, and unusually for historical and geographical work, we vary the book's voice between academic analysis and a more informal, personal recounting of our own self-identifications as well as, in two interludes, our ongoing relations with certain participants.

Our focus on working across boundaries feeds into the second sense in which we use the idea of 'moving histories', referring to the importance of migration in the lives of people who did not necessarily consider themselves as migrants. Central to understanding the importance of migration in individual and collective histories is our rejection of the idea that only permanent migration 'counts' as migration. We also challenge the popular association between immigration and visible minorities, and (like Feldman, 2007) drop the arbitrary academic boundaries between the analysis of migration within national borders, on the one hand, and international migration, on the other. Moreover, we argue it is crucial to render more visible white British *emigration*, and the forms of transnationalism associated with it. After all, the period of which we write saw travel abroad for individuals in the armed forces in the Second World War and afterwards as formal British imperialism across parts of Asia and Africa came to a close, and a continuation of other forms of spatial mobility both within and beyond UK borders. Thus stories of past lives in the estates grounded in the 'local' were often related alongside ones revealing participants' own, or their close relatives', periods spent as migrants. Consequently our contention is that spatial mobility is an important aspect of self-identification: for example, discourses used by certain estate residents about 'race' and contemporary immigration in Britain demand to be understood in the light of their own temporary emigration in the colonial military (Rogaly and Taylor, forthcoming).

Importantly, non-migration too, as much as migration, is connected to identification. Alongside the stories of movement, we also found ones of virtual immobility – individuals living in the house in which they were born, or perhaps a few houses or a street away from their childhood home, still surrounded by a network of extended family and friends. We see how in this phase of 'liquid modernity', fixed identities as well as geographical immobility are often taken as a sign of failure, an inability to move with the times (Bauman, 2004b). And yet, in some of our encounters and interviews, we were presented with the strength, comfort and enjoyment people could draw from being intimately tied to a place. One task then was to avoid the danger of rewriting the history of the area as one of unbridled movement in an effort to destabilize more established narratives of community and stability.[5] As we shall see, they are not mutually exclusive, particularly when we move away from privileging one form of migration over another: one person's move of a few streets from the Larkman to the largely middle class 'golden triangle' of Norwich,[6] or from one part of a street to another over the course of a lifetime, may be of as much personal significance as another's migration to Leicester, to the US or to Australia.

The final sense in which 'moving histories' is used in the book is in relation to emotions. Much of the material on changing identifications is based on in-depth interviews with 73 people, including 25 life histories. The stories people told and the conversations around them were sometimes painful, and often humorous, for the speaker, the listener or both. They were moving histories in the emotional sense. It is an emotional risk to try to reconstruct one's life to tell someone else, even if they are a stranger – it can be harder still if you know them well. We found this to be the case when we wrote about ourselves.

As we shall see, one participant became angry at the title of the research project 'Deprived White Community'? as, due to an error, it appeared without the inverted commas in a public exhibition she attended. Another, a refugee, became upset when telling the story of his clandestine journey to seek asylum in the UK. Again this was triggered by the way we were asking questions, which, in retrospect, we felt we should have avoided. One man was in tears as he spoke of his forced retirement through illness and what he saw as his failure to live up to a kind of masculinity that he would have been capable of in his youth, when he found himself unable to sort out a quarrel with disruptive and abusive neighbours using physical force. More than one woman spoke with quiet dignity while revealing the profound impact of domestic abuse they had suffered at the hands of their husbands. Class identifications were a source of jokes, occasional evasions and, for some, painful memories of moral sentiments associated with class (see Sayer, 2005). Still others spoke of the impact of material poverty and emotional neglect by parents on their lives.

In the following section we will situate the key concepts we use in relation to other recent national and international research. The subsequent section of the introduction sets out our methodological approach, including an attempt to locate our personal histories and roles in the research process. The final section guides the reader through the remaining chapters of the book.

Key concepts

As we have already implied, our emphasis on individuals – including ourselves – is not on them in isolation, but rather is part of an attempt to build an understanding of the relationship between self-identification, social categorization and experience. In turn, we view all of these as being informed by wider structural factors, particularly by shifts in the global and national economy, and the actions (and inactions) of the state. Taking a relational approach, and seeking to understand how individuals locate themselves in and are located by the world, we draw, necessarily selectively, on international academic literatures on identity, class, community, place and belonging. In this section we set out the conceptual terrain of the book, beginning with identity.

Identity, identification and categorization

Identity is 'a relationship not a thing' (Brah, 2007: 141). As Parekh puts it, '[i]dentity basically refers to how one identifies and defines oneself in relation to others' (2007: 132). This understanding of identity as relational (see also Jackson, 2005) means that identity is 'always in process, never an absolutely accomplished fact.... At any given moment, we are positioned across multiple processes of identification which shift and configure into a specific pattern in a designated set of circumstances' (Brah, 2007: 139, 144). It is because identity is not a thing in itself, but rather a slippery concept, that, following Jenkins (1996), we prefer to speak of 'identification'. Moreover, as Jenkins points out, social identifications are made, contested and continually reconstituted through 'categorization' by others, through conscious, even instrumental, choice and through unconscious group affiliations, including affective solidarities (ibid.; see also Brah, 1996; Shotter, 1984).

> We know who we are because, in the first place, others tell us. Categorization is basic even – or especially – during earliest socialization. The foundations of individual self-hood – the sense of 'who one is' that is implicated in an embodied perspective on the 'rest of the world' – are laid in the initial, and continuing, dialectic between the internal and the external.
>
> (Jenkins, 2000: 11)

Keeping this in mind, Jenkins draws on Willis' (1977) classic study of working class white boys in England, and Raban's on dust-bowl migration by American rural homesteaders in the 1930s, to reinforce his argument about the power of categorization by 'strategically-placed others'. We are not simply taught how to see ourselves in the world and empowered to make choices accordingly, but rather face a world in which 'widely shared categorizations such as rough/respectable, undeserving/deserving and unreliable/reliable' influence 'processes of identification... [and] have material *consequences*' (Jenkins, 2000: 12, emphasis in original).

Thus throughout our work we are centrally concerned with the interplay between categorization and self-identification. Crucially for this book, Jenkins draws attention to the inequality involved in this process, stressing that 'the *consequences* of authoritatively-applied identities for individual experience are... significant. In other words, whose definition of the situation *counts*?' (Jenkins, 2000: 9, emphasis in original). As Bauman (2004b) argues:

> Identification is also a powerful factor in stratification.... At one pole of the emergent global hierarchy are those who can compose and

decompose their identities more or less at will, drawing from the uncommonly large, planet-wide pool of offers. At the other pole are crowded those whose access to identity choice has been barred, people who are given no say in deciding their preferences and who in the end are burdened with identities enforced and imposed *by others*; identities which they themselves resent but are not allowed to shed and cannot manage to get rid of.

(Bauman, 2004b: 38, emphasis in original)

This analysis applies to group as well as individual identifications and their interaction. Moreover, in terms of group identifications, Jenkins makes a related distinction between a collective category being identified by others, which he calls social categorization, and a process of group identification which is recognized by the group concerned: 'Problematizing the group–category distinction – put crudely, self-determination versus domination – emphasizes the centrality of power to processes of identification' (Jenkins, 2000: 10). Thus the terms 'working class' or 'from the Larkman' tell us at least as much about the people or institution doing the labelling as about the people being so labelled. Understanding such processes is important because social categorization can be used to justify unequal allocations of state resources. Conversely, group identifications may embody the agency involved in resistance to such procedures. For example, the classed nature of slum clearance and council rehousing schemes is revealed not only when we consider who was planning the moving and who was being moved, but, as James Scott observed, the engrained assumptions driving the phenomenon:

What is striking . . . is that such subjects – like the 'unmarked citizens' of liberal theory – have, for the purpose of the planning exercise, no gender, no tastes, no history, no values, no opinions or original ideas, no traditions, and no distinctive personalities to contribute to the enterprise. They have none of the particular, situated, and contextual attributes that one would expect of any population and that we, as a matter of course, always attribute to elites.

(Scott, 1998: 346)

And as we discuss below, governmental and popular debates over the importance of community and the decline of respect carry with them a strongly classed angle and have significant policy implications.

Jenkins' highlighting of categorization and how it works dialectically as part of the identification process provides an important counter to recent tendencies in the social sciences to emphasize self-identification processes on their own (Goodson, 2006). However, just as analysis of self-identification is incomplete if done in isolation from categorization, so putting too much weight on categorization can lead to the further reproduction of power-laden categories and stereotypes.

Class, gender and 'race'

Such problems have been all too evident in local-level studies of working class 'communities' in Britain, as Steedman's (1986) incisive use of her and her mother's biographies to critique stereotypical depictions of working class experiences illuminates. Steedman insists that by highlighting the idea of a collective identity held in common among working class people in particular places, individual stories, fantasies and desires are missed. The people in the story lose their subjectivities. In Steedman's example, moreover, intra-household relations and identifications based around gender are as important as, and interact with, those based around class. Bev Skeggs' work also powerfully reveals the intersection of gender and class in discourses of working class women (Skeggs, 1997).

Yet the concept of class remains vital to the critique of the production and reproduction of inequalities. Empirical evidence and people's experiences internationally show that class structures continue to be central in terms of positioning within social and economic space (Bourdieu, 1990), and the concomitant differences between people in terms of access to material, cultural and social resources (Sayer, 2005; Savage, 2000; Mitchell, 2008). The pluralist approach we use here builds on other recent work that emphasizes both class inequalities and, simultaneously, the contingency, relationality and ambivalence of class identifications (see for example Crompton and Scott, 2005; Devine and Savage, 2005; Kirk, 2007). Expressions and experiences of class change for individuals both over the course of their lives and within and between particular encounters.

Rather than seeing fluidity as somehow speaking against the existence or relevance of class, we might in fact see it as an intrinsic part of classed experiences:

> both social and spatial mobility are considered to be crucial dimensions in the process of class formation, because they underpin the cohesiveness and permeability of class groups.
>
> (Miles, 2003: 338)

So while, for some individuals, identification with a particular class may be an unproblematic, even a comfortable and affirming, experience, equally for others it may be shifting, contradictory and even painful and bound up with personal social and/or spatial mobility.

As Lawler (1999: 3) has observed, 'class is embedded in peoples' history'. Consequently, we explore changes in the way that class has been conceptualized in the context of historical changes in classed experiences and in intersections between class and gender from the 1930s to the present. Cairns (2008) has pointed to the complicating role of the Second World War in people's biographies, while Brooke (2001) has argued how the 1950s saw the establishment of more complicated and less certain gender identities both at the workplace and the home. An increase in leisure time and real incomes for the majority combined with falling family sizes to reposition roles within the family, with

> the working wife and mother [becoming] a cipher of the new working classes, a complex symbol tying together domesticity and affluence, worlds of work, home and leisure.
>
> (Brooke, 2001: 781; see also Roberts, 1995; Spencer, 2005)

Massive economic change from the 1970s in Britain and elsewhere has led to accounts of the changing nature of work that stressed the accelerated globalization of markets, and increase in service industries and employment in technology and knowledge-based sectors; the feminization of the labour market; growth of self-employment; alterations in the organization of work time; and the rise of multiple job holders and 'hyphenated workers' on part-time or temporary contracts (see for example Bauman, 1998; Beck, 2000; Sennett, 1998). Yet, there has also been continuity. Shift work has been a long-standing feature of factory work, for example, and working class women have long been involved in the labour market (Brooke, 2001; Fenton and Dermott, 2006).

Nevertheless, changes brought about through neo-liberalism have engendered new classed experiences. For Bauman, there has been a gradual shift from 'a society of producers' to 'a society of consumers' (1998: 1–2), while Portelli maintains:

> we need to identify the class differences beneath the veneer of assimilation ... the blurring of class boundaries has eroded the class identity of the workers but not the class power of the bourgeoisie. The promised access of the masses to the master's forms of consumption

has been traded for the master's access to the minds of the workers; but the promise has remained elusive, and its achievements only superficial (lifestyles rather than standard of living; appearance rather than property).

(Portelli, 1997: 234)

Thus, commentators such as Jones and Novak (1999) have tied new economic conditions to a more 'disciplinary' approach to welfare provision, which, in line with neo-liberal thinking, stresses individual responsibility and the need for personal action to guard against misfortune, leading, for example, to the introduction of 'workfare' measures.

Recent work focusing on the changes being felt by 'working class communities' since the 1980s has argued not that class-based identifications have declined in importance, but instead that they are being reworked in a new context. Weis's (2004) longitudinal study of a steel manufacturing town in north-eastern USA shows the continued strong presence of working class identifications in spite of the changing nature of work. Like Walkerdine et al. (2001), she stresses how class needs to be understood as something lived simultaneously at a much broader level and at a specific location 'at a particular time and in a particular place' (Weis, 2004: 2). Thus she emphasizes the importance of moving away from the analysis of some (Gorz, 1982; Willis, 1977; Aronowitz, 1992), who have tended to 'centre the working class as white and male' and wholly in terms of its relationship between white men and the industrial economy.[7]

This understanding of the importance of the spatial and temporal dimensions of class alongside a more nuanced, gendered approach (see also Skeggs, 2004) allows an analysis which, instead of seeing working class identifications as increasingly irrelevant, acknowledges a fluidity suggesting the possibility of multiple reformulations. While Savage (2000: 152) points to a process of 'working class decomposition', Weis argues that the working class of Freeway have remade themselves 'as a distinct class fraction, both discursively and behaviourally inside radical, globally based economic restructuring'. However, 'race' and class are crucially intertwined in this: Weis is not referring to all the working class residents of Freeway but specifically to 'white' working class people. Weis contends that although this group are increasingly divided over changed gender relations, there has also been a [white] 'class reunion', in that men and women have come together against their racial 'other' in the town – the Yemeni population – regardless of any potential commonalities of classed experience (2004: 2–5).

In the British context, Skeggs similarly emphasizes how class, rather than being produced in isolation, is made through the inscriptions going on simultaneously between different symbolic systems, such as 'race' and gender. She highlights how these processes can be contradictory, but can also draw out power imbalances between individuals, stating that examining interactions 'enables us to explore how some people can use the classifications and characteristics of race, class or femininity as a resource whilst others cannot because they are positioned *as* them' (Skeggs, 2004: 4). Thus it is important both to attend to the intersectionality of gender, 'race' and class, and to avoid reducing them into each other (Valentine, 2007). Contrary to what is implied in much British academic writing, working class does not necessarily mean 'white' working class.

In a review of five academic studies on whiteness and class in the US, Bonnett draws attention to the classed nature of the relationship between writer and subject:

> it may be useful to conceive of educated, public or 'helping sector' professionals as a class fraction.... If one does, then the tone of disappointment and disapproval we find directed at working class whites in a number of the books under review begins to take on a class dimension.
>
> (2008: 190)

Consequently we do not reduce the discussion to the identifications and experiences of *working* class people, but are also concerned with the everyday relations between classes, and with people's constructions of class others.

Community, place, belonging and the technologies of rule

The case study drawn on in this book concerns a particular place, one which is defined by the boundaries of three social housing estates. However, we wanted to question the idea that living in close proximity automatically gave rise to a meaningful sense of community. The spatial mobility and emotional senses of moving history are important here. People's feeling of belonging to their place of residence varies, and their connections to other places may be important in explaining this, not only through their own mobility, but through that of their parents, siblings and children, and the connections maintained across space, including transnationally, that this can engender.

Working classness has often been associated by middle class writers, with particular 'places', and with the idea of 'community', particularly in relation to policy. Alleyne (2002) has argued that this classical notion of 'community' is linked to notions of pre-modernity, 'land and homestead', and characterized by dense networks of collective social relations, tied particularly to kinship and religion. In Europe then, 'the death of community' has been an ongoing argument throughout the last century (Alexander et al., 2007; for an early example of this see Zorbaugh, 1929).

Lamenting the apparent loss of community has been especially evident in writing on working class areas of cities, and, in particular, on the movement of working class people from privately rented housing in inner-city areas to mass council housing, notably the tower block estates of the 1950s and 1960s (see Young and Willmott, 1957). Typically, the old 'communities' were located in inner-city 'slum' areas, and, while it was accepted that they were characterized by high levels of deprivation (see for example Chamberlain, 1989; Giles, 1995), they were also seen as embodying a strong spirit of self-help and support networks that were tied to proximity to kin, based around the matriarchal figure of 'our mam' and co-location in a few streets (Kerr, 1958; Rosser and Harris, 1965; Tebbutt, 1992; Young and Willmott, 1957). In one especially nostalgic piece of writing on Southwark in South London, Collins wrote how there was a 'mutual understanding, an implicit code of conduct, and for the most part a mutual respect' (Collins, 2004: 143).

Through this literature there is an ongoing identification of community with place. One classic example is Sheldon's (1948) study of elderly people in Wolverhampton (cited by Fennell, 1997). Sheldon defined a close relative as someone who lived within five minutes' walking distance (this being the measure of the distance a hot meal could be carried from one dwelling to another without reheating). Successive studies of close families and the way they operated followed this tendency of linking locality and important social networks. However, as O'Byrne (1997: 77) observes, there is 'clearly no "real" definition of what actually constitutes such a "working class community"'. At the same time, he goes on to suggest that in traditional definitions, it is 'generally understood that significant "ingredients" include solidarity, close-by family and social networks, shared lifestyles, and limited spatial mobility'. Yet we need to be wary of equating this with any wider identification with 'community'. Research from the 1940s revealed how in working class neighbourhoods, 'interest in the community as a whole is almost completely lacking', particularly among women; and that community centres, where they existed, were 'used by a minority of people only' (Mass Observation, 1943: xxii).

Significantly for this book, and our concern with moving histories, work by Fennell explores people's social and spatial connections beyond their locality with the understanding that 'there is no necessary association between nearness and significance' (Fennell, 1997: 90). A social survey in the 1940s revealed how people did not necessarily drink in their nearest pub, or go to the nearest church of their denomination. This suggests that people had networks and interests outside of their apparently closed community (Mass Observation, 1943). It also highlights the danger of charting a trajectory of increased mobility/decreased 'community' over time, and points instead to the importance of exploring 'links out' in the past as much as 'links within'.

Perhaps unusually for research involving a case study of mainly white British participants in a provincial city, we engage in this book with the international as well as the extra-local national connections made and maintained by the people we spoke with. Taking as central the understanding that places are 'open, porous and the products of other places' (Massey, 1995: 59; see also Keith and Pile, 1993), we challenge the notion that the three housing estates of our case study are socially bounded by their geographical borders. In our living, hanging out and regularly returning to the estates we recorded stories which show, among other things, the complexity of histories of spatial mobility and the relations that emerge from it in shaping individual social identifications and the collective identifications and categorizations of this particular place. This involved discussion of space as well as place. As Massey put it elsewhere, space is

> never finished; never closed...a simultaneity of stories so far...[It is necessary] to uproot 'space' from that constellation of concepts in which it has so unquestioningly so often been embedded (stasis; closure; representation) and to settle it among another set of ideas (heterogeneity; relationality; coevalness...liveliness indeed) where it releases a more challenging political landscape.
>
> (Massey, 2005: 9)

Lefebvre's (2002) work on the 'production of space', though developed out of abstract theorizing rather than empirical study, also emphasizes dynamism rather than stasis and draws attention to the power relations entailed in both the material and the discursive production of space. Lefebvre analysed the interrelation between how a space is conceived and produced by powerful outsiders and 'experts' (representations of space); the perceived space of everyday life and common sense perception – the space of 'inhabitants' and 'users' (representational space) – which is often ignored in the theoretical conceived space of planners and officials; and spatial practice. The latter

embraces production and reproduction, and the particular locations and spatial sets characteris[ing] each social formation. Spatial practices ensure continuity and some degree of cohesion.

Interestingly for our study, Lefebvre provides the following example of 'modern' spatial practice, which may be 'defined – to take an extreme but significant case – by the daily life of a tenant in a government-subsidised...housing project' (2002: 139–40).

In Lefebvre's concern with the interaction between the material and the discursive, and between powerful 'representations of space' and individuals' spatial practices and perceptions of space, we find a resonance with Jenkins' approach to understanding social identity through the interplay between self-identification and categorization. In both cases there is a feedback loop, as illustrated by O'Byrne's study of a south London working class housing estate. Following Willis (1977), O'Byrne argues that people 'learn to be local'. Crucially, he observes that an essential part of being a teenager on the estates is 'hanging out', and knowing how to dress, speak and be while doing so: spending time away from the estate consequently raises questions about their belonging status in the group, so that 'a specific type of cultural capital relates to knowledge of the estate itself: a resource of knowledge regarding the codes pertaining to the physical space' (1997: 82–3).

In this context, behaviour such as 'hanging out' simultaneously signals an individual's belonging to an area through, in Lefebvre's terms, their performance of a degree of 'spatial competence', and reinforces and reproduces spatial practice. Similarly, Savage et al. deploy Bourdieu's (1990) concept of 'habitus' to link social and spatial practices with structural inequalities:

Where people feel comfortable in places, they tend to populate such places, either through permanent residence or through revisiting, but where they do not, they tend to avoid them. Hence, a complex process of the sorting of people's habitus to certain kinds of zones allows a social which is also a spatial structure to be defined.

(2005: 101)

Such making of social space through defining and avoidance goes on as much *within* a particular place or locality as it might between places. One of the consistent ways in which external representations are mediated by residents of an area themselves is through the taking on, and, importantly, adapting, outsiders' narratives of the relative 'respectability' and/or 'roughness' of a place. Hill's idea of moral geography (cited in Modan, 2007: 298) finds that individuals tend to tie notions of respectability to their own place while externalizing roughness. Similarly Harvey (1993: 23) suggests that denigrating the places inhabited by others is a way of asserting the power and viability of one's own location (see also Sibley, 1981, 1995a). In the case of a stigmatized area, such as a 'sink' estate or even a street (see for example Damer, 1989; Elias and Scotson, 1965; White, 1986), this process becomes focused on an 'elsewhere' within the locality – the other side of the estate, the other end of the street or a particular group within the area who are seen in some way as outsiders. In representing 'others' in a particular light, the personal and spatial often become inextricably entwined, so mentioning a street or area is enough to embody an individual with a swathe of ascribed characteristics.

Day (2006) takes this further, arguing, importantly, that these processes do not apply only to so-called 'problem' areas and estates, but rather they represent general features of community formation. He cites Scott (2005) who shows that, in the interwar period and beyond, the development of suburban estates in Britain produced a fine gradation of 'rough' and 'respectable' communities, whose residents came to believe they upheld radically different social standards, styles of living and personal and domestic hygiene. Bourke notes how such distancing combined spatial and social practices with proximity to neighbours, often generating, rather than a sense of community, feelings of being stifled and alienated, resentments, or even simply the desire for privacy. She argues that people deployed a range of tactics in order to create a deliberate sense of distance, such as persisting in using 'Mrs' rather than first names, neighbours not being welcome upstairs in houses, and people taking a pride in deliberately 'not prying' into each other's lives (Bourke, 1993: 143).

This flags up the importance of considering not only the difference between residents and non-residents, but also between people who consider themselves as 'belonging' and 'outsiders' (Sibley, 1995a). And indeed, even for those who 'belong', places are experienced differently. Feminists have highlighted the marginalization of women from public space and shown how fear can often be an important component of women's relationship with place (see for example Valentine, 1990). Time of day/night and seasons in this context are of central importance, with women along with the elderly often cutting short their use of outside public space as a way of managing the fear linked to 'being out' during hours of darkness. Sibley's (1995b) work on childhood and the use of space, building on his own childhood, crucially links the physicality of children's experience of space with temporality.

Thus while place remains for some an important part of feelings of community, people's notions of place and their spatial ties are not necessarily congruent with what might be defined by outsiders as a 'community'. Similarly, an individual's network of social relations may be bound up with a particular place, extend far beyond it, or more probably combine aspects of both. And crucially, people within a particular locality cannot be assumed to follow similar patterns, and hence to have similar conceptualizations of 'community'.

Theorists of community from the 1980s have, for different reasons, increasingly destabilized the link between community and place (for an overview see Silk, 1999). Cohen (1985), for example, argued that community should be understood less as a social practice than as a symbolic structure, thus shifting understandings of community away from the previous emphasis on community as social interaction based on locality towards a concern with meaning and identity. Similarly, Anderson's (1983) idea of 'imagined' communities suggested how community '[was] shaped by cognitive and symbolic structures that are not underpinned by "lived" spaces and immediate forms of social intimacy' (Delanty, 2003: 2). As Day (2006: 163) comments, communities are much like nations through their 'construction of close similarities' and an 'underlying, seemingly essential, unity among those who "belong", and the exclusion of those who fail to meet these criteria'. He goes on to argue that in reality there are often profound internal differences. While these might be recognized, at some level, by residents, they nevertheless:

> join together to perpetuate the illusion that these are of secondary importance or simply do not matter. In the representation of community, it is what people have in common that counts. Unsuspecting observers will find themselves led into taking this proposition at face value, to arrive at the conclusion that communities are marked by deep, unshakeable consensus.
>
> (Day, 2006: 164)

For some, understandings of the constructed and relational nature of community may be seen as part of a wider problematization of the link between society and place. Giddens (1990), for example, sees a disembedding of society: the process by which social activity has become independent of localized contexts, to be stretched across both space and time. Similarly Beck (1992) sees the demise of traditional forms of community, arguing that as ascriptive ties of 'race', gender, class and ethnicity are weakened and people increasingly gain freedom to make their own choices, so the limitations associated with bounded neighbourhoods diminish. However, Skeggs (2004) and Bauman (2004b) have rightly critiqued the unselfconsciously classed production of such analyses.

In contrast to both Beck and Giddens we, like Eade (1997), emphasize the continued importance of place in people's lives. In acknowledging how individuals themselves construct their networks of social relations, we too, though in a different way to Beck and Giddens, are interested in exploring the importance of non-local as well as local networks. Like Harvey we hold that the

> collapse of spatial barriers does not mean that the significance of place is decreasing... as spatial barriers diminish so we become more sensitised to what the world's spaces contain.
>
> (1989, cited by Lash and Urry, 1994: 303)

Neo-liberalist restructuring has not occurred in a vacuum, but rather remains an intensely place-based experience, with global interdependence increasing, resulting in fact in a stretching (rather than negating) of social relationships. Places continue to *be* different, as they are sited differently in terms of local, regional, national and global economies and resources (Castree et al., 2004); are 'represented' differently and thus have different social meanings; and are 'experienced' differently. In addition, each of these elements has a temporal aspect, with change occurring over time and over the course of individual lives. In all these senses then, we understand places relationally, seeing them as contingent, contested and uncertain, rather than as fixed territorial units.

Acknowledging the fluidity of place does not mean denying materiality and structure, but rather setting this in context. The state, though far from the monolith it is sometimes portrayed as, plays a critical role in both in categorization and in the production of space. And, as Rose (1999) further points out, in recent times it has used a discourse of community as part of its technology of rule (see also Huxley, 2007: 199–200). Indeed the concern over the existence or absence of 'community' in areas of social housing can be seen more generally as part of a longer and broader history of debates over the governability of the working classes. While a 'breakdown' in 'community' is never tied to middle class identities – whose new fluid, post-modern flexibility is rather seen as a form of cultural capital (Bauman, 2004b: 53–4) – when identified as part of a 'failing' working class area, it becomes a signal for governmental intervention. Consequently since the 1990s, alongside the apparently unproblematic deployment of ideas of 'respect' (for a critique, see McDowell, 2007), governments, in particular those of the US and the UK, have increasingly used particular formulations of 'community' (for example Etzioni,1995) in relation to working class areas. These ideas stress the moral aspect of community, and depict it as embodying a citizenship of responsibility and participation. In this form of thinking, 'community entails voice, a "moral voice" and social responsibility rests on personal responsibility' (Delanty, 2003: 89).

In the Third Way political context, 'the community' became a key territory for governmental strategies, as for example, according to Giddens:

> community doesn't imply trying to recapture lost forms of local solidarity; it refers to practical means of furthering the social and material refurbishment of neighbourhoods, towns and larger local areas.
> (Giddens, 1998, quoted in McGhee, 2003: 390–1)

Thus, the New Deal for Communities scheme, introduced by New Labour in 1997, with its emphasis on organizations run by residents of deprived areas being granted significant amounts of money in order to solve 'their' problems, was one such product of this form of thinking.

As well as being criticized for propagating 'unreflexive, undertheorised ideas of community' (Alleyne, 2002: 622), this form of communitarianism can be seen as furthering a neo-liberal retreat of the state from public life and from responsibility for social problems. Delanty (2003: 88) argues that it is important 'not to see this as merely the exercise of social control, for it *can* also lead to community empowerment' (emphasis added). However, he agrees that the attraction of community to government can be explained in how the concept carries with it a notion of 'civic obligations and moral commitments to society' which 'produces the political effect of disburdening the state of responsibility and diluting social citizenship'. Rose, taking a Foucauldian perspective on such governmental communitarianism, sees community as having become 'a quasi-governmental discourse that facilitates new technologies of power and of social management':

> in the institution of community, a sector is brought into existence whose vectors and forces can be mobilised, enrolled, deployed in novel programmes and techniques which encourage and harness active practices of self-management and identity construction, of personal ethics and collective allegiances.
>
> (Rose, 1999: 176)

Thus, in this book, we take a critical approach to ideas of class, community, place and belonging. Following Lefebvre, but, in contrast to his work, grounded by an in-depth case study, we are interested in the production of space both materially and discursively. At the heart of our study is a concern with the ways in which the representations and categorizations of powerful outsiders have influenced people's lived experiences, spatial practices and social identifications, and vice versa. Of course, we are not separate from such dynamics ourselves. In the next section we reflect on the process of carrying out this research, especially on the use of life history narratives and the problems and potential of tapping into people's memories, and we write individually in our own 'voices' about our backgrounds and motivations for carrying out the work.

Researching three Norwich estates

The research participants and how we met them

In this book we start from a particular place, a collection of houses and flats built in three estates between the 1920s and 1960s on the outskirts of a provincial English city. Through the course of the text we hear from people who have lived, and many who continue to live, in those houses, about their own individual and group identification processes. Most, but not all, of the residents and ex-residents were working class. Some were middle class. Most, but not all, were white, had been born in Britain and were British nationals. Many had migration histories of their own, including some people who had moved to the estates for the first time in the few years leading up to the interview. Others were indirectly affected by migration through the spatial mobility of close relatives.

As well as grounding people's experiences in the context of their own life histories, we set out to locate them in a wider context: thus, in addition to residents and former residents, we interviewed seven women and two men – mostly middle class professionals – who had worked in the area. In total we interviewed 26 men and 47 women of all ages, though with a bias towards middle-aged and older people.[8] We also spent time in the local and national archives, in order to explore the role and motivations of state actors in the creation of the estates and in daily life there; and we engaged in a degree of ethnographic work and kept regular field notes. Ben spent 3 months in autumn 2005 living in a house on the North Earlham estate, with Becky coming in each day from her home in north Suffolk. Becky continued to visit the estates at least twice a week until the last interview was carried out in October 2006.

We initially made contacts with research participants through three main channels – via the NELM Development Trust (NELM), the organization created as a result of receiving New Deal for Communities money from central government in 2000, which Ben had developed links with, and which led us to the local history group;[9] through putting out a short piece in local newspapers about the project; and in utilizing personal networks. Ben had lived and worked in areas of Norwich adjacent to the estates for 7 years as a lecturer at UEA, and knew people who had lived in the area or who had worked with residents from the area; Becky had friends living on the North Earlham and West Earlham estates. From our initial contacts we used snowballing techniques and took advantage of chance encounters to widen our interview base.

The authors in our individual voices

We want to make visible the way in which the material for this book was produced. We are white middle class researchers – a man and a woman, both parents of young children. The interviews and ethnographic work were themselves relational encounters. Our analysis of class as identity in Chapter 5 writes these encounters in, so that what emerges is about class relations and identities in the plural rather than any attempt to define what it means to belong to a particular class. As Gillian Rose has put it, 'what we research is our relation with the researched ... [the researcher] is situated, not by what she knows, but by what she uncertainly performs' (1997: 315).

'What right do you, middle class outsiders, have to research a working class area'? This is the question that, perhaps surprisingly, no one in the course of conducting our research ever asked us, although it was undoubtedly there, unspoken, in many of our encounters. Is it enough to believe that our identities should never be a bar from asking questions and seeking answers, if only we always understand that both question and answer are not separate from who we are?

Ben writes:

I don't find it easy to create a single narrative that makes sense of who I am. If I talk about myself in any way, it comes with facial expressions, hand movements, hesitancy, anxiety, and will be selective depending on who I am talking to. I much prefer speaking with people one to one than conversing in groups. What brought me to sit here and type my thoughts about identity, the Norwich estates (and briefly about myself) into a machine is complicated and contradictory. It has to do with migration histories, with class and with gender.

My father does not currently answer the question of whether his white South African secular Jewish background was upper working class or petit-bourgeois. This may be partly because he has had Parkinson's disease for over ten years, and partly because he does not feel this is a question he can answer. His reply at the end of 2007 was: "*you* are upper class." He was an only child who witnessed his parents' divorce, and his mother's remarriage to a violent alcoholic. With his own father during school terms, home was various different boarding houses, no doubt for white guests only, in South African cities. In school holidays he would go to live with his mother in Durban, where, one of seven daughters of immigrant parents – cockneys from the East End of London – she now lived with his 'uncle Bill'.

My dad's answer to my class question held the echoes of his own attempt to integrate into not simply British society but the upper-middle and even upper classes and the Oxbridge elite. In one of his early attempts to migrate to England, with very few resources to hand, he was drawn unwittingly into an attempted burglary and spent a night in prison. Later, on his way to becoming a columnist on a national broadsheet newspaper, he met my mother, daughter of the descendants of German immigrants who had founded a merchant bank, where her brothers were learning the business; and, on her mother's side, of a Scottish clan, who had migrated to, in fact invaded, the north-eastern coast of Ireland and ended up with a castle and a title. My mum studied for a postgraduate degree at the London School of Economics and worked for many years as a primary school teacher in North London.

I am as much my father's son as my mother's and grew up in theoretical opposition to class privilege, and actively resisting it, though also benefiting from it through expectations and assumptions that I could do whatever I turned my mind to, as well as a materially very comfortable childhood. The body was another matter. Despite my father's efforts, I did not as a child develop any kind of practical orientation, or much physical fitness. I had multiple identifications, watching Arsenal on the then largely working class North Bank at Highbury, doing a paper round, and going to cubs and scouts, though I kept that a secret as a teenager. I only met my Jewish grandmother once aged 2, taken on a trip to South Africa, but in my forties I was profoundly moved by the letters that she had written to me, as well as my parents, from the time of my birth. Her expressions of all-encompassing, generous love were a revelation. 'My dear, darling grandson...' She died in 1966. While she was alive my dad sent her money from his pay packet each week.

On 29 June 1962, the day of my parents' marriage in London, the person who was to become my Sikh Punjabi father-in-law arrived from India and sought digs in Swiss Cottage. Like many others he had raced to beat the new law which would limit the immigration of Commonwealth citizens to Britain. He had come alone, leaving his wife and their five children in Delhi. They would join him two years later. He moved straight on to the port of Chatham where he worked at the docks, and did not find time to pursue the studies he had dreamed of. Once a worker in the Indian Telegraph Office, he retired in the 1990s from a white collar job with the Inland Revenue office in Romford. My mother-in-law arrived from India against a promise that she would not be expected to have any more children. She promptly became pregnant with a daughter – who I would meet 20 years later as fellow students at Reading University – and later gave birth to a son. When I met her daughter, she was still working as a home-based garment stitcher, receiving batches of clothes from an agent each week for finishing.

At the time of writing, I'm 44 years old. I've lived in India for a total of about 4 years and now live in Brighton, England. My partner and I are still together though not for lack of some serious bumpiness. We have two children and recently moved to a large terraced house – the mortgage is paid from our two salaries – mine comes from an academic job; hers presently from work on mental health with black and minority ethnic people in the city. I've stayed in paid work almost continuously, while my partner took 4 years off and looked after the children in infancy. That's why it's me being paid to write in the attic, itself partly the product of the inherited wealth that helped us start early on the housing ladder several moves ago. Our children go to state-funded schools. We are both ideologically opposed to fee-paying ones. But would we be if we had the money to send our children to them?

We lived in Norwich for 7 years. One of our children was born there. Then employed at UEA to teach and research international development studies, I was bothered by what seemed like the lack of connection between the university and the housing estates that bordered on to it. What was this all about? There was an organization on the estates, funded by the New Labour government's New Deal project. I contacted them and arranged some exchanges between residents and students I was responsible for teaching, mainly international postgraduates. Seen from another angle, I had developed a strong critique of international development practice, felt its strong continuities with British colonial history, and wanted to work in the country I lived in, to be close to my kids as they were growing up....

Becky writes:

Who am I? Researcher, academic and middle class, yes. Also a white British woman, partner, parent, daughter, friend, environmental and peace activist, villager, anarchist, member of a co-operative land project, and gardener. All of these and, like anyone, much more than the labels we give ourselves, or that others give us.

I was brought up in the countryside with my two brothers in south Norfolk and Lincolnshire: my father employed as a manager first in the poultry and then food processing and water industries; my mother our main carer, but also running a small holding, and at various points employed as a teacher. By no stretch of the imagination was my childhood multicultural, and yet without being able to articulate it, issues of insiders/outsiders and (non-)belonging preoccupied me. Growing up, the issue of outsiderness was not based anyway on 'race', but rather on the local/incomer division, which in part revolved around issues of class, but only in part. While I attended the local schools along with other children from the village and played at the rec with them and had my social highlight of the year, the tractor ride round neighbouring villages advertising the village fête, I carried with me the sense that I was an outsider. Other children had their cousins and grandparents living nearby, had been born in the local hospital and spoke with a Norfolk accent – I hadn't and didn't. Knowing no other way of living myself than that of village life, I also knew that as I grew up I would probably go to university and move away. While this, and more, did happen, I also moved back – first to a village 2 miles from my childhood home, and now 15 miles away, dangerously across the border in north Suffolk. With a Polish friend, who lives in Essex, I joke that I too experience the unsettling nature of transnational identities, having lived both in south Norfolk and north Suffolk. And yet this contains a seed of truth: that early on in life (although only now able to articulate it) I became aware that issues of belonging and identity were bundled up in layers of meaning that included who you were perceived to be as much as who you wanted to be; and that identifications can be unsettled by micro-migrations as much as by bigger moves.

Uneasy but relatively undefined feelings of myself as somehow 'not-belonging' crystallized when I became involved in environmental direct action. Living on protest sites, going through (sometimes violent) evictions, being arrested for being in the wrong place at the wrong time, being part of a counter-culture that was largely criminalized as a result of the 1994 Criminal Justice Act showed just how much I had stepped outside the circle of belonging. What has this got to do with my research? Such experiences don't stop me from being middle class, and in fact my middle classness probably gave me much of my confidence to speak out. But, I would argue, they give it another dimension. One which has experienced the physicality of living outside with no fixed home, vilified, ignored or sexually harassed for being identifiably 'the other'. One which understands that the police are not to be trusted, can pull you in and turn your life upside down because they decide to, no matter your accent or background. One which knows that the label given you by others does not even begin to reveal who you are as a person. If I demand the right to be understood in all my complexity, then I also demand that right for everyone.

More pertinently perhaps, activism put myself and fellow activists in the spotlight of the media, writers, and, over time, have made us a subject of academic studies. I, as an (arguably) polite individual, did my best to make people welcome round a camp fire, answer their (frequently to us irrelevant) questions, being recorded, filmed, photographed as 'protestor climbing down from tree' or 'eco-warrior ready to die for beliefs'. Rarely did these outsiders acknowledge that we may be too busy, or simply disinclined, to put ourselves out for them. When we did, rarely did we receive copies of films, articles or photographs, never did we have any control over the final output. My words have been taken out of context, my photograph used as part of articles I didn't agree with, my hand-fasting ceremony was used in a particularly cloying article in *The Guardian*. I could go on. What have these experiences taught me? Mainly not to co-operate with the media and to ignore requests to take part in academic studies unless I want to be misrepresented, objectified and to feel tainted by association.

So why given all this, do I set myself up as an academic researcher? In part shameful practicality – a desire to control my own working time and content, to be able to work from home and in my locality. In part what I can only describe as an innate nosiness, a belief that everybody is interesting, combined with a perhaps politically naive belief that everybody's voice has a right to be heard. And yes, over the years there have been rare occasions of meeting a journalist or photographer who took the time to get to know us as individuals, who created the space to allow us to speak as we wished to be heard, and who somehow managed to capture some of the essence of our time, place and politics. And perhaps arrogantly I want to do the same – certainly it is something for which I strive.

Living on a site outside Weymouth in the mid-1990s next to a council estate, one day a group of Irish Travellers pulled in, and never had I seen such a frenzy of vilification. Asking myself 'Why?' was one strand that led to a PhD looking at the history of Travellers in twentieth-century Britain; which in turn led to work interviewing Travellers in Norfolk about their health; which in turn led to my interest in the Larkman estate where reportedly many Travellers had been housed in the past. Although, as we found, things weren't quite that simple. . . .

Oral history, memory and our research practice

Although the research for this book involved a range of methods, the main body of our empirical material is a number of oral history interviews. It has long been argued that one of oral history's strengths lies in its ability to record the voices and experiences of those whose histories would otherwise go unremarked and unrecorded (see for example

Thompson, 2000). In doing this, echoing the first sense in which moving histories is used in this book, history is in fact remade, as

> by introducing new evidence from the underside, by shifting the focus...by challenging some of the assumptions and accepted judgements...by bringing recognition to substantial groups of people who had been ignored, a cumulative process of transformation is set in motion. The scope of historical writing itself is enlarged and enriched; and at the same time its social message changes.
>
> (Thompson, 2000: 8–9)

Oral history enables us to make the connection between the general and the particular. As Portelli suggests, it asks the question: 'What is our place in history, and what is the place of history in our lives?'(Portelli, 1997: ix–x). For identity studies in particular, this sense of dynamic interaction is also evoked by Somers in what she calls a 'narrative identity approach' that gives space both to the importance of structural contexts (including social categorization) and to the individuality of people's life stories:

> [S]ocial action can only be intelligible if we recognize that people are guided to act by the structural and cultural relationships in which they are embedded and by the stories through which they constitute their identities.
>
> (1994: 624)

Such an approach, like other oral history, relies on memory and the relationality and selectivity involved in its telling. Asking people to tap into their memories to relate a story can connect us to a much more dynamic set of narratives than histories based on documents:

> Memory is life, always embodied in living societies and as such in permanent evolution, subject to the dialect of remembering and forgetting, unconscious of the distortions to which it is subject, vulnerable in various ways to appropriation and manipulation, and capable of lying dormant for long periods only to be suddenly reawakened. History, on the other hand, is the reconstruction, always problematic and incomplete, of what is no longer.
>
> (Nora, 1996: 3, quoted in Burrell and Panayi, 2006: 3)

And, as Portelli puts it, this can be more meaningful to the teller than conventional approaches to history:

> History, we have been taught, is facts, actual and objective events you can touch and see; stories, in contrast are the tales, the people who tell them, the words they are made of, the knot of memory and imagination that turns material facts into cultural meanings. Stories, in other words, communicate what history means to human beings.
>
> (Portelli, 1997: 42)

Often the direction of our oral history interviews was guided by the person being interviewed. For this reason, as Byrne has pointed out (2006: 37), the balance of power 'in an interview' can be even. Moreover, in place-based research in particular, new sites of interpretation can emerge so that the researcher is not the only person with power over the way material is represented. Within their networks, research participants' own accounts of the research, their role in it, their opinions of the researchers and the value of research will be privileged. We might argue that these sites are more marginalized and therefore intrinsically less powerful than, say university networks,[10] yet this underestimates the importance of what might be thought of as subaltern interpretation.

Yet Byrne is right that the writer/analyst has *much more* power of representation than the people who were interviewed (2006: 37). This has disturbed us as writers because it is clear that we are the people selecting how to bring a person's life into the stories being told in the book. We felt awkward talking to each other about people who had taken us into their confidence as individuals. And when we turn our thoughts into print, or stand up in a workshop or conference, the disquiet multiplies. How would that person feel if/when they read this, or were in the room when a discussion of their life took place? What right do we have to prise apart their lives for analysis and to serve them up for public consumption?

However, we want to draw attention too to research participants' conscious agency in the ways in which stories were told, and, thus ultimately in the content of the transcripts that formed a major part of the raw material for our case study. Each transcript was sent to the interviewee to check over and for a second round of consent – this time that the content of the transcript could be quoted from in our writing (see Note 8, above). One participant in particular used the opportunity to read and correct her transcript to change and omit sections that did not fit with how she wished to be represented. She was heavily involved in her local church and wanted to see herself, and be seen, as 'respectable'. Although she said 'yeah' when speaking in the interview, she changed each of her uses of this word into 'yes' in the transcript, and also removed any extraneous 'you know's or 'sort of's. She removed a section of the transcript that referred to a member of her family who engaged in criminal activities, as well as information about how her daughter-in-law came to Norwich to work in a factory, while keeping in the transcript how she was now employed as a manager. The explanation she gave for these changes was that she was now 'happy with the *information* contained in interview' (her emphasis).

The content of the interviews was also influenced by more sub-conscious attempts at self-representation, tailored to what participants thought was expected from one or both of us as individuals (we conducted some interviews together) or from a research project of this kind. This could change during the course of an interview, or more particularly between different sittings of extended life history interviews. Multiple interviews thus provided an opportunity for a story to be elaborated on, though on reflection we realized that even these had an element of false intimacy, opening the door on a person's world, even to a deeper relationship, but that they could never be a substitute for this and some remained quite formal. Signing a consent form, recording the interview, receiving the interview transcript and consenting to the use of that transcript all helped to reinforce the sense in which participants were helping to 'create history'. Many participants remained phlegmatic about the whole process. However, for others, the conscious process of representation of themselves in relation to us as interviewers, themselves as part of a research project or themselves in relation to the wider world were far more obvious.

All the interviews could be read in terms of performances, and what these revealed about the relation between interviewer and the research participant and interviewees. At one stage, Flo Smith talked about her home-baked meat puddings, correctly interpreting from what she read off from Becky's performances that she preferred home-cooked rather than pre-prepared food. However, this example also shows the simultaneity of connections and disconnections (see Valentine, 2002: 120–2) as Flo misinterpreted Becky as someone who enjoyed cooking and ate meat (Becky's partner does virtually all the cooking and she is vegan). Was it dishonest for Becky not to disclose these disconnections alongside the connections? Was it dishonest for Ben, listening to explicitly racist discourse about black people in London one evening in a North Earlham social club, not to reveal that his partner is Asian? Perhaps, though, following Phoenix (1994), it could be argued that the articulation of viewpoints counter to one's own is the whole point of such interviews since they are intended to evoke respondents' accounts rather than to hear one's own discourses reflected back (cited in Valentine, 2002: 123).

Our interpretation and analysis, in keeping with oral history practice, is not only of speech but of silences and hesitations. As Passerini's (2002 [1979], 1987) seminal work on inter-war fascism in Italy revealed, understanding the silences over the impact of Mussolini's regime on the lives of the people she interviewed was central to unpicking its traumatic effect on the population:

> Oral sources refuse to answer certain kinds of questions: seemingly loquacious, they finally prove to be reticent or enigmatic... they force us to reformulate problems and challenge our current habits of thought.
>
> (Passerini, 2002: 58)

An example of this in our research emerged in our interviews with residents and ex-residents of the estates who had served in the British colonial military. Although for people in England in the 1940s and 1950s, living in poverty with no clear route out, this provided important opportunities for livelihood and in some cases social mobility, there was an almost complete silence over the colonialism that made it possible. We have interpreted this as in keeping with the lack of any collective memory of empire in Britain (Gilroy, 2004) and also with the unreflexive use of colonial categories in discussions of 'race' and immigration in the contemporary period (see Rogaly and Taylor, forthcoming). In some instances, particularly in cases relating to memories of poverty, education and housing, we were able to set participants' recollections against findings in the archives. This could confirm and enrich their accounts: in one case, for example, a vivid memory by Tom Crowther of the fumigation of his family's and neighbours' possessions as part of the process of slum clearance was mirrored in discussions in council minutes over the need to fumigate all households to ensure there was no stigma attached to the process. In other instances the archives contradicted memories, or more often, offered another slant, giving 'outsider' and official discourses that we were able to set alongside the 'insider' memories of estate residents.

Now towards the end of the research process what can we say with any certainty? Following Parr (1996) we would agree that research is a 'messy' business: some questions that we had at the beginning of the process have disappeared, others emerged and taken over; relationships begun during the research have not neatly ended with the signing of the final consent form, but have continued in different ways; our own lives too have been the sites of personal dramas and changes that mean that we are not the same people we were at the outset. Throughout the research process we have been aware, sometimes overwhelmed, by the fact that our material is incomplete and partial; also that as outsiders the knowledge and understandings we produce will ultimately be different from the diverse perspectives of individual research participants.

Map of the book

The rest of the book consists of five thematic chapters and a conclusion, broken up by interludes that use a more conversational tone to explore two individuals' life histories in greater depth than is possible in the rest of the text. Chapter 2, which follows this introduction, describes the physicality of the estates, and their everyday sights and sounds, within an international critical literature on place and space. We emphasize not only that places are always in flux, and that the meanings of places change over time as people move in and out of them, but also that such mobility may be local as much as long distance and international. The chapter shows that the internal and external boundaries of the case study estates are social constructions that themselves shift depending on who is doing the talking, where and when. Importantly, we interrogate mythical characterizations of the estates, common to stereotypes about much social housing in Britain, that portray them as housing particular social groups or categories of people with inherent characteristics. We reveal major changes in how the houses and gardens were regarded and used by residents over time, and ways in which this varied for women and men, and for children and adults. The chapter shows not only that the reputation of the estates worked alongside other structural inequalities to keep people in place, but also that people's self-identifications, sometimes used instrumentally, could modify and change how such categorization was experienced.

Chapter 3 is set within debates on changing understanding and experiences of unemployment and poverties. We use poverties in the plural because, although material deprivation has continued to mark some people's lives in the estates deeply, people's experience of poverty has changed, as has its meaning. From a relatively universal experience of poverty among residents, including in the 1940s and 1950s when most men and women who lived there were in paid work, an intensely felt relative deprivation emerged for those who continued to be poor in the 1960s, when this ceased to be the norm. Later, following the economic restructuring that took place in the 1970s and 1980s, many people were affected by long-term unemployment, and poverty was expressed as the stigmatization associated with not being able to afford to be part of consumer society. In spite of dominant stereotypes of council estate residents as 'scroungers' of state welfare, the chapter shows the hard work, resourcefulness and humour that were drawn on at different points in time for people to be able to put together a livelihood.

In the fourth chapter, we delve more deeply into the role of the state in producing categorizations and some of the ways in which these have been variously appropriated and contested by estate residents. This chapter highlights the different levels of state discourse and action, particularly national and local, and their sometimes conflicting agendas in relation to areas defined as poor and deprived. It also reveals the unevenness of states' 'technologies of rule' across space, among them the use of a discourse of 'community', as well as people's responses to that unevenness. The material in the chapter is drawn from residents' direct, everyday experience of the state, for example, in housing and welfare offices. It shows that the state is neither monolithic nor all-powerful, and inasmuch as it has a face that can be accessed, something which we argue is diminishing in the move to a more 'faceless' state, it can, at particular moments, be recruited and appropriated to the advantage of estate residents.

Chapter 5 analyses change and ambivalence in class identifications in a context of continuing inequalities between classes. The chapter draws on interviews with self-identified working class and middle class people, and reflects not only on the relations between classes but also on relations between research participants and us as researchers. It shows that people's way of talking about class can shift according to who they are talking about, as well as who they are talking to. It also reveals how class identifications are formed in relation to historically specific processes of categorization, and that, while in England some people do not want to discuss class or do not see it as a primary self-identification, for others 'within class' differences are often drawn on. This refers not only to the construction of social distance in relation to 'rough' working class people by those who would portray themselves as 'respectable', but also different formulations of middle classness. Education is a key arena where class identifications are made, reinforced and contested, and at the same time often the source of structural inequality based on stereotypes about class.

In Chapter 6, we return to the topic of spatial mobility, first explored in Chapter 2, to examine forms of transnational and translocal living engaged in by estate residents in the past and the present. In this chapter, we argue that life worlds stretched across space influence self-identification, whether the different places to which people maintain connections are within or across national boundaries. The chapter reveals the importance of American GIs in the life of the estates in the 1940s and how subsequent marriages led to emigration. As with other, later, emigration to Australia and elsewhere, experiences of absences, visits and return were suffused with emotion. We also explore stereotypes about recent newcomers, particularly people of colour, and how these may be shaped by national discourses emerging from the middle class media and political elite on asylum seekers and refugees and on Islam.

2
Place

Introduction

If spaces are thrown together and conjunctural (Massey, 2005), they are also imagined. When a class fraction or the residents of a particular locality are categorized as 'deprived' or even 'deviant' or 'dangerous' or of low intelligence, what influence does that have on how they see themselves in relation to others, and on how they live their lives? The categorization of people because of the place they live in and how this shapes self-identification are key themes of this book. In this chapter we draw critically on Lefebvre's concept of the production of space (see also Castells, 1997; Modan, 2007) to analyse how particular physical spaces are conceived by planners, architects, politicians, and other outsider professionals; how they are perceived by residents themselves; and the interconnections between both of these and people's everyday lives.

In combining historical and spatial analyses we argue for the importance of unfixing areas of social housing in order to move away from static and essentializing stereotypical representations of 'council estates'. People's spatial mobility over a life time – their histories of moving – provide insights into what Harvey has referred to as the 'variety of spatio-temporalities'. Like so many other scholars Harvey emphasizes the ways in which '*immigrant* populations . . . internalize heterogeneous spatio-temporalities depending upon how they orientate themselves between place of origin and place of settlement' (Harvey, 1996: 52, cited by Milgrom, 2008: 269; our emphasis). But as Feldman (2007) has shown historically, it is not only immigrants who move. In this chapter we describe different processes by which people have moved or been moved to the case study estates, while in Chapter 6 we explore further the connections that residents maintain(ed) with other places. Thus taking as central the understanding that places are 'open, porous and the products of other places' (Massey, 1995: 59; see also Keith and Pile, 1997), we challenge the notion of these 'deprived' estates as bounded or isolated.

The chapter draws on both archival and oral history evidence to illustrate the diverse and changing range of meanings which the physical space of the estates has had for residents, all of whom have family histories of moving in and/or moving out. We begin by telling the story of the story of the building of the North Earlham, Larkman and Marlpit estates, and explore the influential myths surrounding where the residents came from, what they were like, and the instrumental action of the local state in moving groups of people *en masse* – streets at a time – from one place to another. In doing this we show how representations of space that contribute to essentializing, indeed racializing, council estate residents, can also have the effect of deflecting attention away from the structural causes of social and economic inequality.

The chapter then moves to critically interrogating the stories which surrounded the estates in order to reveal the agency of residents themselves in both reproducing and resisting categorization processes, and the ambivalences surrounding this. It was one thing for residents to use the idea of the estates as being a deprived area to seek large-scale funding from the state in an application to the New Deal for Communities in the late 1990s (see Chapter 4). It was quite another for residents to hear middle class non-residents portray the area as poor, or to indicate that those who lived there were 'thick' or inclined to criminality.

In the third section of the chapter we focus on the sights and sounds of the estates, both in the present and in the memories of different residents and ex-residents. Work by acoustic ecologists has emphasized the importance of the concept of 'soundscapes' as spaces and landscapes which are bound together through the experiencing of particular sounds. It has also highlighted the role of 'keynote' sounds of a space – which may both define a place for its residents, and be almost unnoticed by them – while showing how these might change over the course of a day or with the seasons (Schafer, 1977; Truax, 1978; Wrightson, 2000).[1] Using this approach, we draw attention to the importance of economic change in shaping everyday physical life in the estates as well as illustrating the diverse meanings of the area to its residents.

Drawing critically also on Newman's notion of defensible space (1973), the chapter then moves still further downscale to the private and public spaces of houses, gardens and garages and the boundaries between them. Here our concerns are with not only the relations between households but also within them. As Sibley (1995b) has shown, home can be a source of power and conflict and it is important to understand the 'polar tensions surrounding the use of domestic space' (1995b: 94), which we argue needs to encompass the garden as much as the house. Once again we reveal how the meaning of social housing estates to those who live in them cannot be read off from the conceptions of outsiders. Using an historical perspective also demonstrates the changing use of 'public' space, as we contrast participants' childhood memories of the estates as bordering on and closely relating to, a rural area, with a more urban present. In all this, as Samuel and Thompson (1990) have warned, it is important to be wary of the role of memory in constructing overly rosy narratives of the 'good old days'.

A notion of borders is central to the final part of the chapter, where we move away from looking at all three estates together to bring in spatial practices that marked boundaries between and within them. Boundaries and distinctions between the estates were highlighted in conversations held 'in the estates' with participants. And yet those same participants, in other circumstances and places, might portray where they lived as a single area of Norwich – often, albeit reluctantly for some, 'the Larkman'. This final section of the chapter provides a link to the discussions of poverties, (un)employment and resourcefulness that follow in Chapter 3

Marlpit prefabs and resident (with thanks to Mrs O'Callaghan)

and anticipates the relational approach to class identifications that we analyse further in Chapter 5.

The myths of the 'Larkman'

Many council estates built in the twentieth century were peripheral in relation to the urban areas they were attached to, both spatially and socially, with the two often going hand in hand (Hanley, 2007). The North Earlham, Larkman and Marlpit estates were no exception in spatial terms – being constructed in phases on the outskirts of Norwich (Horsey and Muthesius, 1986; see Maps 1 and 2).

The part of the North Earlham estate closest to the city was built first, in 1927–28. The bulk of the construction in the area, however, took place in the years 1936–38, which saw the completion of the North Earlham and Larkman estates, and the core of the Marlpit estate, located on the other side of the busy Dereham Road. Most of the houses in this phase of building were of brick, with modest front gardens and extremely generous back gardens. After the war an area of prefabricated housing was erected on the Marlpit which remained until the 1960s when it was replaced by newer style housing and flats. This period also

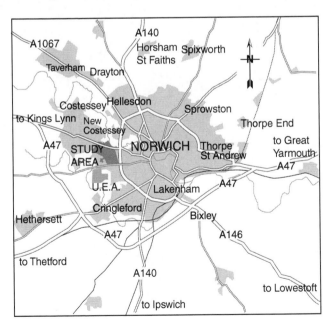

Map 1   Location of estates in relation to the rest of Norwich

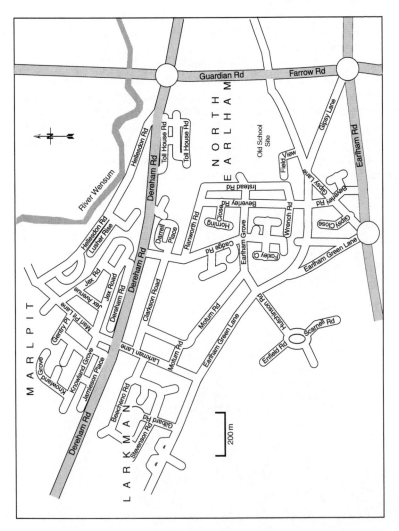

Map 2 The three estates

Street view © Chris Clunn

saw the construction of a small block of flats on the edge of the North
Earlham estate abutting the Dereham Road.

A series of myths grew up about the Larkman estate in particular.
Throughout its history other Norwich residents, including those on the
adjoining estates, have portrayed it as a dirty, undesirable place, characterized by criminality, low intelligence, high uptake of benefits and,
more recently, widespread drug use.

Yet the other two estates have been associated with these to varying
degrees as well, which was particularly irksome to some Marlpit residents, who had been brought up to believe that the Larkman housed
the descendants of its original inhabitants, who were ex-slum dwellers
from the centre of Norwich, and that they were of a 'lower' order:

> I had that instilled in me by my mother.... You don't talk to people
> over there [laughs]...they lowered the tone, you see...most of the

people who live in the Larkman came from Ber Street and all the bad areas, you know the lower class house [s] in the city years ago.

(Diane Kemp)

Another Marlpit resident we spoke to concurred:

the basis of the Larkman was made up of people from very poor areas, like Ber Street... families that were a lot of trouble and that, before the war... and as they cleared the areas, and they built this new estate... in the 1930s, they then moved them there. And I think that's how it got its reputation. In other words, give a dog a bad name, really.

(Joe Hastings)

But other estates in Norwich, like Catton Grove, had also been built under slum clearance legislation. What then made the Larkman keep its 'slum' tag long after it had been lost from the other council estates of the city? In part it was perhaps due to the fact that North Earlham and Larkman together – comprising 1280 houses – made up the largest continuous area of council housing in Norwich, with the bulk of construction and habitation taking place in a concentrated 3-year period, during which a largely peripheral rural area turned into a fully functioning residential area (1936–39).[2] The reputation of the Larkman, however, became more specific than merely being tied to slum clearance. The inhabitants of the Larkman estate, as Diane Kemp and Joe Hastings remembered, were believed to have come from a particular area in the centre of the city – Ber Street – which carried myths of its own.

Two retrospective pieces in a local paper attempted to give a flavour of the Ber Street area, describing it as 'a perfect rabbit warren of yards, alleys and lanes, whose atmosphere was not improved by the stench of a tallow factory. The police patrolled it in pairs, and middle class families made a detour to avoid passing through it'. The pieces also suggested that it was inhabited by various minority groups, including a 'colony' of Italian families and 'drovers, Irish tunnellers, travelling tradesmen and labourers, street musicians, boxers':[3]

To the outsider, they appeared more like slum scenes from a Dickensian novel – rundown and falling down. Yet amid the squalor there was a close-knit and thriving community where the people existed almost in a world of their own and in many ways were a law unto themselves. Such was the slope on which they lived that people spoke about going 'up the city' as if they were no part of it!... It was full of pimps and tarts and there were plenty of fights.... Urchins, left to fend for themselves on the streets, fell into petty crime, stealing food to stay alive.[4]

Such accounts of the origins of the people of the estate were widely believed, and in fact fed into 'official' discourses about the Larkman. If myth had it that the residents of the estate were removed from the Ber Street area of Norwich, itself holder of the reputation as the 'worst' part of the city, it requires a very small leap of imagination to see how the 'roughest' slum dwellers became the 'roughest' council tenants. So, for example a preamble in a pamphlet created in the 1980s explained how

the original population was re-located from the Ber Street area of Norwich during slum clearance and residents retain much of their former rejection of 'authority' and an independence of thought and action. This, combined with strong family loyalties, makes it an interesting and demanding environment to work in.

(Larkman Project Group, c. 1984)

A more detailed account was created for another pamphlet representing the work of 'Project Link'. This initiative, in common with Norwich council's 'problem families' initiative of earlier years (Taylor and Rogaly, 2007), identified families whose children were living in 'a chaotic environment amid emotionally distressful and poor material conditions', and aimed to target support at those families. The report gave an extensive introduction to the history and culture of the Larkman area:

The housing... was part of a large slum clearance programme; so that most of the original population came from families who had been relocated to these new council houses... To be fully able to appreciate the complexities of this interesting community, it is necessary to have knowledge of the social and environmental factors which brought the people to the area. In the 1930s railways systems were developing rapidly throughout England. The shortage of manual workers brought labourers from Southern Ireland... some coming to Norwich and settling in the Larkman area where they were offered housing as an incentive to stay.... [This] coincided with the loss of jobs for farm workers in the rural parts of Norfolk.... These hardworking labourers flocked to the city looking for work and inevitably were housed in the most rapidly expanding part of the city – the Larkman Area. The 'country' people and the 'townsfolk' found it difficult to mix because of their entirely different cultural backgrounds. They remained separate; which led in the 1950s and 1960s to inter-communal violence. During the 1950s many authentic gypsies [sic] (known locally as diddy coys) settled in this area of Norwich.... At this time it was the general policy of Local Government to house like people together, and this resulted in small 'ghettoes' being established. For example, Motum Rd housed mostly travellers [sic]; Stevenson Road, city folk; and Ranworth and Irstead Rd, country people.

(Docherty, 1989: 5)

A narrative thus developed whereby the Larkman was seen as being inhabited by people from the worst slum area of Norwich, who were immigrants, casual workers and 'roughs', and over time they were added to by other long-stigmatized groups – Irish labourers and 'gypsies' (see Munt, 2007: 3). In a quasi-anthropological analysis of life on the estates, these antecedents are seen to feed into particular anarchic attitudes towards authority and work. All these categories contained elements of truth – we did speak to people who had been cleared from slums, or whose families had migrated to Norwich from the countryside or from Ireland. And yet, as we shall show, these identities were far from fixed, were often partial, and never expressed to us as speaking of a wider collectivity of experience (see Valentine, 2007).

In Docherty's formulation, which both fed into and was informed by popular attitudes towards the area, it was the *people* rather than the place that were the focus of the myth. Yet it is important to acknowledge the representations of space contained in narratives about the slums and the estates even before the estates had been built. The Labour council and its officers believed that the creation of healthy, well-designed housing estates would erase problems associated with the slums.

As with national Labour Party policies, the built environment was seen as the key to, not only removing the slums, but also in eradicating the 'slum mind' of those removed from crowded inner city areas. Cllr Mabel Clarkson, a pivotal figure in Norwich's slum clearance programme, spoke optimistically of the new housing:[5]

(1) Repairs will be kept up, the houses are well spaced, allowing free access of the general public, who will soon cry out about any serious delinquency.

(2) All the houses have gardens, thereby giving free circulation of light and air and avoiding the dreadful depression produced

by street after street with dismal houses built right up to the pavement.

(3) The educational effect of having reasonable dwellings and surroundings will, it is hoped and expected, produce some housepride in the occupants.[6]

And yet the areas set aside for rehousing people from the slums were not a set of blank canvases, but rather countryside on the edges of the city, with its own history and character. Before the construction of the North Earlham and Larkman estates the land had been farmed, with the adjoining Earlham Park confirming the pleasant, rural nature of the landscape. In line with national trends this area was becoming suburbanized by the 1930s, and it had seen some building of private homes for ownership. The following is an extract from a letter from the owner of one such home to the council protesting against the building of the estates. In it, the writer reproduces pejorative categorizations of residents of the Ber Street area:

> The Building Committee of the City Council of Norwich is removing slums from Ber, Oak, etc., Streets, and causing teeming colonies of streets of cottages in Earlham here, to *the utter disregard* of the health and comfort of inhabitants of some seventy-five...bungalows and houses.[7]

Five other owner-occupiers wrote a letter of protest over 'the proposed erection of a public house', which asked that it might be sited in a more northerly location (and hence further way from them).[8] In Lefebvrian terms, the spatial practice of protesting reveals the collision of the perceived and lived spaces of the two different sets of residents, the suburban owner-occupiers and their dream of a little Eden, and ex-slum dwellers being offered short-distance migration to a new (and cleaner) life. And yet, when we looked closer into the archives and into the oral accounts of the early years of the estates we found spectra of experience, expectations and behaviours that challenged the representations of the space of the estates as divided into solid binary categories with clear internal boundaries.

First to take the idea of a 'slum dweller'. If we are to begin to destabilize the myth of 'the Larkman' we need to begin by questioning the role of Ber Street in the story. Exploring the construction of the idea of this inner city area of Norwich (Mayne, 1993) we might start with this response sent in by an ex-resident, entitled 'An insult to the people who lived there', to one of the newspaper articles written about Ber Street. This writer retrospectively resists the negative categorization of the area and its residents:

> Far from being 'run down and falling down' the majority of the houses...were in tidy terraces. Most had small front and back gardens, usually kept neat.... Sure we spoke of going 'up the city' – it was not the 'city centre' in those days – just as people talk of going into the city today. That does not mean we 'existed in a world of our own'. As far as 'law unto themselves' it was a very law-abiding area. I don't remember hearing of burglaries or shop-keepers being attacked by knife-wielding youths.... My father had two lorries and a car which had no locked doors or ignition keys required for starting them. They could be parked outside the house for hours and be driven away...we were safe walking the streets, and were certainly not accosted by prostitutes.[9]

In a similarly prosaic vein, John Burnett's father, who had lived in Ber Street before being moved to the North Earlham estate, had been a small trader who 'sold a bit of fish down there and that sort of thing', before branching out as a greengrocer. The lurid picture painted by certain middle class outsiders with such enthusiasm, and in particular the painting of Ber Street residents as the 'other', was more the result of a desire to exoticize the urban poor in a tradition stemming back to Henry Mayhew and other Victorian social investigator journalists, than it was grounded in reality.

If Ber Street then failed to live up to its reputation as a den of iniquity, what of the broader idea that the inhabitants of the area were moved onto the newly created North Earlham/Larkman estate out of their slum dwellings? Detailed archival investigation bore out McKenna's (1991) observation on the importance of periodization in understanding the process of council house building. As was common under the 1919, 1923 and 1924 Housing Acts, those initially receiving council tenancies were from what might generally be described as the lower middle classes and the skilled ('respectable') working classes.[10] Prospective tenants needed to prove that their income was regular and stable, and that the Town Clerk made an effort to ensure that those in arrears were evicted.[11] So, for example, over the issue of arrears of one tenant, the Tenancies Committee 'could not agree that poverty was a justification for non-payment

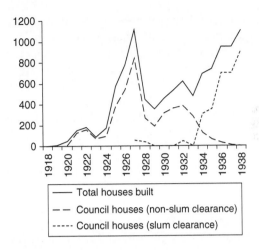

Figure 1 House building in Norwich, 1918–38
Source: NRO: Medical Officer of Health Annual Reports, 1931–39, Appendix F1.

of rent'. An analysis of occupations of head of households receiving tenancies in this period shows there was a preponderance of what might be seen as skilled working class jobs represented among council tenants, and a smattering of higher grade/white collar workers living on the newly created North Earlham estate.[12] A move to a council house would confirm their relatively secure economic status, which was consistent with national patterns of council house tenants for the era (see Burnett, 1993; Ravetz, 2001).

Figure 1 shows how house building in Norwich was concentrated in two periods – 1926–27 and 1933–38. The first of these periods which included the building of 248 houses in North Earlham thus *pre-dated* the major slum clearance programme of the 1930s, with 'tenants being allocated houses as individuals and not *en masse*', and tenancies granted with terms that required tenants to be able to cover the full cost of the rent and to be of a certain character.[13] Matters changed following the 1930 Housing Act which allowed councils to provide rent subsidies, and the following year the council attempted to open up its housing for those on lower incomes (particularly those with more than three children) by lowering the minimum income requirements for its prospective tenants.[14] By 1935, aided by the consolidation of power within the council of the city's Labour Party (Doyle, 2004), building new council houses under slum clearance legislation had become the most significant aspect of the council's housing programme.

In contrast to the myth that tenants of the slum-cleared areas had been moved *en bloc* to new council houses, as had happened in areas such as Sheffield (Frankenberg, 1966: 222), nowhere did we find evidence of wholesale removal of families from a particular area, or even street, to the North Earlham and Larkman estates. As Eva Garland remembered:

> And, they cleared all the area and... some people went to Lakenham, some went the Larkman, some went North Earlham. All different...

Importantly, housing built under slum clearance legislation was not necessarily allocated to people removed from particular slum-cleared areas. Even if housing was designated for a particular group on paper, others could end up living there. In Norwich, a certain number of houses were built for families containing tuberculosis sufferers,[15] including 50 houses on Larkman Lane. However, this did not mean that a 'colony' of tuberculosis patients was created. Rather, these houses were thrown into the common pool, with tubercular households being allocated tenancies throughout the city. The process of dispersing the population of the slum clearance areas from central Norwich to all of the new estates being built around the city's fringe was reinforced by the officially sanctioned concept of 'decanting' – whereby families living in overcrowded accommodation anywhere in the city could be allocated housing built under slum clearance legislation, leaving smaller households cleared from slum areas to move into the properties thus vacated.[16]

Other myths too failed to stand up to closer scrutiny. So, while we did meet *individuals* who either were, or had descended from, Irish migrants or former rural dwellers, we found no evidence of the kind of *group* migrations or identifications suggested by Docherty. This, for example, is Lily Haley talking about her experience growing up in the estates as the daughter of an Irish Catholic and using her own agency to avoid feeling singled out as a result:

> *BR:* Were there other people who were daughters of Catholic parents?
> *Lily:* Not that I knew.
> *BR:* [at same time] So that would have been a singled out thing and you would have been actually not going to the same assembly?

Lily: Yes I think this was the same out of school, Sunday school . . . you don't want to be singled out. You want to be with everyone else.

BR: Yeah, yeah so were you not aware of other Catholics around you at all?

Lily: No I wasn't.

BR: Or people with Irish backgrounds?

Lily: No.

If not then populated by the distinct groups of popular myth what caused the development of stereotypes about the area? One thing we can say for certain is that by the eve of the Second World War, the inhabitants of the second wave of building on the North Earlham and Larkman estates were, on average, demonstrably poorer than the other residents of Norwich's council housing. In 1939, only a year after the estates had been completed, they contained a fifth of the city's council housing. Yet, they received over a third of the rent rebates.[17] In part this was due to the fact that along with the three bedroom houses which made up most of the estate, larger houses had been built specifically to deal with cases of overcrowding, and were allocated to larger families. As we discuss further in Chapter 3, evidence from the post-war period demonstrated the continued and engrained nature of poverty among young large families in which there was just one breadwinner (Abel-Smith and Townsend, 1965; Gazeley, 2003).

The issue of larger families also became entwined with that of so-called 'problem families' (Taylor and Rogaly, 2007). For the 20 years for which we have evidence, council committee minutes record that disproportionately high numbers of families they defined as 'unsatisfactory households' (later referred to as 'problem families') were housed in the estates – typically a third of all those in the city. These families were often clustered into two or three particular streets.[18] Jane Knox, who had worked with people from the estates when they sought NDC funding, explained how this practice had continued under the later Area Seven policy:

> The idea originally was that you shove everyone who needs to have social work support and you can do it with far fewer social workers in a much more effective way. So you have one area that gets bad rent payers, drug addicts, ex-alcoholics the whole lot, you get them all in one area and you can throw a social services team at them and do it all really quickly. Very Machiavellian.

Overall, the effect was to ensure that the estates, and a few roads in particular, came to be associated with 'rough' families. An ex-policeman who had worked in the area in the 1960s and 1970s described how:

> you had to be flipping rough and tough to deal with some of them, because they were, the Clarkson Road, the Motum Road, the Beecheno Roads and that and Stevenson, they were thieves. And they'd break-in their own mates if they were hard up.

So far we have seen how the categorization of residents and the representations of the estates in which they lived became so inextricably entwined that people were often simply characterized by the reputation of the place. While we have shown that the 'Larkman' was not populated by subgroups of people with strong collective identifications, we can see how, as a direct result of council building, rehousing and social policies, certain streets within the estates became associated with deviant behaviour. However, in tune with a long tradition of essentializing and racializing poverty and the residents of low-income neighbourhoods (Lister, 2004: 72; Mayne, 1993), what stuck in popular and official imagination was the image of the slum – itself often condensed into the idea of 'Ber Street' – the Irish and Gypsies – the archetypical marginal 'others' of so much of the nineteenth and twentieth centuries. And in perpetuating the idea that the poverty and reputation of the Larkman was the result of the 'slum' inhabitants, whose characteristics were somehow handed down between generations – the poor are another country, they do things differently there – it shifted the blame away from the structural causes of poverty and the attitude of the council and outsiders to the area and onto the residents themselves. In the next section we draw on everyday life in the estates, its temporal and spatial variations and the changing perceptions and uses of public and private spaces.

Everyday perceived and lived space

Sights and sounds

Walking through the estates in the middle of a sunny autumn day, with bright yellow leaves against a clear blue sky, watching a grandfather wheel along his toddler granddaughter in a buggy, stopping to chat with a neighbour leaning over the gate in front of their solid brick semi-detached house, it is hard to think of the estates as anything other than a quiet suburban area. None of the visual signs which serve as a shorthand for 'deprived council estate' immediately jump into view: no threatening concrete alleyways, no swirling litter and plastic bags, no boarded up shops or houses. Look a little closer and you will see the crumpled cars in a number of driveways, the occasional front garden full of old white goods and sofas, and the number of older male teenagers hanging around in particular pockets across the estates.

Visual signals, as well as sounds, shift over the course of a day and across the year(s). For example, the sound and presence of children play-ing in the street, and teenagers hanging out, became prominent during out of school hours, and throughout the summer holidays in particular. John Burnett evoked the voice of his father going about his work as a mobile grocer, encapsulating both a time in the estates' life, and a strong childhood memory of the sharp division between the cultures of home and school:

> My old man used to shout out 'new po-ta-to'. You could hear him at school on summer day. And I wouldn't do nothing [at school], would I. I would just leave it and when he come round, he'd say, 'you ain't done nothing'. Well I said, 'I don't need it for fruit and veg, do I?' [All] I wanted to do is fruit and veg, and I won't learn up there, and I was right.

In autumn 2005, when we were based in the estates, there was a period of around three weeks during the Halloween/bonfire night period when each night the estates resounded with the sound of fireworks being set off. Similarly, during the 2006 football World Cup, several houses were festooned with St George crosses, while the Christmas period saw some houses emblazoned with lights and decorations. If we are able to expand our consideration of the keynote images and sounds of the estates from the time they were built, we might find some continuities, such as the sound and sight of children playing in the street, but also a number of changes: an increasing number of cars driving around the streets; the replacement of wooden with uPVC windows, especially among houses bought under right-to-buy policies; shifts in the use of gardens, includ-ing the arrival of conservatories; the proliferation of TV aerials and, later, satellite dishes.

Such changes, while apparently superficial, also speak, albeit subtly, of deeper structural processes. Moreover, the 'meaning' of the space

Kids on bikes © Chris Clunn

contained within the estates, how it has been used, experienced and represented over time has shifted. Further, individual residents and ex-residents perceived the spaces of the estates and changes in them differently. Harry Collins used a combination of images, sounds and smell to evoke his memory and feeling about the road on which he was brought up:

> they were very close community...on a Sunday morning you could walk down Stevenson Road and at eleven o'clock you could smell all the dinners cookin', that sound a bit silly probably to yer...you could smell the roast beef or whatever meat they had cooking and all the old people or mothers used to be standing in the gate talking to each other and the fathers would be cutting the hedges.

Cars in gardens © Chris Clunn

If the meanings and symbols of a place which make it home for an individual change over time, and can be invoked, as in Harry's case, to reveal a sense of loss, they are also relational, being deployed to compare the estates with other parts of the city:

> As a friend so nicely put...it, 'you've made it into a white trash neighbourhood, but that's a step up from a white vermin neighbourhood'.... So that's an external perception of the area I'm now in and the area I was formally in: more nasty Christmas decorations, but at least people who cover their house in nasty Christmas decorations are probably not on smack.... I mean apparently this house once had tenants in it who sold the tiles of the roof, so [laughter] I think you can assume if somebody's put up a flashing Santa, then skag [heroin] is not their drug of choice.

These two quotations indicate the importance of understanding the multiple meanings of the space of the estates. While dominant discourses in the city have continued to represent the estates as 'rough' or 'deprived' – most recently in order to win funding as a New Deal for Communities area (see below and Chapter 4) – we now use the example of gardens to explore how, in the context of individual life courses, the production of the space of the estates must be read as far more complex and ambiguous.

Moving histories and gardens

Central to the building of the new council estates was the belief of the planners in the importance of gardens in providing healthy and pleasant surroundings for the working class inhabitants moved out from the slums.[19] Houses built between the wars were provided with large enough gardens for families to produce a substantial portion of their vegetables, fruit, and sometimes livestock. Embedded in the memories of many older research participants were narratives of well-tended gardens, typically by their father, but sometimes with themselves as children having a role in the process:

> *Fred Hall:* Once the boys got old enough, I mean, you had to...feed the chickens and...you all had your little jobs to do. Not like...
> *Yvonne Hall:* Remember bees, and peas and sprouts.... And the gooseberry bushes were all up each side, up to the top. I mean I ain't got so much room now 'cos the conservatory there, but it used to be all the way up there.

In order to encourage pride in their gardens, all council tenants were eligible for entry into the annual garden competitions held on every estate and judged by the council.[20] These competitions clearly tapped into the enthusiasm of at least some of the residents. Valerie Draper remembered how her father 'was proud of his front garden. Years ago they used to give him prizes for gardens. I can remember my dad getting a third or something'. In contrast, the competition between Harry Collins' stepfather and his neighbours appeared to be rather more informal:

> They used to have competitions...and one day my father said to me 'I'll give you sixpence if you can go up the yard and find a stone in my garden that's as big as a sixpence. And if you find a stone big as a sixpence, for every one you find I'll give you sixpence'. I couldn't find one!... That was raked so beautiful and all the stones he used to put

on the garden path... and we weren't allowed to go up that garden. If we were outside here playing with the ball, outside the back door and an accident, a ball went on the garden it has to stay there until them vegetables had grown. He wouldn't even walk on it to pick it off!

But not everyone could look after a garden. In 1948, a national survey by Mass Observation suggested that lack of time – through having young children – and poverty were common reasons for not maintaining one. Planners may have envisaged the children playing in gardens alongside the fruit and vegetable beds, but instead the absence of public play space[21] contributed to them playing in the streets and surrounding fields.[22] Such conflict is implied in Harry Collins' tale of a football being left in the vegetable garden until after the crop was harvested, which could well have been profoundly frustrating for a young child: adults and children wanted different things from gardens. Internal domestic politics also influenced the care of outside space due to pressure on resources:

> I never had the money, this is the thing. I still don't have much. But, you know, just something like having a lawnmower. I mean we were in, or *I* was, *he* wasn't in poverty, because... he would just spend it, but even the simplest things would be just out of my reach.... But I certainly... never spent any money on the garden whatsoever.
>
> (Lily Haley)

Gardens were also one of the sites in which neighbourhood relations were enacted. In some cases this could be the result of positive relations: Gail Steadman, among others, related how the bottom half of the exceptionally long gardens in her row as a child were all joined together, with neighbours keeping all their chickens in the same large, shared run.

Gardens might alternatively become the space in which conflicts were played out. Liz Barnes and her family were housed on the North Earlham estate in the late 1990s and initially felt very positive about the move, and especially about the gardens of the estates – 'the garden's fantastic you know and that's what's really good about this area is the amount of green spaces'. When they first moved in, their garden had been a central play and meeting space for the children of the street, which was welcomed by the couple:

> we had just a picket fence and all the kids would come and play in the back garden which was lovely if not a bit harrowing sometimes 'cos

they'd all be in there all the time... we had a big back garden... and also we had ride-ons...

However, as Valentine has shown (2007), a person's acceptance in a particular set of social relations may be contingent on fitting into particular implicit categorizations. In Liz's case, as a result of an accusation – completely unsubstantiated – that she and her partner were paedophiles, not only did people's attitude towards them shift dramatically, but this was mirrored in the use of, and their feeling about, the garden:

that summer... our immediate neighbours didn't speak to us... people that had known us for yonks, really sort of got into the malicious, and it was horrible and... I, in the end, got a fence put up, a big fence put up which I don't like and haven't liked it ever since... we've completely lost energy for doing anything in our garden.

Liz's narrative is a moving history in the sense that it reveals the emotions which were intimately tied into her use of the garden. It is also an example of the intrusion of 'the public' into what conventionally might be thought of as 'private' space.

Representations of council housing in place and time

In the context of negative contemporary representations of social housing,[23] it is interesting that the positive features of the gardens in the case study estates, as well as the design and layout of the houses more generally, were often highlighted by residents. Although such inter-war council estates had been criticized by outsiders for the pseudo-cottage housing and monotonous appearance,[24] they provided people with a popular form of high-quality housing. It was the post-war housing developments of the 1950s and 1960s, such as the estates described by Hanley (2007) and Collins (2004), that received the most sustained attack. But there was much variation in housing design within the case study estates too. Although less ambitious than many other places, Norwich's post-war housing programme nevertheless saw council houses being built of nontraditional materials, attempting different house styles: blocks of six storey maisonettes around communal courtyards, high rise towers, and houses sited around shared 'greens', with clusters of garages and connected by pedestrian alleyways. Residents of the North Earlham and Larkman estates contrasted the housing there (built mainly in the 1920s and 1930s) in positive terms in relation to the more modern flats on the western part of the Marlpit estate, and more particularly to the adjacent Bowthorpe development.

More than one research participant recalled with affection the prefabs that had stood in the western Marlpit from the end of the war until the 1960s. Gina Malley remembered them as being far preferable to the houses that replaced them. They had been put up on vacant land which was intended to form the next wave of the Marlpit estate, and represented an attempt by the council to house some of the thousands of bombed-out families in the city. As Gina remembered:

> they weren't what you would call attractive, to look at. But they were quite ... sought after. ... The kitchens were fitted, which was unheard of then. You had an inside loo, and separate from the bathroom, which was, then, quite luxurious ... for ordinary working people. And you also had a refrigerator. ... And cooker. That came with the house. You never had to buy them separate ...

Her memories resonate with Kynaston's (2007: 102–3) national-level findings that while planners and architects dismissed prefabs as 'fungus-like outcroppings', with their gardens, modern appliances and the fact that they were semi-detached or detached, they were in fact highly sought after by tenants. When Gina moved into her present house, built where the prefabs had once stood, the daily reality of living on the Marlpit was impaired for her by its design and construction. Her house, which was on the end of a row, abutted an alleyway and a set of garages:

> I mean I've had trouble with boisterous young boys. ... I'd get rubbish thrown over the wall into the garden all the time ... there's been very little done on this estate, even with the houses themselves. I mean we've still got wood window[s]. They're as drafty as hell ... they're not double glazing. So you do get condensation as well in the winter. You know dripping down the windows ... [and under the] windows, I mean, you got like holes there. That's just a board up there [indicating wall beneath window] ... pull that off, it's just a hole. Yeah ... in the winter, you get a draft come through there ... if the wind blow, that lifts the carpet up!

One key to understanding some of the limitations and failures with new designs of houses and flats, in contrast to the design of the prefabs as well as the older parts of the Larkman and North Earlham estates, is

Newman's concept of defensible space (Newman, 1973, cited in Ravetz, 2001: 188). His hypothesis was that particular types of building and lay-out could induce either social or antisocial behaviour. The latter resulted when design precluded any sense of personal ownership, control or surveillance over the immediate surroundings of the home. As Taylor and Brower put it:

> Keeping the house freshly painted and in good repair, the lawn and shrubs neatly trimmed and the flower beds brightly planted, one is telling one's neighbours 'I've invested in where I live, I like my neigh-bourhood, and I can be counted upon to help out if there is any local emergency'.
>
> (cited in Sibley, 1995a: 99)

By the 1970s there was more of an acknowledgement among planners and architects of the need and desire for private garden space, which was reflected in a move away from the provision of purely public gar-den space and a return to private gardens, albeit significantly smaller than they had been before. For residents living in other parts of the city where, prior to the change of policy, council maisonettes had been built around courtyards, the issue of public/private space remained a very live one. Jenny Ridley, who made an active choice to move to the North Earlham estate in order to leave such an area, painted a vivid portrait of the differences in how people and space interacted in her previous inner-city flat and on her new street:

> Globe Place was an area where actually the quality of the housing was arguably higher... it was a more modern flat which was more spa-cious and in better condition.... [Outside though] there's an element of territoriality that used to go on... there'd be a... pecking order and people would make themselves known as... the people who got away with things.... I think the communal courtyard was really... a no man's land. [Here in North Earlham, there is] a social convention about how you use the street and the road. And although you might get streets and roads that have a bit of a kind of gangland atmo-sphere... you've at least got the social convention to fall back on. And like people's gardens have an understanding of how they're used.

Here Jenny pinpoints the importance to her, a lone parent, of defen-sible space, and how the North Earlham estate, although far from

the centre of Norwich and as we have seen in many ways a stigmatized place, in fact offered her a far more attractive housing prospect
through its 'traditional' house-with-private-garden design. The more
recently built Bowthorpe housing to the west of the Larkman estate
also included such 'defensible space' and had been conceived as 'for
everyone' (Camina, 1980). However, the lack of space between the
houses was derided by several people. Take Harry Collins, once of
the Larkman, now the Marlpit, who had lived in Bowthorpe with his
family:

> *Harry:* You ask a policeman, that's like tin pan alley the Bowthorpe
> estate. If a policeman run after somebody he'd lost them because
> the designers who built the Bowthorpe done it all wrong any rate.
> It's too many little alleys you see, too many little pokey holes...
> Bowthorpe is a maze. When you get over there, I mean I can go for
> a long walk and people say 'where's So-and-so Road?', and I haven't
> got a clue, I don't know.
>
> *BT:* But some people say that it was meant to be much better designed
> than...the Larkman...
>
> *Harry:* [at same time] No
>
> *BT:* because they had better services...
>
> *Harry:* ...if you look at the Larkman estate there's more open space
> than there is at the Bowthorpe. I mean there's bigger gardens, the
> houses...are detached but then you have a break. There's about four
> or five in blocks in the Larkman estate...that's more open space.
> You've got the Bowthorpe you've got a garden about big as here to
> that window, a back garden. That's like little rabbit hutches over at
> the Bowthorpe...they're too close.

All the foregoing confirms that we cannot read the multiple and situated
meanings of the estates from the opinions of outsiders. While the houses
and the layout of the estates had built into them the representations of
space of architects and planners, and *their* intentions and expectations,
it was and is through the lives of the residents that the spaces and places
gain(ed) their layers of meaning. Building on this, the final part of this
section explores residents' own spatial practices in sometimes subvert-
ing the space and its meaning – in part through living out their lives in
contradiction to the idea that they are living in a stigmatized space, and
partly through how they use that space, particularly through children's
play.

Residents' narratives and spatial practices

White's work on the model tenement blocks of the East End (2003) demonstrates the importance of taking account of the narratives of tenants themselves for understanding the experience of living in the buildings. Yet at the same time, as we pointed out in Chapter 1, we need to be wary of the role of myth-making in people's telling of their individual life histories. Thus the memories of research participants, who had ambivalent or negative views of the estates, have been as important to us as those of residents who have challenged prevailing images of the area. The stigmatizing effect of the negative categorization of the estates and their residents were deeply felt by some research participants, whose associations with the area have been profound and unsettling: Lorna Haley's overriding memory of the Larkman is the feeling of 'shame' it induced in her; similarly Sharon Finn, a resident of Motum Road, spoke of how when she went out with an accountant from a local market town she had been so wrapped up in being overwhelmed by the fact that *he* wanted to go out with *her* (because of the difference in social and financial status), that it had taken her a long time to work out that he had 'no personality'. Living on the estate 'did that to you. It made you feel as if you weren't worth anything'.

In contrast, those who remembered moving to the estates from over-crowded housing in the slums of central Norwich in the 1930s generally narrated positive memories of moving in. In common with other evidence of slum clearance and resettlement in new council houses,[25] the analogy of 'feeling like a queen' or moving into a palace was used by more than one research participant:

> I mean when we came to that house it was like going to Buckingham Palace. It was a real event, to turn, put a switch on, you know, and you got light where otherwise... in the old house we'd strike matches to get the candle or the gas to light so it was quite a transformation really...Oh it was marvellous! God! New bricks!... New paintwork! Oh great, you could even see through the windows, what you couldn't do before. [laughs]
>
> (Tom Crowther)

One participant remembers walking out of the city on a summer evening with his parents, when surrounding the estate was 'just woods', and when he saw the house they had been allocated he was 'overwhelmed by it. Because it was brilliant compared with what we had. Absolutely brilliant...we'd never had a bathroom or anything like that...it was amazing' (Joe Hastings).

For young married couples, it was often less the electricity and inside toilet that made an impression, than the simple fact of finally having somewhere of their own. The housing shortages of the 1940s and 1950s meant that it was common for newly-weds to live with one set of parents, sometimes for years, before being allocated a house of their own:

> it was delighting in thinking we'd got...a three bed-roomed house, with two little ones at the time, and away from all the hustle and bustle of poor Mum's house. And all the agro with my sister cos we didn't get on. Oh! we used to fight like cat and dog.
>
> (Marjorie Lovell)

In these instances, people's reaction to being resettled might be seen as being remarkably congruent with the official discourse of Labour's resettlement programme – for both council and tenants the estate was not a stigmatized space, but rather one which offered a new life and hope.

Moreover, some residents, particularly women, articulated life in their houses on the estates as part of a narrative of personal achievement, which included bringing up their children to be decent and hardworking adults, and being good wives and neighbours. As Diane Kemp emphasized, 'I mean none of [my children] ever got into trouble, none of 'em have been to prison...they've just had ordinary lives, grew up and got a job and got married and gone'. For one woman, a migrant from the Republic of Ireland who came to England to escape poverty and family abuse, and whose move to Norfolk was part of her recuperation from tuberculosis, the allocation of a house on the estate was central to establishing her identity as a mother and a housewife. She, as with virtually all the women interviewed, remembered, and could describe, the layout of the domestic space in great detail and the amount of work it took to keep it 'immaculate'. Woven into her memories of the house were a strong sense of belonging – neighbours keeping an eye out for her children, 'nearly all' the street on holidays at the coast – and that, despite the reputation of the area, she had made a success of her family.

For those born on the estates with no memory of slum living, the physical space of the estates could still encapsulate a world in which immediate and extended family and neighbours provided a network of security that provided a framework for their lives:

> I was brought up on there, lovely place to live... soon as you walked on the road, in my day when I was a kid, it was like going into someone's house you, kind of go through the door and the doors shut, you felt secure all the way along the road you knew all the neighbours, by 'auntie' and 'uncle' and they were all looking out, they're all snugging out the window... [laughs] we used to think they were nosey but they were all looking after you all.
>
> (Mark Fry)

For those who shared Mark's sense of belonging, it could act as a buffer to the hostility – real and imagined – experienced by residents of all three estates when they went out of the area and faced the negative attitudes held about the estates by the rest of Norwich's population. However, others experienced a sense of exclusion *within* the estates. As Sibley suggests, a person may be seen as 'in the "wrong" place' if there is a 'stereotype that locates [them] elsewhere' and vice versa (1995a: 100). Among the relative newcomers were two Filipina nurses, Rose and Josephine.[26] When they were interviewed together, they talked about their own and another Filipina friend's experiences of hostility in the estates:

> *Rose:* We have a friend from the Philippines... while she was walking, some bunch of children said to her that 'you go back to your place.'
> *Josephine:* Yeah, I remember too, I met a young adult. And he asked me, 'oh, do not step on my garden.' But I couldn't find any garden there, it's really a road, it's a public use. I couldn't find any garden ...
> *Rose:* I think sometimes it's better for you to walk [these streets] in the uniform. While you're on your uniform, in this place, rather than on your own clothes.
> *BR:* That's interesting. So how do you think people see you when you're in your uniform?
> *Rose:* ... during night time, from the hospital, [I] usually remove my jacket. And let them see my uniform. They just shut up.

For others, there was an element of self-exclusion. Soon after Liz Barnes moved to the estate, she and her partner co-founded a toddler group in the centre of Norwich, rather than joining an existing one in the estates. Several years on, she has continued to use the same group as a source of social support. Although she very much appreciated the quality of her house and garden, she felt at home with what she referred to as 'alternative' culture and had only a limited sense of belonging to the place she lived in:

> There was a few people to do with Quakers that had little ones and they were all a bit alternative and didn't quite fit into ordinary things that were going on so we very much sort of had our own thing which was great. There was only about ten of us and it's completely continued. I think my support network was right off the estate really.

Children who did spend most of their time in the estates and the surrounding area developed spatial practices that both reinforced and subverted official and popular representations. As we have seen, the provision of gardens did not automatically translate into child-centred play spaces. So the streets and the surrounding fields and rivers were central to childhood memories for all of our interviewees growing up before the 1960s. The vivid stories we were told of sliding down haystacks, wading in the river, and being sent off all day with siblings and friends and a bite to eat, in one sense resonate with council aims to provide a healthy environment for children. Harry Collins' memories of play are closely tied to the seasons, and give a flavour of the strongly 'rural' nature of childhoods on the estates in the first 30 years of their existence:

> *BR:* You were born as you say in '46 and you were living on Stevenson Road. Do you remember playing out there as a child?
> *Harry:* Oh yes a thousand and one times. We were like Tom Sawyers and Huckleberry Finns. [laughter]
> *BR:* What sort of things did you do?
> *Harry:* In the summertime we used to have popguns and things like that. When they wore off we used to play hooples and bows and arrows and go bird nesting...adventurous.... Down the end of Stevenson Road where the Fourways centre is now there used to be one big field, corn field and we used to play it on there. And that's so lovely you know? And harvest time we used to run behind the combine and get the rabbits.

Yet, many of the stories also demonstrate how such adventures became a source of conflict between children and householders or the authorities. As Sibley points out, children's 'conceptions of time and space' are often 'at variance with those of controlling adults' (1995b: 99). And while older people tended to construct the play they engaged in as 'harmless', often in contrast to the activities of today's young people, it is clear that others construed their activities as a problem. The council's housing committee minutes are peppered with complaints from tenants, owner-occupiers and officials of children using space in ways not intended by adults. From the early days of the estates there are records of youths being prosecuted for damaging trees, children playing in the streets and complaints 'about the nuisance, and particularly noise, arising from the use by children of the unfenced woodlands in Larkman Lane'.[27] The problems experienced by Gina Malley on the Marlpit due to children playing thoughtlessly or even maliciously in the undefined areas of the estates can be seen in this light. Outside the boundaries of the estates themselves some of the complaints were from owner-occupiers of private houses abutting the area, who no doubt felt that their fears of the tone of the area being lowered by the presence of 'slum dwellers' had been realized. Accounts by some research participants suggest, however, that some of these complaints might have been more than justified: John Langley remembered how he and his friends would 'set fire to the cornfields... and we used to gather all the bales up, and make dens out on 'em. And, and cos you tried smoking, don't you. Up goes the field!'

In what might be seen as a continuation of this tradition of (not unproblematic) rural and 'free' play on the edges of the estates, teenagers currently use areas of wasteland – the 'fields' – to ride their motorbikes. In the following extract, one revealed his feelings over the way in which his activities were viewed:

> Like they, like people bring dogs out, they just shit everywhere and don't pick it up. And same with, on horses.... We're going right slow, right slow past the dog. They just attack us. And they're complaining about us!
>
> (Dean Bradey)

It is clear that there are competing definitions of what might be seen as an acceptable use of space – and, as we have seen, such conflict is not recent but part of a continuing struggle. While such behaviours and conflicts have become associated with 'rough' areas, we must also accept that they may be a source of joy for the children concerned. Just as a tenancy on the estates might have been experienced as a step up, and the chance to establish an independent family home, so too might a childhood on the estates have provided a level of freedom and play now associated with Huckleberry Finn and other fictional childhood characters. The 'Larkman' may have been stigmatized by outsiders, but for those living there it could generate multiple, and sometimes positive meanings. For other residents, as we have seen, the ways in which space was lived in by the majority could generate a sense of exclusion.

Spatial practices of boundary making

It might be clear by now that rather than being clearly bounded and divided from the rest of the city, the place of the three estates is, and always has been, in fact far more complicated and blurred. Children play(ed) between gardens, streets and the fields around; the increasingly busy Dereham Road cuts off the Marlpit estate from the Larkman and North Earlham estates but also provides one of the direct bus and road routes into the city; families such as Harry Collins' move between the Larkman, Bowthorpe and the Marlpit, creating webs of personal networks and intimate geographies that bind the areas together and, as is the case with newcomers like Liz Barnes, tie them with other places. And yet, as with other areas that have been defined as materially and socially deprived, the estates are seen as being isolated from the rest of Norwich, as well as from society more generally: spatial proximity is not the same as social proximity (Lister, 2004: 70). In this final section of the chapter we consider what boundaries mean to residents, and reveal the importance of perceptions of the micro-geographies of an area in individual and collective identification processes and spatial practices.

In speaking about the estates, research participants referred as much to the people who lived there – the 'big families', their own relations and friends, or, in the case of relative newcomers, longer-term residents in general – as to the physical space and architecture. For people who had lived in the area a long time, the idea of respectability and personal distancing was crucial and was reflected in portrayals of particular streets, even portions of streets.[28] Thus, for example Flo Smith, who lives surrounded by one of the 'big families' of the estate and who has had problems with them in the past, was nevertheless at pains to stress how 'you often get riots up the top. You know what I mean, *further up the road*'.

Intimate associations of individuals with their surroundings can be, sometimes simultaneously, empowering and disabling. Perhaps the most extreme illustration of this we found in our encounter with Donna Carswell. Part of one of the 'big families' of the estate, she was born and has spent the majority of her life living on Motum Road:

Donna: Nine of us, yeah.

BT: Do they all still live quite close?

Donna: Quite close, yeah. There's one next door.... There's Kirsty who lives opposite. And then Leanne lives there. Two doors down my dad lives.

BT: So he's moved back to the area?

Donna: Yeah. Then you've got Malcolm who's with Gail – my brother. And then you've got Wanda, just over the road from them. Crystal is round about here somewhere. Sandra's on Irstead Road. There's only Melanie who doesn't live in the area.... I've actually lived in nine houses on this road. And I've lived up the top, and in the middle bit, what I'd call, straight to the top and then down here and that sort of thing.

She spoke very positively of the street, citing how she had felt it was a safe place for her children to grow up, and how in particular she enjoyed the experience of barbeques in 'the summertime, yeah, that's good... even if you don't invite them, you'll always end up with half the street round here anyway'. However, in the course of our interview with her she revealed how she suffered from panic attacks which were very place-specific: 'I'm OK from the corner [to] where I live.... But even now, I couldn't venture up the top of the road on my own.' Her story illustrates the profound, and sometimes troubling, link between space and individuals and the importance of invisible, personal boundaries in understanding place.

We have seen already how the estates, often referred to in shorthand as 'the Larkman', have continued to be designated by many in the city as 'the other', a place apart. Yet, when we interviewed people, what we rapidly found was how many different definitions of 'the Larkman' there were; for the people who had lived there, or in the neighbouring estates for a long time, the lack of consensus over the boundaries of this apparently notorious estate was striking. One local business owner told us that he regarded Motum Road as part of the Larkman. Another man defined the Larkman much more tightly as just Beecheno, Gilbard and Stevenson Roads. A third participant, who was brought up in Stevenson Road but now lived in the Marlpit estate, emphasized that that estate too was 'classed as [part of] the Larkman'.

For Harry Collins, the idea that the Larkman estate was confined to three streets with limited exits suggested a deliberate approach to managing residents. This strengthened his identification with an imagined collectivity of Larkman residents:

There's only two roads out from the Larkman. That's Stevenson Road, Gilbard Road and Beecheno Road, there's the Good Companions [pub] on the Earlham Green Lane and Larkman Lane.... So, if the police had problems they know they contained our people.... No one can leave that estate off them two roads unless they go down Monkey Island across the Bowthorpe or down to the Oval ...[29]

The micro-geography of the estates could be particularly important to young people, who themselves produced space in their boundary-making practices, for example if they become involved in gangs. Such practices are not confined to the Norwich or even the English context as this insightful passage from the study of a US town anonymized by the authors as Townsville attests:

As with all Western inner-city areas, the young people of Townsville are also actively involved in a diverse range of practices that sustain a sense of belonging and self-definition through making claims to public and private spaces as their own. These practices include walking, talking, gathering, shopping... the favoured spaces to gather during daylight hours are in either streets or public parks of the inner-city or shopping malls.... Actions and ideas of a teenager's subjectivity are often aligned along border-making spatial practices that hem their movements into particular places.

(Waitt et al., 2006: 231; see also O'Byrne, 1997: 83)

Here, and with great relish, Gail Steadman who as a teenager lived on the Marlpit estate, relates how in the 1970s she was involved in gang-fights with the neighbouring area of Costessey:

you hung around with 'em at school and that was all alright, but by the night time you'd be all up in arms. I can remember lay-ing underneath a caravan in some woman's garden seeing all these people walking past thinking 'oh shit', cos I thought they were all Costessey. [I was thinking] 'I'm going to get the crap kicked out of me, I'll stay here', and next minute I know I can hear rustling beside me and there's some boy standing there, right. And I thought, 'oh no!' So he's like, 'which one are you?', I go, 'where are you?'. He go 'Costessey', and I say, 'so am I' [laughing] and we lay still and I'm lay-ing there thinking 'oh shit!' [laughter] He thought they were Marlpit out there, you know and I thought they were Costessey ...

Gail's account highlights the importance to young people in the 1970s of territorial identification. At the same time she revealed its con-tingency on time and place: during school hours estate identity was relegated, while after school it became of central importance, but only, as Gail explained, at particular albeit unspecified times.

In discussing differences between the Marlpit and Larkman estates in 2005, Darren Harrison, a homeless young person, simultaneously revealed just how artificially constructed and ambivalent he felt those boundaries were:

BT: Is there much mixing between this side of the road and over at the Larkman and stuff?

Darren: No.

BT: Why not?

Darren: We just clash. Even though ... all my good friends live on that side. But they're all alright. They're the only actual people on there I do like. The rest of them are knob heads. Even little thieves ... and little toe rags. ... You see a group of us [from the Marlpit], you're going to be scared, ain't ya, but we're not that sort of ... but like, up on Larkman ... a group of boys if they see, they'll just terrorise them. They'll just be really out of order to them, we ... don't do that. We wouldn't go round terrorising people. I hate bullies.

What is perhaps most striking in Darren's account is his instance on the respectability of the Marlpit youth in relation to those from the Larkman. Seen in reverse, one resident (from North Earlham) portrayed Marlpit people as seeking to project themselves as superior: 'they spell fuck with a capital F over there.' As Pauline Jones, Marlpit resident, remembered:

we were always sure to say that we live *this* side of the Larkman. Always say, 'no, I don't live *that* side of the Larkman'. We always felt that that side of the Larkman was rough ... we would ask for Larkman Lane when we got on the bus, we wouldn't ask for the Larkman.

Pauline's everyday spatial practice – doing her best to make sure the bus driver and other passengers did not think of her as from the Larkman proper – shows how boundaries could be both constructed and deliberately blurred by residents. A different, more formal kind of construction was characteristic of another set of actors – social activists and professionals who were trying to win funding for the estates. In the following conversation Penny Langley, who had been involved in setting up a health action area during the 1990s, revealed how she played an active role in the representation of space:

> *Penny:* I had done an analysis of the 1981 census figures to show how the ward figures for Henderson Ward completely obscured the reality of life in the Larkman... the employment figures, the single parent figures, free school, all those things.... I looked at single parents which were huge in some tiny pockets there was thirty, forty per cent, you know at the end of Beecheno Road there's a little place there, but, but around the Larkman it was very high, unemployment was very high... and we included the Marlpit... the [medical] practice [was] there... there were high numbers of single parents. There was a big drugs problem in the Marlpit.
>
> *BR:* So that's, did you make the distinction between the new area of the Marlpit round the [Knowland Grove] bit and the Jex Road?
>
> *Penny:* No it was all one... it's peppered with middle class housing at the other end of the Marlpit up towards the pub but we did put the whole thing... it was to do with the [GP] practice, it was to do with getting more money and so we were using the practice area.

This was thus an attempt to construct the idea of the three estates as one, in spite of their different histories and physical characteristics. As Penny made clear, a range of social indicators revealed how deprivation across the estates tended to be concentrated in certain pockets, which along with the internal divisions within and between the North Earlham, Larkman and Marlpit estates, meant that experiences of life and understandings of the area were far from uniform. Yet, attempts to draw a line around the area and define the space within it as 'deprived' was a necessary step in order to receive attention and funding from outside agencies.

Crucially, the boundaries chosen by Penny were those that were later used in the definition of the area covered by the NELM (North Earlham, Larkman and Marlpit) Development Trust in order to win the New Deal for Communities funding that came on line in 2000 (see Chapter 4).

During the preparation of the bid, in order to ensure there were enough households to fit the criteria outlined by central government, Marlpit was included, despite the fact that a survey revealed a far greater proportion of owner occupiers there, and a higher level of people in work than the Larkman and North Earlham estates. With the success of the bid, lines which had in many ways up to that point only existed on paper developed a material reality of their own. As an area-based initiative, schemes, opportunities and activities were targeted at those living within the boundaries, while largely excluding non-residents.

In perpetuating the idea that the poverty and reputation of the estates was the result of the 'slum' inhabitants, whose characteristics were somehow handed down between generations, representations of the space of the estates shifted the blame away from structural poverty and the attitude of the council and outsiders to the area onto the residents themselves. The most recent construction of the area as deprived, in order to get funding under the New Deal for Communities scheme, reinforced the prevailing stereotype of the area as bounded and poor, and hid the ambiguities and fluidity of people's understandings of their area. The fact that residents themselves were forced to accept, and indeed to emphasize, their boundedness and deprivation serves to underline how agency operates within profound structural constraints. In the rest of the book we move on to consider in more depth how inequalities of material resources and power have affected the lives of the residents of the three estates, and some of the ways in which residents have responded.

Interlude 1: Tom Crowther (1929–2006)

Ben Rogaly

Tom was one of the first people Becky and I got to know when we started the research. He belonged to the local history group that was being backed by the New Deal for Communities project and had a collection of cuttings, photographs and writings that he was planning to put together into a history of the Marlpit estate. Tom had undertaken many moves in his life, but felt particularly positive about his two moves into the Marlpit: the first as a child in 1939, into a new house that felt like 'Buckingham Palace'; and the second – 'the best move I've ever had' – into sheltered housing in Knowland Grove, just months before we met in 2005. One of the reasons why Tom was so pleased to have returned to the Marlpit was that to him it was also known as the VC estate – several of the roads were named after men in the Norfolk regiment, who had received the Victoria Cross for bravery. Tom organized and completed the restoration of a plaque that had been put up to commemorate the men. 'I don't care what it takes me', he had told us, 'that *will* be finished.'

As I got to know Tom more, I felt he was genuinely seeking ways to help us with the research. At the same time, he made me aware that, on particular occasions in the past, doing things for people had made him feel foolish, sometimes resentful. Tom's telling of this aspect of his own life history had veered between anger and self-deprecating humour. At one point he told me about the time he had agreed to drive his ex-wife up to Scotland to visit her sick relative: 'talk about a mug, but...anybody who's in ruddy trouble I'll help.' He talked also of his resentment of the circumstances – obstacles to formal education, and a terrible accident at work – that had led him, as an adult, to *need* to run errands for people to earn money.

It had been one thing as a child growing up in 'what they call the slums' of Norwich to have been able to use running errands for people to earn cash for himself and his family:

I'm the eldest of [six siblings] but...we used to do all sorts of funny things, run errands for people...to get our sweets and that kind of thing or we used to buy five Woodbines and get a ha'penny box of tip top matches.... [My Dad] was jealous because he couldn't afford cigarettes and I could. [laughs]

It was quite another thing, as an adult father of four, at a time of less generalized poverty in the 1960s, to be so desperate that he *had* to run errands:

> I'd had several bits and pieces to do before... jobs which I absolutely detested but I done them because it was a way of getting remuneration, you know and getting money into the family. That was all I could do but the wages were very rock bottom.

This was a period – after his accident at work – during which Tom had faced extreme poverty. He felt that his individual experience was akin to the general dog-eat-dog competition between workers that his father's generation had faced in the 1930s:

> you had to watch your back as well because people would try and do you out of [your] job... they would tell the governor that... 'I could do the two jobs for you for the price of one' sort of business.... Get a little boldness and the other chap would be hoisted out... back on the street again, so I mean it was quite a desperate time.

The war had rationed the formal education available to Tom, and, fascinated by military marching bands from early childhood, he spoke bitterly of his mother, who had prevented him both from joining the forces and taking up an offer he received to join the choir school attached to Norwich Cathedral. Her priority, he said, was that he earn a wage for the family. Yet in spite of his frustration at not having been able to join up as early as he wanted, Tom was able to take up some of the work opportunities the war brought along, both in terms of money and, as a teenager, the potential for fun. He told us he found work building the new US airfield near Hingham:

> I found that quite hilarious 'cos it meant getting your hands all dirty... and the money was good. Worked... oh seven days a week 'cos the war was on and they wanted these places ready.... I used to start these blessed [tractors] up and then it got so at lunch time I used to go get in one of these lorries and I'd hare round this blessed track as if I was a racing driver...

But Tom's work experiences were rarely so benign and, in 1960, one job in particular caused an accident that multiplied the challenges he already faced in feeding his family. The job was with an agency that was going to cover the floor of a Norwich department store with linoleum:

I was getting this [roll of lino] off of this lorry this day and was about to swing [it] onto my shoulder and my mate says to me 'hang on Tom' and with that I looked round to see what he was at. I didn't know if I was going to hit him...and I overbalanced and that shot my back out...it wasn't very pleasant.... Anyhow I managed to get home and have my tea...I sat in my chair that night [in] somewhat more than discomfort, went to bed and in the morning I couldn't get up.

The doctor Tom sent him to the Norfolk and Norwich hospital where he was put into a plastic corset. Becoming agitated as he remembered the pain, Tom described to me what happened after he was discharged:

I came back home and...I went to sit in a chair similar to this, and jee whiz, oh, I nearly decapitated myself. The corset, which was plastic, shot up under my ribs, dug into the tops of my thighs there. Oh god, and I had to yell and ask her to help me up. I was alright in a vertical but by jingo, when I went to sit down it was a different kettle of fish altogether.

Tom described how he was subsequently classified as incapacitated and was not able to get employment. He started a one-man painting and decorating business but it was hard to get it off the ground: 'I haven't got the head of a business man to...charge people...for my holidays coming up and all this sort of thing which you should do.' He told the doctor he couldn't move without 'real agony'. The business teetered:

After that I hit a rough patch and work...dropped off.... I think it was coming up towards the Christmas period...I done anything that I could get hold of then...to sort of get us over the Christmas period and through the winter months...it was rather desperate.

It was often via such struggles and pain that Tom came to make friends with middle class professionals. One was the doctor who had treated him after the accident, who Tom said he often visited and shared many laughs with. He also stayed closely in touch with one of his school

teachers until the latter's death aged ninety-one. By contrast, his connection with Catholic clergy had made him both hostile to the church,
and, eventually, atheist. His encounters with clergymen began when the
same doctor encouraged him to convert after a nun had visited the family following the birth of one of Tom's sons. Tom remained Catholic for
15 years and became involved with the church, helping out with practical jobs, including consecrating a church – St George's on Sprowston
Road – by burying 'the bones of the saints in a little tin box on the top of
the altar'. But later when he became sick and could not work, he asked
the canon of the church, whom he had got to know, to come round and
advise him, and was so shocked when the man did not contact him that
he decided to give up religion altogether:

> I'd been down there called out the bingo numbers to get money to
> go towards the church. I didn't want him to give me money, I just
> wanted him to give me advice as to how I could get money or if he'd
> lent me the money I would have paid the beggar back.... I thought
> 'bloody hell, if that's religion', and I'm as good as he is, after all I
> come into the world the same way he does and I shall bloody well go
> out the same way he does.... And I've been an atheist every since....
> If there's a god well he must be bloody redundant.

This time of his life with young children had already been challenging
enough when, in 1957, after the family had been unable to keep up hire
purchase payments on their cooker, his wife had taken off back to her
parents' place in rural county Fermanagh with three of the children,
leaving him to do the caring of one son who was sick in hospital with
a skin infection. Contrary to images of supportive extended family in
working class 'communities', Tom said he had received no help with
childcare from either his own parents ('my mother had done with child-
minding') nor his far-off in-laws. Tom eventually saved up, took his son
and followed his wife, ending up staying in Ireland for over a year. Even
in comparison to his own experiences, Tom emphasized what he saw as
extreme deprivation:

> That is a god-forgotten country. By jingo I used to think I lived in
> the back of beyond when we lived in the slum but that was the
> end of everything...that was still on oil...lighting...there was not
> telephone or anything like that in the village.

Tom was also moved by what he saw as the plight of Catholics in Northern Ireland. He once told us how he had been recruited into the police because of his weapons training after 'two chaps had been blown up'. He said he eventually left because he objected to the completely different ways in which the two communities were policed:

> If it was a Protestant you turned your back; if it was a Catholic you done [them] for everything except for murder... that was what got me... I do like to be impartial. I treat everybody alike. I don't like to segregate people.

Yet Tom held strongly hostile views about Muslims, something, which as we explore in Chapter 6, he shared with certain middle class media commentators and politicians as well as with some other estate residents. Given that he also told me disparaging things about Indians in Britain – 'they're just swelling the ranks of unemployment and they are taking over essential houses' – I was anxious when I bumped into him in a café just as I was about to meet with an old Nepali friend, Mahesh, who had recently set up a community allotment scheme in the area. I needn't have worried. I went off to order some food, returning to find Mahesh deep in conversation with Tom, who turned to me and claimed: 'I've discovered he's a Gurkha'. This probably reflected Tom's sense that his true community was the military. When I had to leave for my next interview 45 min later, Mahesh and Tom stayed back. There was still much to talk about.

It was the same day that Tom told me his ex-wife had just died and that he felt like he'd had his legs knocked away from him. When Tom himself died a few months later, I took two of his sons a copy of the digital recordings of our interviews as well as printouts of the transcripts. They appreciated having these but were still completely stunned by his going, and had been frightened by the speed of his decline, as they and their other siblings had nursed him through the last two weeks. In spite of his capacity to make the best of things, Tom struck me as someone who had been knocked back many times in his life. It seemed grimly in keeping with this that, though he had needed round-the-clock nursing, social services had not designated him for terminally ill treatment until two days before he died.

3
Poverty

This chapter moves on from considering the construction of space and place in resident's lives to explore how living in the estates combined with material circumstances to produce particular categorizations and identifications around notions of 'poverty' and 'deprivation'.[1] We saw in Chapter 2 how from early in the estates' history the area housed a disproportionately large number of poorer council tenants, but how this had micro-spatial variations. Further, partly through the concentration of 'problem families' on a relatively small number of streets and parts of streets, there existed pockets of deep deprivation alongside relatively more affluent households. Thus through unpicking outsiders' image of the poverty of the area, we began the process of understanding the complexities and nuances of the experiences of estate residents themselves.

In this chapter we go further, exploring how people remembered material deprivation in their own lives and on the estates more generally. Within this we engage with the 'new paradigm of welfare' (Lister, 2004), with its emphasis on the

> capacity of people to be creative, reflexive human beings...to be active agents in shaping their lives, experiencing, acting upon and reconstituting the outcomes of welfare policies in various ways.
>
> (Williams et al., 1999: 2)

Lister believes that this approach offers a means of highlighting the 'agency of individuals in poverty without losing sight of the ways in which their agency is constrained by lack of material resources and power', and it consequently allows us to explore 'how far people in poverty are able to be authors of their own biographies' (Lister, 2004: 127; see also Chamberlayne and Rustin, 1999; Leisering and Leibfried, 1999).

Overlying the spatial specificity of deprivation within the estates were the broader contexts of welfare policy and economic change. Official discourses on post-war poverty stressed that the problem of deprivation had been solved through the construction of the welfare state (Coates and Silburn, 1983: 179). In this light, while being poor was 'normal', extreme poverty or rather 'failing to cope' with multiple deprivations led to the labelling of individuals or families as 'problem' by welfare officials and society in general (Taylor and Rogaly, 2007; Welshman, 2006). Paradoxically, the 'rediscovery of poverty' in the 1960s (Abel-Smith and Townsend, 1965; Titmuss, 1962), and official recognition that the welfare state had not removed deprivation, came at a time of full employment, overall increasing prosperity and equalizing incomes and life chances. While absolute poverty became less widespread, existing evidence suggests that those who remained poor felt increasing shame and marginalization from more prosperous neighbours and emerging consumer society (Roberts, 1995).

Growing economic and social inequalities from the late 1970s in the context of neoliberalist restructuring and 'deregulation' reinforced this process, with the gap between winners and losers being well documented and theorized (Bauman, 2004a; Harvey, 2006; Townsend, 1993; Townsend and Gordon, 2002), and with discourses shifting away from 'poverty' to that of 'social exclusion'.[2] Pahl observes how these post-war decades, while often thought of as 'normal' and the benchmark by which later shifts in the economy are understood, were in fact 'unprecedented', as, over the past 250 years, economic and social insecurity have been a far more consistent feature in people's lives (Pahl, 1984: 313; also Bauman, 2004a: 67).

Given the time frame of over seven decades within which we work, it might be more helpful to think about different 'poverties' rather than 'poverty' which perhaps implies a degree of stasis of meaning and experience. Work from the 1970s highlighted the importance of accepting the existence of relative as well as absolute poverty in an attempt to acknowledge the continued existence of deprivation in the context of very real improvements in general standards of living (Beresford et al., 1999; Lister, 2004; Townsend, 1979). However, while over time poverty may have been increasingly defined in terms of lack of access to certain consumer durables and lifestyle opportunities, evidence also reveals the continued existence of engrained material deprivation in the lives of

Britain's poorest residents (Beresford et al., 1999; Cohen et al., 1992; Gordon et al., 2000; Kempson, 1996).

As well as shifts in the meaning of poverty, extensive research has testified to the different causes and forms of poverty in relation to individual life courses (Barnes et al., 2002; Dewilde, 2003; Thane, 2007). Thus just as a family's experience of poverty had different manifestations and social meanings in the 1930s as compared to the 1990s, the same is true of an old age pensioner and a young family at any particular point in time. Equally research suggests that gender is a crucial factor in poverty. Childhood disadvantage has deeper effects into adulthood for women than men (Hobcraft, 2003), and within households women generally experience greater financial deprivation than men (Goode et al., 1998; Pahl, 1989; Vogler, 1994). For some women domestic violence further deepens their experiences of poverty and constrains their abilities to cope with it (Tolman and Raphael, 2000). At the same time, other work reveals the historic and central role of women in working class households in terms of their part in creating and sustaining social networks (Roberts, 1995; Young and Willmott, 1957); in relation to the feminisation of the labour market (Pahl, 1984); and in the context of challenges to 'traditional' working class masculinities (McDowell, 2003). Thus, in this chapter, we move on to consider how the personal biographies of poverty of individuals intersected with wider structural changes, in order to explore different experiences of deprivation over time.

This chapter is also centrally concerned to explore continuity and change in the ways people have *responded* to poverty. It has been recognized globally and historically that people living in marginal situations manage to juggle resources in innovative and complex ways (Datta et al., 2007; Fontaine and Schlumbohm, 2000; King and Tomkins, 2003). Accepting this, researchers in a range of national contexts have highlighted the importance of diverse household strategies with livelihoods increasingly viewed as multidimensional, dynamic and based on a range of factors beyond income alone. Here we consider the wide range of strategies of resourcefulness deployed by individuals on the estates. In terms of Lister's taxonomy of agency we consider people's means of 'getting by' and 'getting (back) at' that form part of their everyday strategies of survival (2004; see also McCrone, 1994). In order to avoid romanticizing people's resourcefulness in the face of disadvantage, we also consider the very real costs of such strategies.

Getting to the heart of understanding the nonmaterial effects of poverty allows us to explore responses to deprivation that move beyond simple economic 'rationality'. Helpfully, Mary Chamberlain's historical

study of Lambeth residents reveals the central importance of 'being seen'
to be dealing with poverty as a key coping mechanism, suggesting how
where

> poverty is circumvented, culturally and emotionally, if not eco-
> nomically, life becomes in part a pretence but pretence is central
> to survival... the gap between appearances and reality, the decep-
> tion, was relentless and year long. It was part of the culture, of the
> armoury of survival, part of the rhythm and structure of life. Decep-
> tion became reality, at the same time as it was a symbol of how life
> should be lived... Keeping up appearances was a point of pride and
> a rallying call for the family's morale... Deception became a form of
> resistance, a form of protection for the family when intrusions from
> outside could all too easily disrupt the equilibrium (1989: 11, 51).

In this way, we can see how coping with deprivation becomes deeply
entwined in self-identifications, and we reveal the moving (emotional)
history of poverty, for as Coates and Silburn recognize:

> you can reason with impeccable rigour about the condition of the
> poor, and still you will remain miles from understanding it, until your
> own feet can feel the ache that accompanies the proud display of little
> John's 'new shoes' from the reachmedown shop. It is these emotional
> and moral consequences of being poor that are hardest to grasp for
> those who have never experienced such deprivations themselves, but
> they are at the very heart and substance of poverty.
>
> (Coates and Silburn, 1983: 67)

In what follows, the first section narrates trends in unemployment
and changing conditions of paid work. It reveals growing inequality
not only between people with and without jobs, but also among those
in employment, as Norwich's manufacturing declined and the service
sector expanded. The second section traces changes in the experience
and meaning of poverty across the period. In it we show the shift
from widely shared experiences of poverty in the early part of the
period, to stigma and exclusion of the poorest people when prosperity
was generally rising in the 1960s. The lack of secure employment and
widespread long-term unemployment following the Thatcherite reforms
of the 1980s continued to produce poverty in subsequent decades. The
final section of the chapter examines people's resourceful responses to
such changes, which were definitely not conditions they would have

chosen. This included the use of humour and careful management of material resources.

(Un)employment

Although we repeatedly came across the assertion that multiple generations of families on the estates had experienced unemployment – feeding off and feeding into the 'fixing in place' stereotypes we explored in Chapter 2 – the stories we collected suggested a far more complex picture. While long-term unemployment was a clear cause of household deprivation, being in work was often no guarantee of financial security. Throughout the lives of many estate residents the struggle to make ends meet was enacted in the context of at least one adult household member being in formal paid work, with them and often other household members engaged in other income-generating strategies.

In the early 1930s, the economy of Norwich was based on a range of manufacturing industries (Clark, 2004), with a government inspector noting the existence of

> large mustard and starch works and boot and shoe factories and several foundries. Other industries are brewing, brick-making, tanning, chemical work and the production of malt vinegar and crepe, gauze and lace.[3]

Despite the first wave of municipal house building in the 1920s, the majority of workers in these industries were unable to afford council rents: in part this was the result of the seasonal and cyclical nature of many of the industries of the city which led to irregular employment. As Eva Garland remembered, her father, 'being in the shoe factory...had...six months work...on full time, six months unemployment'. Such seasonality was compounded from 1929 by the onset of the 1930s' depression, which led to long-term unemployment for many, despite direct employment schemes actively run by the council.[4] As Tom Crowther remembered of his father:

> He came out of the Forces...late 1918...and he worked for Porters the timber merchant as a circular sawyer. And from then when the depression set in, in 1929, he was out of work and you just couldn't get a job. Everybody would stab somebody in the back to stop them from getting the job in place of them. Oh! It was a very cut throat

business and my father was out of work from 1929 in the depression until 1939 when the airfield started up.

For external observers the long-term and engrained poverty experienced by some residents was largely invisible, as the absence of a single dominant industry masked the widespread and long-term unemployment of some. As a government inspector visiting in 1932 recorded:

the City does not bear the aspect of the depressed areas, though at the [Infant Welfare] Centre I visited I was surprised at the number of women who stated that their husbands were out of work.[5]

This inspector also noted the high proportion of women employed in many of the city's factories – particularly in the food processing and footwear industries – and the gendered and age-related nature of (un)employment:

There is no difficulty in finding employment for women and lads but . . . in the boot trade the latter are apt to be displaced at 18 years of age, a result attributed to trade union restrictions. There is little employment of married women; estimated to be not more than 15% of the total female employ.[6]

In line with Todd's (2004) work, this suggests the prominence of unmarried daughters within household finances, while research participants also pointed to the importance of married women's role within households. Bill Fussell's father experienced extended periods of unemployment in the inter-war period due to workplace injuries, leaving his mother to construct a livelihood based around her range of domestic skills:

Bill: Well, she was good at sewing. So she'd do a lot of that.
BT: So she'd do that at home would she?
Bill: Yeah. And she used to go and do a bit of cleaning . . . go and cook if anyone wanted. . . . You know, these big families, their big dos. Oh, she'd run rings round some of these what think they're clever, I can tell you. She could make things out of nothing that woman.

As Tom Crowther's earlier account suggested, the onset of the Second World War opened up new sources of employment: not simply for his father, as his mother was also able to take advantage of changed circumstances, and began to take in the laundry of American soldiers stationed around the city (see Chapter 6). This shift in the Crowthers' economic fortunes mirrored changes within the city and nationally, as Britain moved towards a state of full employment which lasted until the late 1960s.

In tandem with memories of work in this period, people spoke of a profound sense of spatial and social continuity between home and workplace, as work colleagues were often family or neighbours, and places of employment were close enough to go home for their dinner break:

> Well, at first I worked at, in shoe factories. Then I went in a brewery, with my aunts and my uncle, down King Street.... And we used to just cycle down Dereham Road and St. Andrew's Hill, and cycle across Prince of Wales Road, and glide along, and we used to do it.... Everybody came home at dinnertime.
>
> (Eva Garland)

For those who didn't work in factories, social networks were still important, particularly in finding work. Harry Wrigley for example, began his career as a car paint sprayer through using his wider family networks:

> my brother in law and his mate ran a car repair business. And from the age of twelve I got fed up with school and I wanted to work. So instead of going to school, I used to walk down their workshop.

And yet, there was a reverse side to this communality, as Fred Hall acknowledged: 'you were classed as an outcast if you didn't work'. Unlike the 1930s where unemployment was commonly experienced and bore little personal stigma, by the 1950s there had developed a sense that unemployment was *outside* rather than *within* collective experience. This was certainly the memory of Greta Fawcett and Jean Holmes, whose father was frequently unemployed:

> *Jean:* All of the neighbours, they all worked. He was about the only one who was permanently unemployed, weren't he, in our road?
> *Greta:* Yeah.
> *BT:* Did that make you feel a bit different?
> *Greta and Jean:* Yeah.

Despite dominant discourses of the male breadwinner and stay-at-home wife in the 1950s, the memories of our research participants also revealed the continued importance of women's incomes, not simply as supplementary to male incomes, but as an integral and crucial part of household livelihood strategies. However, the Hastings' discussion below shows, women's work often took place within a context in which its importance was minimized or even denied:

Joe: No, I wouldn't let her go to work. Although it was desperate I wouldn't let her go to work.

Rita: ... All I did, I did a lot of odds and ends.

Joe: Yeah, you did, sewing and that.

Rita: I used to go out and do housework, I used to go out and do supervising on the school playground lunchtime, I did loads and loads of dressmaking. I more or less taught myself dressmaking.

Other female research participants similarly revealed how their wages were a critical part of household finances and how they might take work against their husband's wishes. They also showed the importance of informal female networks in finding work and helping with childcare, as notes from Ben's interview with Marjorie Lovell demonstrate:

Marj said that the job 'came about through an argument'. She said you can't expect total agreement in every marriage though 'I know you're supposed to be Minnie Mouse'. James had needed a new pair of shoes. 'I said to my husband, "can I have extra to get them?" He said "you'll have to take it from the housekeeping." ' She told him she couldn't manage all the food, clothes etc. if she did that.... [She] asked a friend who worked there whether there were any jobs at UEA. She came back from work the next day and told Marj 'you've got an interview on Friday morning'. So when the day came, 'I didn't say anything', saw the children off to school. She saw the housekeeper at UEA: 'She was very nice'.... After returning from the interview she waited for her husband to come home. 'I gave him his evening meal. He was a calm man most of the time but when he did get angry he could explode.' Then she told him 'I've got a job.' 'Where?' 'At the university.' 'You're not going up there with them young lads.' The rowing went all weekend 'but I started work on the Monday'.

In Marjorie's account we can see how although her husband was in work, it was not sufficient to meet the needs of their growing family.

Roberts (1995) and Spencer (2005) have been among those showing how shifting gender norms from the 1950s in combination with growing consumerism changed women's working patterns. As we can see here, this did not mean that gendered attitudes within the household made the same transition.

One expression of both women's work and the need to supplement formal wages can be seen in the long-standing engagement of estate residents in casual work. Until very recently casual employment was largely based in the agricultural and related sectors, particularly seasonal harvesting and food processing work. Both archival sources and oral evidence suggest that although this work tended to be dominated by women, children and teenagers also took part in this work as did men who were working 'on the black'. Many of our participants remembered going fruit picking locally either with their mothers, or, when they were older, in groups of friends. This was a common activity, and not one confined to the poorest families on the estate:

> *Harry Wrigley:* Oh you'd do spud picking, strawberry picking, anything that was going.
> *BT:* Would that be in the school holidays or?
> *Harry:* Yeah, yeah. Because you could eat them as well, couldn't you.

However, for some, active involvement of children in income generation was vital, not simply a supplement:

> *Jean:* He was always, unemployed.... And unemployment was very unsociable to be.
> *BT:* So how did you manage for money then, did your mum go out and work?
> [laughter]
> *Jean:* I was one of the original flower girls, because he also would come home armed, with all these violets.
> *Greta:* Don't know where he got them!
> *Jean:* We never asked where he got them from. My mum would then do 'em in little bunches. And Greta wouldn't, so I had the dubious duty of going up the big houses up, well, they seemed big in those days, Earlham Road, selling, my flowers. And that weren't for pocket money, that was for the next meal.
> *Greta:* And he used to bundle up kindlin'. Didn't he?
> *Jean:* Oh yes.
> *Greta:* He'd get any wood he could find anywhere. (Greta Fawcett and Jean Holmes)

So then, even in the context of 'full employment', unemployment and deprivation existed, despite the presence of a male breadwinner; and other incomes, especially women's, were very important. Yet for many research participants this period was often depicted as something of a golden age in the life of the estates, sandwiched as it was between the depression of the 1930s and a gradual but inexorable decline of the core manufacturing industries of the city from the 1960s (Townroe, 2004). Unlike northern and Welsh industrial towns for example that saw an absolute rise in unemployment as the result of the closure of major industries, in Norwich the shift was hidden by the massive growth of the service sector over the same period. The council was active in supporting the expansion of the service sector in the city, through, for example, encouraging the creation of the university, but it was unable to prevent the decline of the boot and shoe factories and the closure of the Mackintosh/Rowntree factory and other food processing plants.

While the existence of large service sector employers, such as Norwich Union and UEA, have had an impact on residents of the North Earlham, Larkman and Marlpit estates, this has often been ambiguous and by no means unproblematic. Residents frequently assert that the former, as well as other large, employers in the city maintained a policy of not employing anyone from their NR5 postcode area. When they were employed by these organizations it was largely as builders, cleaners or security staff (see Chapter 5).

The personal experiences of our interviewees can be put into a wider context. Dinneen (1994) identified the changes in Norwich's economy as being part of the wider trends of globalization, casualization of the labour force, technological changes and the massive shift towards the service sector in employment opportunities. Figure 2 shows how at the same time as a levelling off of employment in the manufacturing sector in the 1970s and a steep decline from 1981, the financial and business service sectors grew rapidly. The years 1981–91 saw a rise in full-time employment in the Norwich area by 2.5 per cent, but in part-time employment by 51.6 per cent.

Dinneen further identified a trend of the workforce of Norwich becoming increasingly divided between 'information rich' and 'information poor' (more generally see Bauman, 2004a; Castells, 1997). This polarization of the workforce meant in practice an increasing gulf in life experiences between an 'expanding group of highly paid professionals' and 'an underclass of generally low skilled individuals who are unable to find stable employment, many of whom constitute the long-term unemployed'. As a result by 1991, while the UK average of unemployed people who were considered long-term unemployed was 26.8 per cent,

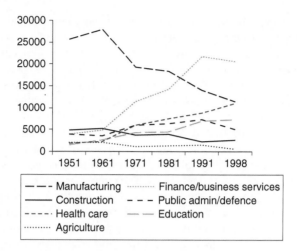

Figure 2 Norwich employment in selected sectors
Source: Clark (2004: 403).

in Norwich it was 32.2 per cent. In contrast the British average for the increase in managers and professionals as share of total workforce for the years 1981–91 was 26.8 per cent but for Norwich it was nearly a third (32.9 per cent). This led Dinneen to conclude that the 'Norwich area workforce is becoming polarised more rapidly than the UK [as a whole]'.

Consequently the estates, which up to the 1970s had acted as a vast reservoir of labour for the factories of the city, now became pools of high unemployment. The 1981 census figures showed the ward in which the estates are located had 17.5 per cent of men of working age registered as unemployed. However, a voluntary worker in the area in the 1980s and 1990s who did her own survey of the estates found that the ward statistics 'completely obscured the reality of life' as there were 'key little intense corners of both the Marlpit and the Larkman' where figures for unemployment and of lone parents reached 30–40 per cent. Thus, by 1999 over one quarter of households on the three estates were in receipt of Income Support and a third of households had no one in work (NELM, 1999).

In this new economic context there were continuities with earlier decades. The informal sector and casual work, which had always been a factor in many people's households, grew in importance, as did female support networks and employment (Pahl, 1984).

For those leaving school from the 1980s onwards, the world of gaining employment in factories with the help of family or friends had disappeared (Willis, 2000: 86), and what was left for those with few or no qualifications was a world of temporary or minimum wage 'McJobs'. Darren Harrison, who had left school with no qualifications at 14 and, when we met him, was living in a friend's shed:

> *Darren:* I need a job, it's just not as easy as everyone makes out it to be.
> *BT:* And do you think that if you get a job everything will be alright?
> *Darren:* Yeah, if I get a house and that as well. I can't get a job without accommodation, that's impossible, I tried it before... I just can't get up and go out. I've got to have a bath, after being in the shed I stink... I've worked everywhere, KFC, Burger King, Fat Cheese. I've just had dead end jobs, really... I think high school's a load of rubbish... my brother got... all his GCSEs, good GCSEs. And he's working at Morrison's.

In this section we have seen how the employment opportunities open to the majority of estate residents have changed over the period as a result of wider structural factors. We have also indicated that for many households it is important to move beyond looking at the formal employment of a primary breadwinner in order to understand their livelihood strategies. The role of casual and temporary work, sometimes in combination with claiming state benefits, and wider (often gendered) social networks in order to gain employment and provide necessary childcare and other support remained crucial factors for many people. In the following section we go on to consider more specifically different experiences of poverty over time.

Experiencing poverties

> *BT:* So did it feel like... it was poor when you were growing up or did you not notice?
> *Fred Hall:* You didn't notice.
> *Yvonne Hall:* Well, you didn't know different, because everybody was the same, if you know what I mean.

Without exception the early memories of older research participants centred around material poverty. While not coping with the challenges brought by poverty might have been stigmatized, poverty itself was not. These memories were set in the context of the 1930s depression, the war and austerity years when the whole tone of British society was pervaded with a 'make do and mend' mentality. However, for participants who had grown up in the 1960s and 1970s there were two main differences with the previous generation: not everyone described their upbringings as 'poor'; and for those who did feel themselves to be 'poor' this was linked to a specific reason – such as being the child of a lone parent, or having an alcoholic parent – and was tied to memories of stigmatization and marginalization. Since then, it has been poverty itself that has been stigmatized and resulted in 'exclusion' rather than particular 'poor' ways of managing poverty.

These older participants, who had experienced life in the 'slums' of central Norwich in the 1930s, remembered poverty as a combination of material deprivation and extreme uncertainty of income and housing:

My family was in and out of properties like playing a game of in and out windows. I remember we never settled anywhere at any one time … we had some funny meals but we never went hungry. I mean bread and butter and jam for Sunday night tea was a luxury or if you've got custard it was an added luxury. [laughs]

(Tom Crowther)

Well into the 1950s, council records demonstrate that some households routinely had no, or insufficient, beds and bedding, mattresses and furniture, with some families sleeping on the sitting room floor covered only in coats. In some cases furniture had been 'chopped up and burnt in the cold weather' and then not replaced for several months.[7]

The sleeping arrangements for this family are very poor. There is one single bed with a mattress on it and one blanket. There are two double sized bedsteads with springs partly broken in both, but no mattresses or bedding of any kind. Mrs Edwards states that she and her husband sleep in the single bed and the children in two prams and a carry cot. … The three youngest children are usually scantily clad with bare feet.[8]

This archival evidence was borne out by the memories of participants who had been children during this period. At the same time, the following discussion between Valerie Draper and her husband John, about how their respective families dealt with their circumstances points to the importance of understanding the differing experiences of poverty in this period:

BT: Were there any people you knew who were a bit richer than?

Valerie: Yeah, yeah, 'cos I suppose, well, although there's only three in your family, but...

John: Three children, yeah.

Valerie: 'Cos there was eight in mine.

John: You were still better off than me.

Valerie: Yeah, 'cos I had a good mum, a good manager. Your mum weren't a very good manager.

John: No, she was a lovely woman really, but you give her £50 Friday night, Saturday morning, she'd go and borrow some off someone. Just go through her fingers, you know. Mind you she never had fifty quid. Friday night, we'd all be sitting round waiting for my dad to come home. . . . He used to go like this, he'd turn his back, 'here you are, here's her money'. *He* used to have about a tenner, *she* had eight quid...

BT: And he'd drink it?

John: And drink was only a shilling a pint. So that's twenty drinks for a shilling, for a pound. . . . He could drink twenty every night. . . . My dad used to go busking, King's Lynn, playing the piano, and his mate'd be on the guitar. . . . Put all the money, pennies and ha'pennies and that in the middle of the table after the weekend and we'd count it all out.

BT: So would that be . . . on a Saturday . . . he'd do that?

John: He might be gone three days. Saturday, Sunday.

BT: What, when he wasn't working or?

John: Yeah, he'd take the Monday off work, he never bothered about it. My father worked in every boot factory in Norwich. He got the sack in the morning, he'd be somewhere else in the afternoon . . . come Sunday, she'd have [no money] so my aunt Iris . . . I went there, 'cos . . . she'd give me a half crown to give to my mother, you know, she'd borrow half a crown. Well, one week I come home. And I'd lost this half a crown. Well, I got a whack! And my brother and sister, me, my mother and father, we all went up there to look for this half a crown, I mean.

John here articulates the bundle of factors that led to the extreme poverty he experienced as a child. Unlike Valerie, whose family poverty was the simple result of one wage having to stretch to support a family of ten, John's resulted in part from his father's drinking and refusal to hand over an adequate amount of housekeeping money to his mother. This was further exacerbated by his mother's inability to budget and his father's to keep in regular work. His account also points to other coping strategies used by his family in order to manage their poverty – as well as using busking as an informal means of income generation, borrowing from family members was sometimes a vital means of getting through the week.

In the 1940s and 1950s, those most susceptible to poverty and the consequent attentions of council welfare workers were elderly people and large families with many young children, often very close together in age, where there was no stable wage earner. Mothers of young households struggled simultaneously with pregnancy, toddlers, one or more children at a bed-wetting stage, in addition to older children playing out on the street or in neighbouring fields, or beginning to engage in courtship and sexual adventures. The influence of a family's life cycle was acknowledged in part by officials working with such families:

> the general standard of living remains poor, though it has much improved with better living conditions, Family Allowance, the Health Service etc., *and the family are growing up* [emphasis added].[9]

This finding resonates with the work of Abel-Smith and Townsend, whose analysis of family expenditure data revealed in particular the poverty of families with large numbers of children, even in the context of a male breadwinner in full-time employment. They found that of all people 'in the low-expenditure households as many as 34.6 per cent were in households whose head was in full-time work' (Abel-Smith and Townsend, 1965: 30).

An important theme to weave into the overriding narrative of the communality of experience of poverty in this period is that of the emotional cost of deprivation (Giles, 1995). Margaret Brooke, who was one of nine children had a key memory of her mother – 'I mean I never used to think my mum used to go to bed because when I used to go to bed she was at the sink and when I got up she was at the sink' – and spoke about the lack of attention she received in relation to her brothers. Others spoke more generally about how attention to physical survival overrode emotional needs:

> I don't have memories of being cherished and loved. I have memories of being looked after... I don't think my mother had time to cuddle and I think that then had a knock on effect with me and my own children. I started a family thinking the main thing to do was to look after them in a very physical way, that they were clean and fed and

warm and, but by the time you realise maybe you should be doing
something else that's often too late really.

(Lily Haley)

For some families, even being 'looked after' stretched resources too
far. Issues such as mental health difficulties and domestic violence could
overwhelm families already struggling with material deprivation:

I know the lady who lived next door to us she got a lot of children,
and her husband used to really be unkind to her. Especially when
that came time to go in to have another baby. And she was very, very
poor.

(Eva Garland)

Thus, rather than portraying the unproblematic celebration of working class community rightly critiqued by Steedman (1986), we highlight
the importance of understanding variations in causes and responses to
poverty, and concurrent experiences of isolation and emotional trauma.
If this was true for the immediate post-war years, accounts from the
1960s and 1970s were marked even more by feelings of marginalization. These years saw both the continuation of easily obtainable work –
with the building of UEA providing an additional source of employment – and declining average family sizes. Many of those we spoke to
who were bringing up their children during this period saw these years
as cementing a sense of well-being and material comfort. Eileen Donald,
who spent her childhood in abject poverty in Eire, remembered:

Eileen: We were one of the first couples to ever have a television, 'cos
my neighbours around the corner, their two sons used to come over
every Friday night and sit on the pouf watching Tony Hancock and
they thought that was great.
BT: And compared to your child it must have felt like you'd moved
on?
Eileen: Oh, yeah. A hell of a lot. I mean, my poor mother, she never
had nothing.

For those whose circumstances meant they were unable to take
advantage of these changes, often from one of the social groups
reliant on inadequate and increasingly stigmatized national assis-
tance/supplementary benefits – lone parents, the able-bodied unemployed, the disabled and the elderly (Walker, 1993) – poverty was not

something remembered as being part of a collective experience. Leah Price's memories of growing up in the 1970s, as the child of a lone mother with an alcoholic absent father, reveal a shift in the experience of deprivation from the previous generation. What comes through in Leah's account is the isolation of her position from her peers:

> *Leah:* We didn't have money as a kid.... I can remember break times not having a packet of crisps, whereas all the other kids had crisps and I had to go from breakfast in the morning until dinner time... just little things like that, you know, and having the frumpy shoes that mum could only afford.... I used to nick from the shop on the way to school in the mornings so I had some food 'cos otherwise I'd have to wait until dinner time... and I'd be starving and all the other kids would be walking around with their crisps and their chocolate and I'd be scabbing off them probably saying, 'oh, give us a crisp', or 'give us a drink'... they're all the things I suppose that stick in my mind.... I had a great aunt who was like the fairy god mother who sort of three times a year would take us out, like go in a restaurant whereas I'd never gone in a restaurant with my mum or my dad... she'd take us to Wimpy or Macdonalds and you'd have a big knickerbocker glory.
> *BT:* What about, did you used to go on holiday?
> *Leah:* No, no.
> *BT:* What about day trips to the coast or anything?
> *Leah:* Yeah we used to do that with nanny and granddad, used to drive us to Eccles, we used to go to where there's nothing to buy, no shops or nothing, I think there was one little shop there near the toilet that sells you buckets and spades and one ice cream and that was it, you never went to Yarmouth or Hemsby or anything like that 'cos we just didn't have the money.

Not only do Leah's memories reveal how she felt difference in relation to her peers, but they also crystallize around particular consumer experiences from which she felt excluded. These themes also come through in Lorna Haley's narrative – growing up at the same time she remembered the starkness of her childhood poverty, and again it was as a consequence of specific circumstances at home:

> We were very poor, definitely but also there was an alcoholic who drunk all the money. So we were poor and then we were extra poor.

When Lorna went to university and received a grant:

> it was the first time [my Mum] had a phone. Because I couldn't contact her I paid to have a phone installed and she didn't have a washing machine until [then either].

Again, part of the way in which poverty in this period was remembered by Lorna was through the absence of owning certain consumer durables which were becoming 'normal' in wider society.

Thus narratives of community solidarity and intimacy ran parallel with individual experiences of deprivation and isolation. From the 1940s to the 1970s the dominant culture of the estates moved away from one in which material deprivation was a central part of many households' lives to one in which poverty became increasingly residualized in certain types of households which were unable to attain the modest comfort and engagement with consumer society achieved by many living in the estates.

As we have suggested, from the 1970s more people found themselves in long-term unemployment, induced by deep structural changes in the economy. The consequent increase in levels of material deprivation over time led to the three estates being awarded New Deal for Communities funding at the end of the 1990s (see Chapter 4). Yet long-term unemployment did not affect everyone. For those with jobs these years were not marked by any particular changes in personal circumstances. And paradoxically, because houses in Larkman and North Earlham estates became harder to let as the estates' reputation as a 'rough' area hardened, tenancies were granted to anyone who was willing to move there. David Carwadine, whose wife had been granted a three-bedroom house as a single university student, commented that this led to there being a 'tremendous variety of people living here' with very different backgrounds and life trajectories.

Nevertheless, for those people who were structurally disadvantaged within the economy and society, the period from the 1970s to the end of the century were ones of increasing difficulty. One consequence of this was that 'being poor' once again became a central part of the dominant culture of the estates. However, unlike the post-war period when material deprivation was part of a wider national experience of austerity, this was at odds with the prevailing ethos of consumerism, success and individualism that characterized the 1980s and 1990s. Increasingly the estates themselves became seen as cut off from the rest of Norwich, particularly nearby affluent areas such as the 'golden triangle' and the university.

Thus individuals who are from very poor households now have to cope simultaneously with material deprivation alongside the more nebulous, but just as significant, problems associated with being marginalized from consumer culture. This combination of difficulties was discussed by the area housing manager, who had previously worked in East London:

> She was very open about how 'shocked' she was when started work there, and said that she had seen 'more poverty' there than in Newham. She clarified this by saying that the living conditions and social skills of people were far worse, in the sense that she had gone into people's houses and been 'shocked' at people's perception of 'what's a reasonable way to live...it's depressing and sad. They don't see it's wrong' – houses with no beds, just mattresses on the floor, no bedding 'yet there'll be the TV in the living room, the CCTV camera and the car outside...white goods in the kitchen are grey'. She spoke of 'dog excrement' on the floors where there were toddlers crawling around. She reflected that it was an indication of different priorities over what was important to spend one's money on.

While the case of Darren, who was sleeping in a shed when we met and had been homeless on and off since he left home aged 14, was more extreme than most, housing difficulties were a recurrent theme. Most common was offspring or siblings moving (back) in following personal difficulties such as relationship breakdown or overwhelming personal debts. Interviews also revealed the prevalence of full-to-capacity/overcrowded housing:

> *Kyle:* Yeah, there's seven of us.
> *BT:* Do you live with your mum then?
> *Kyle:* And six other brothers and sisters.
> *BT:* Wow. You got a big house?
> *Kyle:* No. Three bedroom.
> *BT:* How do you all fit in then?
> *Kyle:* Well, four in one, three in another bedroom. Just my mum in one, the other bedroom. We need a bigger house, but...(Kyle Thompson)

Similarly Charnelle, aged 16 and a classmate of Kyle's, told us how in her household of eight, she shared her bedroom with her two sisters, where 'the bedroom's like [a] little box'. Given the fact that each of them only had one pillow case and duvet cover, she was fiercely protective of who she allowed onto her bed – 'Like if anyone lay in my bed, when I'm like out, I'll go mad' – as she felt they made it smell funny, and invaded what was the only space in the house which was hers alone. While this level of overcrowding was very common in earlier decades, Kyle, Charnelle and others now experience it in a context where children having 'their own bedroom' is the norm.

With her friend Kelly, Charnelle spoke about going into the city centre to go shopping. As with many young women they liked to buy new clothes, and in their discussion they revealed their desire to engage fully in branded, consumer culture:

> *BT:* Someone said Chapelfield [shopping mall] was really expensive? Is it?
>
> *Charnelle:* Yeah. For like little things, a t-shirt, that's about a tenner.
>
> *Kelly:* That's like what I paid for a scarf. I paid fifteen quid. For a scarf! I was in Jane Norman. But that's worth it. I think it was.
>
> *BT:* What do you think about...going into the charity shops and getting clothes kind of thing? Or do you always get stuff new?
>
> *Kelly:* No.
>
> *Charnelle:* I always get something, stuff new, I would.
>
> *Kelly:* I usually get stuff new.
>
> *BT:* Why's that?
>
> *Kelly:* Skin allergies and stuff.... 'Cos people might have skin diseases or something. That's what I'm scared of.
>
> *Charnelle:* I prefer wearing new ones. No one I knew had wore 'em.... But I will say at the same time I go to Poundland...to get my shampoo and that there. Make my hair lovely and soft and shiny.

This extract also shows the ambivalences within their position, what Bauman (1998: 1) characterizes as the 'plight of a flawed consumer': Kelly's uncertainty over whether 15 pounds for a scarf was worth it; the ambiguity in Charnelle's statement over second-hand clothing, suggesting that new clothes were in fact an ideal rather than matter of course; and her acceptance that Poundland was a good place to buy things, despite lacking the prestige of shops in the mall.

While neither of the young women talk directly about being poor, the ambiguities revealed in their positions here need to be placed in the wider context of the major shift in the meaning of poverty since the 1970s. Whereas in the past 'being poor' was not stigmatized but rather the inability to cope with poverty, now simply being poor was enough to be labelled a social failure. Lister (2004: 135) observes that coping strategies adopted to survive poverty are not limited to managing inadequate material resources, but also include dealing with attitudes of 'othering' and stigmatization. Being able to engage in consumer culture is one crucial means of signalling one's full and successful relationship with society. Given this context it is not surprising that we recorded a number of stories in which self-identifications involving low esteem and a sense of personal failure were connected to the categorization of the estates as being 'poor'. One voluntary worker in the area during the 1990s ran a health and self-esteem group for local women. She told us how when the group first started she tried to get the participants to tell her something about themselves:

> I said to her 'So can you just say a little bit about yourself?' and she didn't say anything and I said 'Something?' and she just looked down and she said 'I'm a slug in the mud' she said 'you don't get lower than me'.

In this section we have discussed the changing faces of poverty over 70 years, suggesting that while the area has always contained people who are poor the form and context of that poverty has changed profoundly. In the following section we move on to consider in more depth the various tactics and strategies deployed by people in order to 'get by'.

Resourcefulness

Official and popular categorizations of poor people in general as 'scroungers' dependent on the state were prevalent in Norwich with regard to residents of the three estates. Yet, people's narratives suggested something quite different. We have already shown how the distinction between employment and unemployment might be blurred through a range of casual and informal work practices, sometimes embracing all family members – creating what we might think of as an 'economy of makeshifts' (King and Thomkins, 2003). In this section, taking on Lister's (2004) taxonomy of agency, we explore different means residents employed to 'get by' and sometimes to 'get (back) at'.[10] In doing this we do not intend to minimize the enormous difficulties faced by people in poverty, both material and emotional, but rather to demonstrate the extent to which they are able to 'exercise "generative power" to control their lives despite their subordinate position in wider "hierarchical" political, economic and social power relationships' (Lister, 2004: 125).

While in most of this section we consider 'material' forms of resource-fulness, we begin by pointing to the role of humour and dreams. Some of the anecdotes related to us were recognizably well worn, having been used by the narrator possibly countless times over the years in order to, not only amuse listeners, but also perhaps reveal the narra-tor's ability to meet life's challenges head-on. Occasionally participants were explicit in stressing the importance of humour as a life skill. For Gina Malley, who in the course of her life history narrated to us extreme domestic violence, the difficulties of living with a criminal husband and severe health problems, humour and laughter were central to her way of managing:

> Life is the most precious commodity, you can have as much money as you like, that won't buy you health … happiness is what you make yourself, with your own group, with your own family. I mean, with my sons we have a laugh, we have a joke, we have fun together…. My sister is always buying, but that's all materialistic…. That's like a status symbol. And I don't see that as very important at all.

As Gina's words testify, taking this approach to life is very personal, with some people having the skills, including humour, to meet the chal-lenges caused by structural and individual disadvantage. Dreaming (or fantasy) is another less tangible mechanism that can also be important. While it may not be 'helpful' in a rationalist sense, nevertheless it is another way of individuals asserting their agency within the one world where they have full control:

> BT: So what would you like, say in ten years time, what would you like to be doing with your life? Or do you not think that far ahead?
> *Dean:* Live my life of luxury … get a house, big field, couple of Crosses, that'll do me. Nice car.
> BT: So you wouldn't stay at West Earlham then?
> Dean I'll probably move out of Norwich or a different part of Norwich, well just get out of Norwich or something. Definitely.
> BT: What about you?
> *Kyle:* Yeah I want to, I want a big house.
> [laughter]
> *Dean:* Somehow get the money.
> BT: Where are you going to get the money from?

Kyle: Hopefully win the lottery.
 [laughter]
Dean: I've been dreaming years win the lottery. Buy like sixty lottery
 tickets or something at once.
Kyle: Yeah.

While the character and experience of poverty may have changed over time, many of the means of dealing with it have not. In the course of our interviews we came across a range of means used by people to manage situations caused by structural disadvantage. Though in practice different individuals within a family might deploy a range of strategies, and indeed over the course of their lifetime an individual may use strategies from across the whole spectrum (Leisering and Leibfried, 1999), residents' narratives used differences in means of dealing with poverty to mark out categories of 'respectable' and 'unrespectable' people.

For example, avoiding debt was something that some people saw as a marker of respectability. While Tom Crowther knew there were people who 'get things on the knock', he had been warned against it: 'I've always been brought up if you can't afford a thing then you can't have it, when you can afford it you can.' 'Respectability' was often strongly gendered, so that typically for men it would involve working hard, and perhaps taking on a second job in order to make ends meet. Margaret Brooke remembered how throughout her childhood her 'dad was doing various jobs. I mean he was a crane driver and in the evenings he used to go and drive the buses'. Bill Fussell asserted his ability to pay for a better grade council house despite his low wage:

I said 'I don't want an old house I want a new one. I'm entitled to a new one.' I said 'I've done my bit I want a new one.' 'You can't afford a new.' I say 'I'll be the best judge of that...if I have to get another job I'll get another job.'

Classically for women respectability was couched in terms of rigorous household cleanliness. Archival reports of the health visitors and home advisers repeatedly based their judgements of the household on the enthusiasm (or lack of it) of the mother of the family, and time and again we were told in various forms, 'we were poor but we were clean':

She was clean, we had nothing. But you could come in, you could eat off my mother's floor. Never had no carpets, we didn't have no bed linen or nothing. She'd have us in off the road, you had a bath in front of the fire, and everything you took off was put in this bath-water, she'd wash it, get it dry. And always patching and ironing. You know, she'd patch your sleeves of your overalls.

(Eileen Donald)

If this was one means of constructing an image of coping, there was another way too, as Rita Hastings suggests:

There was a couple used to walk down from the Larkman to meet my mum, Mr and Mrs Horn. And he was really dapper, well dressed, so was she.... Always looked lovely. And when my mother took me to their house, I was absolutely amazed. There was lino with holes in it. There was old furniture that was really, I mean we didn't have much, but ours was fairly reasonable, but I mean!... really scruffy inside their house, and yet they walked out as if they were royalty! [laughs]

For those who wished to signal themselves as 'respectable', as well as middle class outsiders such as council welfare officials, this type of strategy could be frowned upon as fecklessness. For this reason, one family seen as a 'problem' by the council were criticized for indulging in 'much mis-spending', noting in one case how 'several pounds [were] recently spent on colour photographs'.[11] And yet, while the poor were, and continue to be, criticized for spending on anything other than essentials, it takes a certain type of person to do nothing but live on basics year after year. This tactic might, in fact, work against the thrifty. Bill Fussell, who worked hard all his life, and as we have seen, took on extra work in order to pay for his house, shared a story with us that revealed the shortcomings of his approach:

Bill: I mean the time I'd paid the bills we had no money left. People [who] lived next door, they used to go off on holidays, could never figure that out. I used to sit here and try and work out, 'I don't know how the hell, they manage it.' Well weren't till years later I had to go round there for something one day... fella's wife said to me, 'you never go on holiday, do you?' I say, 'I can't afford it.'... 'Fff!' she say, 'Well, can't afford! Fff!' she say, 'Well, why don't you do like we do?' I say, 'What's that?' She say, 'Use the rent money.'

BT: So they used to not pay their rent and go on holiday?

Bill: Yeah. Yeah, what she used to do is spend the rest of the year paying it back. I wouldn't want, that weren't my cup of tea.

As Chamberlain has observed, 'thrift was more than a simple question of book-keeping. It was a refined evasion' (1989: 11). The creative approach to budgeting adopted by Bill's neighbour shows us that just as people's material experiences of living on the estates and of deprivation could be very different, so too could their responses to it. While often depicted as a sign of the improvidence of 'the poor', various forms of debt often form an active and central part of individual and household financial strategies (see Rogaly et al., 1999).

John Burnett, a local fruit and vegetable trader, gave a telling view of changing forms of credit and debt over the course of his and his father's lifetimes, as well as considering the classed implications of different forms of borrowing. He told us how his father used to give customers credit, but how now he rarely gave, or was asked to give, people goods 'on tick':

> *John:* That's not an old fashioned thing really, because, what you've got to remember in them days was, you didn't have such a thing as credit card, did ya? Not the normal Joe Blogg, what would be then a cheque book. And people who had cheques books, they live down on Newmarket Road, ain't there?[12] ... So, I wouldn't like to say that they had more credit than what they do today, 'cos if they had fifteen quid, they were really in dire straits. But today, they got thirty, forty grands worth, ain't they, round their own neck, so they're not any better off than people were in them days when they used to go round the butcher shop...
>
> *BT:* So, people are still living on credit, it's just a different sort?
>
> *John:* Well, they're living on bigger credit now, ain't they?... it's obviously more money about now, but yeah. But there's still, they got more problems than what they had in them days. 'Cos they didn't have no problems keeping up with the Joneses, 'cos they were all the same up there.

Here John suggests that credit has long been an important way of dealing with a limited income, and what has changed over time is rather the form credit takes, and the amount borrowed. He also understands how all classes use credit, they simply use different kinds. John implies that over time there has been a shift in the wider cultural context in which people make their decisions – gone are the times when social status could be signalled through hard work and a clean house, now the imperative was to 'keep up with the Joneses'. This made Flo Smith feel there had been a significant change in the culture of the area: 'we worked and aimed for something.... They just want everything yesterday on a plastic, the easy option'.

It would be wrong, however, to suggest either that over time people have moved from using debt to pay for necessities to using it for conspicuous consumption, as evidence points to the continued importance of borrowing to cover daily essentials. One survey showed that among low income people, 'necessity' rather than 'convenience' was a more important reason to use credit: overall 36 per cent said they used credit out of necessity, but for those with a weekly income between £50 and £100 the percentage giving 'necessity' as a reason was 45 per cent; for those unemployed for less than six months it was 52 per cent, and for those unemployed for more than six months it was 64 per cent (Pantazis and Gordon, 1997: 174). Nevertheless, from the 1950s the archival evidence points to an additional pressure on poor families, with the advent of a range of consumer durables which signalled the end of post-war austerity. From this time references to both cars and televisions being owned by families were not uncommon, but typically these would be bought on hire purchase at considerable cost and sometimes anxiety to families, particularly when in addition to other purchases: 'Mrs Jenkins is in debt for about £100 for kitchen furniture, beds and bedding ... she finds difficulty in paying rent arrears.'[13]

If the context and availability of debt changed over time, with financial deregulation during the 1980s combining with an increase in real incomes for the average household leading to an increase in both the supply and use of credit, many of the forms of credit on offer have remained remarkably consistent. The types of credit predominantly used by 'poor' households include Social Fund loan, mail order (club catalogue), credit, tally men, money lenders and 'cheque traders' (Rogaly et al., 1999). And as Pantazis observes: 'All these are used exclusively by those living in, or on the margins of poverty' (1997: 178).

As Bill Fussell's story indicated, consciously deciding not to pay the rent in order to pay for something else, while perhaps seen as improvidence by council officials, within the constraints in which many residents lived, was in fact a sound strategy. Unlike other forms of borrowing which involved paying (often high) interest, this was cost-free, and given the fact that the council only evicted tenants as a last resort, it was also a low-risk strategy. Similarly, borrowing from family, while potentially containing costs in terms of strain on relationships, could offer a flexible interest-free means of getting money without having to take recourse to outside sources.

Lumpy expenditure, such as on expensive clothes or household items, might be paid for in instalments, which over the decades have taken different forms from 'tally men' to buying in instalments from catalogues:

> There was one winter time, my brother and I – ah it was great! – we got Crombie overcoats.... Well, when I was about ten or eleven.... And [my mother] got the money to buy it off a Mr Knights, and that was thr'pence each, a week. So that was sixpence, right. We'd hear him come, we used to dive on the floor and hide up. He never got his money, poor sod. He used to come all the way from that Heartsease to get sixpence!

As John Draper's memory here indicates, his mother simultaneously used two forms of debt/borrowing, first through paying for the two coats in instalments, and then through hiding to avoid payments.

> They would because the loan people, those loan companies went round.... I mean it was awful they would say you know you can have a free pair of school shoes, you know, the offer this month is a free pair of school shoes and I was just amazed at what people, if they borrowed a hundred and fifty pounds by May you were pay, then paying back something like five hundred pounds... it was phenomenal but the imperative of it was to have the money for Christmas. That was a hugely important driver.
>
> (Frances Bailey)

If loan companies are frequently criticized for their extortionate interest rates, cynically preying on individuals and areas where other forms of credit are more difficult to come by, this does not mean that 'in-community' credit should be seen as automatically more 'benign'. John Draper and Leah Price's stories show how we must be wary of making such assumptions:

> I'll tell you a story, shall I? This used to happen most weeks, she'd get paid Friday night...and Saturdays, the fellow what she used to get the groceries off, used to come round with the van, and this is how my mother was, she'd have a small tin of salmon. He'd come round with the bill, 'large tin of salmon', double the price! She used to just pay!
>
> (John Draper)

Leah: I used to when I was younger get a lot of stuff out of club books. Unfortunately my friend's mum was a Provident agent, and I had bleedin' loans when I was sixteen. She used to sign them for me 'cos she was the agent so I was in debt from sixteen to about nineteen.

BT: Was that quite a lot of money?

Leah: Well hundred quid's there, I mean when I was sixteen, which we're talking, I'm thirty four now so that was quite a few years ago, was a lot of money a hundred quid weren't it. And she used to take the first payment of that! I mean that was a right rip off. I mean you have to pay like fifty percent back or something.

BT: Did you realise that at the time?

Leah: No, no, I really, like sort of swear under my breath now when I think about it because you know I thought she was doing me a favour but she wasn't was she. She was doing it to get me... 'cos obviously she was getting commission off it... and I spent years in debt.

Equally, while mutual aid of various types was a recurrent theme in the memories of research participants, we must be alive to the costs – often gendered – and limitations of such aid. Many participants remembered staying or eating with relatives, being given clothes or other material aid during periods of household stress:

I don't think I had the clothes, I mean my mum was a single parent, my dad was an alcoholic so he never sort of supported my mum throughout us growing up, so we never had much. If it weren't for our extended family we would have been really poor, you know, our extended family really supported me and my brother as children and my mum.

(Leah Price)

what strikes me now is how unofficial everything was so that... my Aunt June could be handed over the fence and... brought up by the neighbours and we could just sort of shunt around from house to house. It all seemed to be contained within that world. There was wasn't a kind of official, there was wasn't this sense of social workers or any kind of official authority taking a hand in any of this.

(Lorna Haley)

Lorna's Aunt June was informally adopted by this family and remained with them throughout her childhood. This story, as well as giving testimony to the depth of support available to people living on the estates, reinforces our understanding that despite images of people from the estates being dependent on state support, in fact their own networks and resourcefulness was vital to their livelihoods and well-being (Bourke, 1993). Such memories were sometimes held up in direct contrast to what were depicted as the officious and brutal methods of formal aid:

But everybody seemed as though they helped Vera. You know, I think you grew up like that, because even as a teenager, and I [wasn't] earning a lot of money, when she had had her babies, I would always buy something for that baby. She had to give me her coupons, but I would get something for the baby. My mother'd knit something. But I think that was a, a different community. I mean, face it, if you didn't work, you didn't get any money... And the Board of Guardians which, I hope God class me as a Christian, I like to think I'm a Christian. They were Christian people, but they were so horrible to the people who had to go and ask for help... people used to come round the house, and if you had a radio, that had got to go, no luxuries nothing.

(Eva Garland)

Eva's memory here reveals the existence of differences between neighbours – some neighbours were in the position to offer substantial support while others could not. The tension between feeling isolated through domestic violence and feeling part of a supportive community was expressed to us by Gina Malley about her experiences in the 1960s:

We would always talk, have a little chat, you know, when we passed. Not in and out of one another's houses, but you know, if I passed to go over the shop or she did, you know, we'd stand, have a little chat... most people what sort of spoke about [her husband] thought he's a really agreeable person you know. And in years, they said they'd, 'Never of thought you two what have got divorced, we thought you were inseparable.' But I said, 'well do you know what goes on in my house when I shut my door?'

In Gina's case, when she really needed help, she turned to her mother. And in fact, for all the assertions we heard from people about the supportive nature of the estates, this generally came from those residents who had family members living close by. It was family which was most valued, and it seemed, from where most practical and emotional support was found. This has profound implications for those who live with the compound disadvantages of being poor in a poor area without family and other support. This may occur for a range of reasons from insensitive housing allocations or breakdown in personal relations to the diverse circumstances of newcomers: their different migration histories as local, national or international migrants; their legal status, ranging from British nationals on the one hand to asylum seekers on the other; and the length of time they have lived in the area.[14]

For those with nearby relatives, one central tactic for many households was for the family home to be seen as a resource to be used by all family (including extended family) members. The post-war housing shortage meant that for research participants who had married during this period, living with one, or both sets of in-laws was the norm, sometimes for a period of years, until they were allocated their own house. As we showed in the previous section this is not simply a historical phenomenon. Children or other relatives continue to come back to the family home during periods of personal crisis, such as divorce and debt. As with other informal 'in-community' solutions to problems, it is not without its downsides. Women in particular bear the extra burden of care and domestic work caused by people living in their homes. For some, like Lily Haley speaking to Ben in the extract below, greater perhaps than the practical strains, is the lack of freedom to say 'no', the fact that their house is *assumed* to be a family resource rather than their own private space:

Once I was by myself with two children, it seemed I was the place to go if you didn't have anywhere to live, because there was no man to say [no]. So at various points, I've had all my brothers, I think, most of them, stay at my house.... Because I was the one without a partner so I was dumping ground for family ... my father by this point came to me when he was, had had a heart attack. So he had a bed in the living room.... And brothers at various points, they would just sleep on the floor or whatever.... And even a brother who was married, and had had a child at the same time as my second child, they lived with me for some months as well, with their baby ... I think the wife didn't want to live with her parents. Because she probably knew that they would be taken over ... whereas I didn't have time to take over anybody else's baby. So they were there. For about four months.... And drove me up the wall actually ... I've never wanted to live with anyone since. I just so value my own space.

(Lily Haley)

The costs, limitations and opportunities provided by forms of mutual aid and action are also revealed in the range of activities that straddle the line between 'getting by' and 'getting (back) at'. Extending across the spectrum of semi-legal to clearly illegal, we found a range of examples, which while providing income, also offered opportunities to get back at either the state or richer individuals. The majority of these operated within close personal networks, with opportunities arising through 'knowing somebody' or being able to work with a trusted group of friends. In the course of our research we came across a number of older residents who admitted having been involved in burglaries and selling on stolen goods in the past.

> I knew a friend of a friend of a friend who knew someone, who knew where certain items were and we done it, done it for about a year.... That was like arranging things [to] get stolen, things get sold and they'd sell on. Yeah. And all five went, we all went down.

This participant ended up spending a couple of years in prison. Unlike others, this man, who ran his own business, admitted to continuing to 'do a bit of dealing' on the side, saying 'life's all about dealing'. Someone else was engaged in selling smuggled tobacco to people living in the area, which offered the twin advantages of providing an income and getting one over the state through avoiding paying taxes. A similar combination of satisfaction comes through in one man's account to Ben of the opportunities he had to make extra money while working in a garage:

> Hundreds of ways of earning money out of cars, hundreds of ways ... I used to charge fifty quid a month for cleaning his Rolls Royce. Yeah, and just take it down to the cleaner boys, give them twenty, keep thirty myself.... When you're delivering a new car and you're picking the old one up. You take the old one home and take all the good stuff out, like the radio, any good tyres, seat covers. Empty the fuel. Make sure you've got enough to get back so that, well, just whatever's in the car, is yours ... if there's a new battery on the car, put an old one on, keep the new one.

Overall we have shown how the structural constraints and opportunities within which estate residents have lived their lives have changed profoundly over time. The availability of different kinds of work interacted with individual life courses and personal circumstances to produce different poverties at specific times for particular people. Central to this was the change within broader society towards consumerism, resulting in the stigmatization of 'being poor' rather than of particular ways of managing poverty. However, estate residents have continued to be actively engaged in a wide variety of forms of resourcefulness, despite dominant stereotypes of them as dependent 'scroungers'. Tactics range from taking on extra employment, having other household members work, engaging in the casual, informal and sometimes illegal sectors, using forms of credit, and family and local support networks. All these take effort and time and are often not without limitations or costs. In the next chapter we consider the complex roles of the state in both producing and responding to poverty, unemployment and marginalization.

4
State

In the previous chapter we focused on the causes of poverty and some of the ways in which individuals have responded to it. In this chapter we explore how the state, at its different levels and over time, acts on, for and with people, and how, both individually and collectively, they respond to state actions. Veyne points out that 'there is no universal object, the governed, in relation to which a body of governors proceeds to act. The governed vary over time'. Equally how government conceives of its people also changes, for, as he asks, are 'we to be governed as members of a flock to be led, as children to be coddled and educated, as a human resource to be exploited, as members of a population to be managed, as legal subjects with rights...' (Veyne, 1997, in Rose, 1999: 40–41)? Changing conceptions of 'the governed' are of course partly informed by shifts in the (perceived) functions of the state over time and, as Rose (1999) observes, in the 'technologies of rule' available to the state at any particular time.

Central to this argument is the importance of disaggregating the state, for as has been widely demonstrated, the state is not monolithic. Rather, it operates at different scales, including at the city, regional and national levels and it is situated, through the individuals who work for it, in society. Instead of thinking of states as 'discrete or singular entities' it is more helpful to think of 'dispersed practices of government. States are best thought of as bundles of everyday institutions and forms of rule' (Corbridge et al., 2005: 5; see also Fuller and Harriss, 2001). Such an approach throws open the workings of 'the state' to scrutiny, suggesting the existence of dynamic and potentially conflictual relationships between different state actors. This points to the importance of understanding how different actors within the state engage with individuals outside it, perpetuating or challenging certain categorizations. Ferguson and Gupta (2005: 105), following Anderson (1983), go further in arguing that the state, as much as the nation, is 'imagined'. In this sense both are 'constructed entities that are conceptualised and made socially effective through particular imaginative and symbolic devices'. In this chapter we adopt a close-up and critical approach to the state in order to ask how, over time, state practices are experienced and responded to by individuals, including through identification and categorization processes, and consequently what they signal about an individual's status in relation to the state.

Rose uses the term 'translation' to describe how policy moves from 'government in great buildings and capitals' to the 'myriad of micro-locales'. He suggests that in the 'dynamics of translation, alignments are forged between the objectives of the authorities wishing to govern and the personal projects of... organisations, groups and individuals' so that linkages in 'aspirations, judgements and ambitions' are assembled between the different actors. Critically, because disparate agencies are involved in this process, he suggests that it is 'an imperfect mechanism' and 'one that is subject to innumerable pressures and distortions'. Thus policy is 'a matter of fragile relays, contested locales and fissiparous affiliations' (1999: 48, 51).

Historical work on the extension of the British state in the twentieth century certainly points to the importance of understanding the contested nature of the process of translation, with 'the brittleness of the accommodation between government and governance... fully exposed... through the evolving relationship between central and local government' (Lowe and Rollings, 2000: 99). Understanding the material relations between different levels of government is key, as finance played, and continues to play, a vital part in mediating intra-state dynamics. While local authorities traditionally enjoyed 'considerable scope for initiative', this was eroded during the interwar period, as local authorities' increased responsibilities were not matched with an increase in independent income (Dupree, 2000: 388; see also Taylor et al., 2007). White (2006: 3) points to the nationalization programme of 1945–50 and the privatizations of 1979–97 as confirming the 'immiseration of local government', with the later twentieth century marking a shift towards a centralized 'command and control' form of government which left local authorities with only 'residual environmental and regulatory functions'. Over the same period state actors such as teachers, the police and social workers saw their roles continually contested, shifting in meaning and function.

Along with stressing the dynamic and temporal specificity of 'the state' we acknowledge the importance of developing an understanding of the spatialization of government (Ferguson and Gupta, 2005: 107). Building on Corbridge et al.'s (2005) questioning of the assumptions of Giddens and others that power is exercised uniformly across a defined and exclusive modern territory, Painter (2007: 605) remarks that there is no reason to suppose that the uneven development of state capacity identified by them is only a feature of their Indian case study: 'There is plenty of evidence that state institutions and practices exhibit marked unevenness in all countries.' This points to the importance of understanding how the practices of the state in Britain, and the ways in which it constructs its presence have varied across space and time. Indeed, Huxley suggests that through

> investigating the ways in which spaces and environments are invested with causal powers in programmes, projects and plans for the government of individuals and populations, we can begin to trace how particular specifications of spaces, buildings, environments, suburbs, cities and regions enter into unstable, heterogeneous, assemblages of technologies of rule.
>
> (Huxley, 2007: 199–200)

Using Foucauldian terminology, Knowles (1999) suggests that the disciplinarity of the state is spatially (re)produced within the local micro operations of welfare practices. Also deploying insights from both Lefebvre and de Certeau she considers not only what the state 'does' to its subjects, but how they actively engage with everyday manifestations of the state. This resonates with Corbridge et al.'s argument that microspatial practices are central to how the state is 'seen' by its citizens in the context of its own enacting of categorizations, asserting it is not simply what the state does to poor people:

> it also matters to people how the encounter is structured and performed.... We can learn about the practices of government by attending to the diverse ways in which 'the state' is experienced and understood by differently placed individuals.
>
> (Corbridge et al., 2005: 8)

Thus it is the very mundane ways (Painter, 2007: 606) in which individuals and groups encounter particular faces of the state (or its absence) which help to shape individual attitudes to, and relationships with, 'the state' more broadly. Jones and Novak argue that the signal sent out by state welfare organizations – described variously as 'austere', 'shabby' and 'hostile' – is that they are 'places for losers', with people's lives 'taken up in endless waiting and queues, in being shunted from office to office as if their time was of no importance' (Jones and Novak, 1999: 78; also Beresford et al., 1999; Knowles, 1999). This suggests an unseen and underlying moving (emotional) history of individuals' relationships with the state, one imbued with a range of feelings including shame:

> Waiting is a shame, and the shame of waiting rebounds on the one who waits. Waiting is something to be ashamed of because it may be noted and taken as evidence of indolence or low status, seen as a symptom of rejection and a signal to exclude.
>
> (Bauman, 2004a: 109)

Anticipating arguments we develop more fully in the next chapter, we suggest that encounters between state agents and estate residents are intrinsically classed. Moreover, since the 1990s, there has been a flowering of the discourse of 'community' as part of the technology of the state (Burchell et al., 1991; Rose, 1999), with consequent reworking of the relationship between central and local government as well as the emergence of the idea of the active and participatory citizen engaged in a 'workfare' rather than a 'welfare' culture. Even when taking on board the Foucauldian implications of these developments, we suggest they have opened a space for residents, in Lister's (2004) words, to 'get organised'.

We use two cases at the beginning and end of the chapter to illustrate the temporal and spatial specificity of 'the state' in order to fully comprehend its actions, inactions and consequent impact on lives of estate residents. In a sense the historical material in the first section, relating to the building of schools on the estates, acts as a backdrop for the final part of the chapter. In this, through exploring the genesis and outcomes of the New Deal for Communities (NDC) project in the area, we see that issues of the 'translation' of policy, and the contested nature of governance have continued to be a feature of the British state, and its relationship with a marginalized area. In the central section we explore the importance of face-to-face encounters and micro-spatial factors in mediating relationships between 'the council' and estate residents, and suggest that over time there has been a move towards more 'faceless' encounters.

Lost in translation?

> The Lord Mayor said '...the City Council and the citizens in general were interested in the educational developments taking place on the Earlham estate. The Education Committee were planning very carefully and with foresight the provision of schools for this large body of people who had been removed from the centre of the city and must feel some sense of isolation.... Parents and citizens alike must be impressed with the care which had been taken by the architects, the education staff and the contractors to make these buildings and their furniture and equipment so fitted to their purpose and so pleasant to the eye...[these schools] stand for the development of human personality and the fostering of the qualities needed for good citizenship.'[1]

Behind this statement, what do we really see? Was the council as committed to good education for the population of the new estates as this extract suggests? Is it helpful to consider 'the council' as a single body, or do we need to consider the actions of individuals? What was the role of central government in the creation of the schools? And finally, were the estate residents and their children simply 'done to', or did they themselves play a part in the story?

By 1933 Labour's control of the council was firmly consolidated and it used its power to develop a twin approach of rehousing and improving educational facilities to raise living standards within the city. This was in tune with the national party's emphasis on social welfare (Whitemore, 1986; Thane, 2000), and yet local conditions were also important, most notably perhaps the relative weakness of trade union interests and opinion of key council officials. The strength of the Labour Party in Norwich, as with some other city boroughs, stemmed primarily from individual membership rather than the trade unions (Taylor et al., mimeo; Tanner, 2000).[2] Doyle (2004) sees this as allowing space for women such as Dorothy Jewson[3] and Mabel Clarkson to become prominent in the local party, and for social issues of housing, welfare and education to gain prominence in both local party and council agendas.

The commitment of the Labour Party, as well as individual members, to education was shared by Mr Woodhead, the city's education officer. Running through his plans for the schools on the new estates was a desire to provide up-to-date 'experimental' classrooms and the best equipment. In his vision, schools, rather than being isolated, separate buildings, were to be part of larger complexes incorporating community centres and infant welfare clinics.[4] The North Earlham nursery, opened in May 1939, was to be a living example of this new approach:

> The Nursery section contains two large play rooms facing south, each having its own bed and toy stores, together with carefully arranged toilet and cloak accommodation adjacent. The playrooms open direct on to an open veranda.... Within the open court is a paddling pool surrounded by grassed play space. Two large sandpits and a brick doll's house are also provided. These, and a large grassed area, are to be used under supervision as a play centre in the evenings and during the holidays.[5]

How did these aspirations translate into educational experiences for the pupils? Did high-quality facilities, informed simultaneously by Labour philosophies and modern educational thinking, result in the provision of good-quality education? The Larkman Lane infant and junior school opened in April 1939, admitting children from the new estates including John Draper and Tom Crowther, who previously had been bussed to one of the old inner city schools. Yet, just over 18 months later severe problems with overcrowding led to the council asking for prefabricated classrooms in order to accommodate the extra numbers, an issue that was not resolved until the early 1950s.[6] One result of overcrowding was that the council introduced part-time schooling:

> I was coming on six, my school days started. And instead of going for the week...we'd go to school Monday morning, miss Monday afternoon, miss Tuesday morning, go Tuesday afternoon. Then we'd miss Wednesday altogether. Then we'd go Thursday morning, and then Friday afternoon. That would be my school days.
>
> (John Draper)

How is it that the visions set out so carefully in correspondence with the Board of Education resulted in memories of overcrowding and part-time schooling? In part it was a misfortune of timing: while provision for younger children was completed before the war, the planned secondary schools were delayed through wartime shortages. But beyond historical contingency we can trace the active role of the council, and Woodhead in particular, in establishing the roots of the problem well before the war. Despite the Mayor's claims regarding the careful foresight of the Education Committee, the evidence reveals the systematic failure of Woodhead to project the number of school children likely to be resident in the new estates.

As early as 1936 he was forced to revise upwards his estimated number of school places,[7] with later comments by the Board of Education revealing that these figures were still only half the national and city-wide average.[8] Despite the fact that the majority of houses being built had three bedrooms or more, and were thus intended for families, Woodhead believed that the population being transferred would 'not to any great extent [be] young married couples [with children]'.[9] We can only infer the reasons for Woodhead's opinion. It was not the result of inexperience or limited information, as Mile Cross and Drayton estates provided him with local bases for comparison, and the board gave national data for the same purpose. And we cannot accuse him of lacking vision – he was central in arguing for up-to-date facilities and building designs for the new schools. Yet, this might provide the explanation, as, in order to ensure that the schools were built to the highest standard, Woodhead had to concentrate resources in relatively few school places. If he had a choice between a larger number of schools with limited facilities, and a smaller number of schools with excellent facilities, he chose the latter.

While it is important to understand the role of individuals in the development of particular policies, it is vital to understand the context in which they acted. The massive slum clearance and estate building programme embarked upon by Norwich council took place during and just after the worst depression in living memory. There was thus an engrained tension between the aim of developing projects targeting the poorest in Norwich, and an ability to be able to afford to do so. The interwar period has been characterized as the 'zenith of responsible local government' (Mackintosh, 1953: 131); however, more recently this perspective has been tempered by an understanding of the influence, and often interference, of central government in the actions of local authorities (Lowe and Rollings, 2000; Taylor et al., 2007). There is conflicting evidence over the role of central government in limiting the spending of local authorities (Lowe, 1986; Peden, 2000: 186–7), but research on Ministry of Health[10] officials' dealings with local government suggests that they saw fiscal prudence rather than costly social reforms as their primary role (Savage, 1996).

Our research into the construction of the schools reveals both the tight control over apparently insignificant detail combined with an overriding concern with parsimony within the Board of Education. While the board approved of the design of the North Earlham nursery, it had a number of micro-suggestions directed at reducing the overall cost of the project, highlighting for example, what it saw as 'excessive' expenditure on music facilities and the plans for 'too many mirrors': 'bearing in mind the number of children which the Nursery school is to accommodate... the provision contemplated is too costly.'[11]

The Board's detailed intervention into the design of the schools on the grounds of economy suggests that its failure to press Woodhead on his projected number of school places should be understood in this context. Certainly, after the outbreak of the war, the Board was focused heavily on balancing demands for materials and expenditure nationally. As early as November 1939 in discussions over construction of the senior school, officials questioned plans which required the use of a large amount of timber, arguing that in wartime this could 'have a serious effect on our nation and react unfairly on other schemes'.[12] Only after the council had managed to source a synthetic substitute and put all other building projects on hold did the Board accept that there was an 'urgent need' for the senior school, and that building might go ahead.[13]

So far we have seen how 'state' failure to make adequate schooling provision for the children of the estates must in fact be understood in terms of a dynamic interaction between individual officers, local and central government all operating within a specific bureaucratic and economic context. But what of the parents and children for whom the schools were being provided? Tom Crowther's memories suggest he was more than happy with the shift-system of schooling, although it had a negative impact on his later life:

BT: When you weren't at school... you must have had quite a lot of spare time?

Tom: Yes we did, oh yes.

BT: What did you get up to then?

Tom: Oh! All sorts of things. We used to go fishing... used to be two of us with a sack and we would dredge the bottom of the river... you could paddle... we used to take a jam jar with us and bring that home with fish.

Others used their time less benignly, generating 'local discontent' and subsequent complaints to magistrates and the police.[14] Parents, in contrast, were far less happy about the situation, objecting to the fact that if they wanted their children to go full time, they had to walk to inner-city schools:

The residents are... in the main poor. They cannot afford to spend much on shoe leather. Few of the children have overcoats.... For them a walk of one and a half miles, four times daily, means expense in shoes and clothing, wet clothes and illness. These are plain facts which must be faced even in time of war. . . . The parents are also very naturally unwilling to allow their children to go very far from home in case there [should] be an Air Raid.[15]

This combination of practical difficulties in sending children to other schools and the problems caused by some children on the estates led the parents to organize a strike in the autumn of 1939. This ended quickly with the Board of Education accepting how insisting children 'walk to these town schools might lead to a recurrence of the strike'.[16] It was the threat of further strikes, in combination with the compromises on materials made by the council, that led the board to authorize the building of new secondary schools in early 1940.

In this section we have shown how 'the state' acted on multiple, contradictory and sometimes very personal levels. 'Translation' needs to be understood, as Rose suggests, as a bumpy process with different actors infusing it with their own agendas. In the following section we take this analysis further, as we focus our gaze at the personal level, and consider how the micro-actions and interactions of council officials affected residents' relationships with the state.

State on the ground – from face-to-face to facelessness

Thrift (2000) and others have shown that for the majority of the population 'the state' existed primarily at the level of the personal. It is through encounters with particular police officers, social workers or housing officers that the state is formed in the minds of individuals, and through those encounters that their place in relation to the state is located. Bourke has observed how people's experience locally

> was essentially their experience of national politics, institutions and structures. People did not experience the 'Education System', they experienced neighbourhood primary schools: they did not experience the 'Health Service', but local clinics.
>
> (1993: 166)

As this suggests, these encounters do not simply occur between certain people, but also in specific, meaning charged, places. In this section we begin by considering the attitudes displayed by council officials towards a particular fraction of estate residents in the decades after the Second World War, before exploring the response of residents themselves. In the second half of the section we consider residents' relationships with the council, and how they might have changed over time.

The 'classic' welfare state has been criticized for being top-down in its approach, for creating passive recipients of benefits and services, and for failing to move away from the old poor law dichotomy of the deserving and undeserving poor:

> social security policy has been managed, not with the needs of poor people to the fore, but within a framework of ideological, economic philosophies, which have often been anti-poor both in sentiment and application.

> (Walker, 1993: 1)

It is undoubtedly the case that there was an institutionalization of attitudes relating to the deserving and undeserving poor, with benefit applications from certain groups such as immigrants, Travellers, and unmarried mothers being viewed more unfavourably than those from those seen as 'deserving', such as the elderly (Hill, 1969; Taylor, 2008; Walker, 1993).

Characteristic of the period up to the 1970s at least was the importance of face-to-face encounters with particular officials – perhaps hostile, perhaps sympathetic – in relatively informal settings. Typically these might take place in the house of an individual, or at a clinic or school based in the estates themselves. Thus while there were institutionalized attitudes towards particular 'classes' of person, these were mediated through the individual officials concerned, often in places outside welfare offices. As we show below, we can make no easy equation between 'home' encounters and sympathetic officials, nor between office-based encounters and negative relations: visiting an office may be viewed daunting and alien, or a neutral professional space, while official visits to an individual's house may be taken as being intrusive:

> When I called Mrs Ibbotson opened the door and said, 'Nurse Coe has been, Mrs Thurling [the home adviser] keeps calling and I've had the Sanitary Inspector and two Welfare Officers in the house, my husband says I'm not to let anyone else in.'... She went to say that neighbours are beginning to talk about her.[17]

One feature of welfare–client relations in this 'classic' period of the welfare state was the expectation that recipients of benefits would be passive, with those who tried to assert their rights roundly criticized, and sometimes actively obstructed in their attempts to receive welfare benefits (Hill, 1969: 82). This was particularly apparent in the treatment of households defined as 'unsatisfactory' or 'problem families'.[18] In such cases council employees dealing with these cases held simultaneously contradictory views: on the one hand families were deemed as being in need of focused attention and resources, and on the other they were criticized if they actively solicited such help. Mrs Fairly, for example, was particularly unpopular with staff in part because she spent

> her time gossiping and trailing around the city seeking advice and help from one Welfare Department to another, complaining about her husband and asking for the children to be admitted to a home... [she] complains that her husband leaves her without money and that he 'knocks her about'.[19]

Reports of the Fairly household, spanning 13 years, reveal how they suffered from a number of interrelated problems: Mrs Fairly had a poor, mutually antagonistic, and sometimes violent, relationship with her husband; he was frequently unemployed and she often resorted to casual work or begging; she had a cleft palate which made it difficult for her to communicate; she had mental health problems, and struggled to look after her three children. Yet, as we see in the above extract, through using words such as 'gossiping', 'trailing around' and 'complains' the health visitor implies that not only were Mrs Fairly's problems somehow not genuine, but also that she had no right actively to solicit help. Significantly, as suggested in Ferguson and Gupta's (2005) work on how hierarchy is embedded in spatial practice, while the health visitor and home adviser felt able to visit the Fairly's home whenever they felt fit, this right was not seen as reciprocal: Mrs Fairly's visits to the welfare department and other offices in active attempts to solicit help counted against her, and merely confirmed her status as one of the undeserving poor in the eyes of officials.

Mrs Fairly, like other mothers on the estates who were on the unsatisfactory households list, was frowned on in part because while they received state attention, nothing in their behaviour demonstrated that the resources directed at them had had any effect. The health visitor expressed her frustration on this matter with reference to another mother, Mrs Walters:

> They are typical of an 'over-cared for' unsatisfactory household. They are improvident, much in debt (in spite of this Mrs Walters is arranging for television to be installed). They have, it seems had an

abundance of material help for many years. They are known to every social welfare society in the city. It is a 'poor' home with a standard of living much below average. Mrs Walters thoroughly enjoys our much attention and looks upon herself as an 'interesting' case.[20]

Other estate residents exhibited a range of responses when confronted with the barrage of officials on their doorsteps. Some of the individuals concerned were able, at least at the micro-level, to use the attention of the council to their advantage. Mrs Topley, for example, although living 'within two minutes of the Welfare', expected the home adviser to collect her milk. Similarly, when the home adviser took clothing to Mrs Topley, the home adviser 'was told to take them back as they were not good enough'.[21] Others clearly appreciated the help and advice given, particularly it seems by the home adviser. Sometimes she took on the daily shopping, and in one case was entrusted with buying Christmas presents by a father while he was in work, knowing he was likely to be unemployed over the winter.[22] For those who found it harder to tolerate the incursions of welfare officials, responses ranged from abuse, outright and rude refusal of entry, to semi-compliance or evasion:

> generally [she] will not answer the door.... If by any chance she should do so she resents the slightest complaint and will stand and shout abuse. If I am very persistent, the Welfare windows will be smashed.[23]

The ongoing frustration of officials at their inability to change the behaviour of these households gives us an insight into the limitations of the state to control the behaviour of families, even those receiving intensive attention. While the home adviser, health visitor and others may have had aspirations to change the daily practices of households, these officials were commonly forced to confront the fact that, as Knowles (1999) suggests, their clients were agents able to deflect the disciplinarity of the state.

Not only were the recipients of the attentions of the council active agents, but it is equally clear that neighbours of these families were also actors. As we suggested in Chapter 3, neighbourly intervention could be benign, through lending or giving food, clothing, money and child-care services, as has been documented for many poorer neighbourhoods over place and time (see for example Bourke, 1993). Yet, this was not simply the cosy world, sometimes portrayed, of working class self-help networks existing in isolation from officialdom: neighbours proactively engaged council officials to allow them to cope with problem neigh-bours. This could take the form of concerned parents informing the health visitor of neighbouring children or babies who they saw as under-fed, underdressed or coming to some kind of harm. In other instances, however, clear undertones of malice and deep animosity broke through, particularly when individuals were seen to have violated neighbourhood norms, as suggested in this anonymous letter:

> Dear Sir,
> This [Mrs Carlisle] who you had at your office this morning about her house and two children which are dirty. People have helped her and given her clothes which she has sold again.... She is a disgrace to other women who are clean to what she is.... I hear the children have no bed to lay on. She has been working at Pearl Laundry now and don't care. Pictures and a smoke is all she care. Her legs are awful and smell too. So I trust this letter of advice help you. Woman at laundry have helped her but it's no good. From one who has given her things.[24]

Although mediated through the observations of outsiders, the very exis-tence of such complaints demonstrates how even marginalized estates such as the Larkman could engage with services offered by officialdom. It is too simplistic to depict estate residents as being 'done to' by outsider officials. Thrust into a world of mass council housing, working class ten-ants expanded their existing support networks to include officialdom in their range of strategies for accessing the services of the welfare state and for managing problem neighbours. Officials may well have been resented, but they were also seen as potentially useful, with encounters varying with context and the individuals involved.

We find similar ambivalence surrounding memories of one of the central characters in many of the older respondents' stories: the 'rent man'. Until the early 1970s the council collected its rent weekly through rent collectors, who visited each house, not only to ensure that money was paid promptly, but also to keep an eye on properties. In some ways as emblematic as 'the matron' in 'failing' hospitals, the rent man was remembered as an individual who embodied the authority of the council in the estates, and who 'got things done' unburdened by the bureaucracy of today:

> But that was a really lovely estate...it had no stigma at all to it. But you had the rent man come and collect the rent. You were only

allowed to do so-and-so. And if you put a lean-to in your garden, that would be ripped down ... And you couldn't have cats and dogs in certain places. Chickens, that was all kept properly. And it's really strict. And of course, when the rent man stopped coming, that got a bit lax.

(Hilary George)

Yet Hilary's memory ignores the realities of the rent man's role, the limitations on his power and influence and the fact that many residents could well resent the restrictions imposed by him in the course of his duties: as John Burnett phrased it 'the rent man, he used to do most of the spying'. His choice of the emotive word 'spying' suggests that for some at least the days of the rent man were not a golden age: as we shall see below John had good reasons to resent his presence.

In part John's resentment stemmed from diverging perceptions of the function of local authority housing. For those granted a house on the estate, a council tenancy was viewed as for-life (and beyond, as tenancies could pass down families), and thus long-term residents naturally saw and treated their houses as their homes. In contrast, the council, embodied here in the rent man, saw the houses as public property over which it had a long-term duty to maintain, with a right to ensure that certain standards were kept (Ravetz, 2001: 123). Council housing might provide freedom from the uncertainties of the private sector, but independence gained in this sense carried with it a certain loss of autonomy.

The tension over the council house as private space or public property is epitomized in the Burnetts' decades-long conflict with the council over running their fruit and vegetable business from their house. Records of the conflict in the housing committee minutes show two things – the level of council surveillance and officials' detailed knowledge of individual properties; and the Burnetts' persistent resistance to outsider interference:

[In] April the tenant was asked to remove two sheds erected by him in his back garden without permission, and from which he was believed to be trading; and to cease parking his lorry at the side of the house, and to reinstate the front garden fence. Fence was fixed, but the tenant erected gates, and continued parking his lorry at the side of the house; the sheds remained, for storing 'vegetables, etc'. Committee resolved that provided that no trading is being conducted no further action be taken.[25]

[Tenant] has always maintained that he does not trade from his house but he has two sheds adjoining the house which he uses for storing vegetables etc.... the chief public health inspector... feels that the sheds are too dilapidated and break food hygiene regulations. Tenant has always maintained that as long ago as 1954 he was given permission to use his sheds in connection with his trade. Resolved – to require him to demolish the buildings and allow Housing Committee to erect a suitable building, if he signs an agreement saying he is not trading from his home.[26]

When asked about the attitude of the council to his business, John remembered: 'I used to get threatened every year, with eviction, yeah. Then we used to just tell the people [customers] to be a bit careful. And they'd go away for a year'.

What does this saga, insignificant on one level, tell us about estate residents and their relationship with this local manifestation of state? The rent man and public health inspector noted the erection of sheds without permission, and we can infer perhaps that they knew that trading was conducted from the house despite a lack of hard evidence. Yet, over time, despite their efforts, it was the Burnetts and not the council who won. Even in the hey-day of the 'rent man', his influence was not as extensive as memories portray: yes, he was a presence on the estates, he might have known what was going on, but what, in fact, were his powers? Only in the most extreme circumstances did councils evict tenants, and while the warnings of the rent man may have influenced the more law-abiding, those who kept up with their rent but chose to ignore some of the myriad of restrictions placed upon them as council tenants would probably find that they would prevail. The Burnetts' autonomy may have only been confirmed in law on the day John finally bought his house, but in fact it had been established many decades before.

John Burnett's memory of being threatened with eviction 'every year' is not supported by evidence from the council minutes. It may be that the rent man, with no authorization, used verbal but unsubstantiated threats of eviction as a tool to try and influence their behaviour. It might also be a simple exaggeration, a means to portray himself as the savvy estate resident able to outwit the impotent official. For, although in general we found that people's memories were poor when it came to remembering their use of different aspects of what might formally be thought of as 'the welfare state', there was one particular area which commonly elicited tales. This was the genre of story of the 'little person' standing up to bureaucracy, and most often related to the allocation of council housing (see also Portelli, 1997). In these stories often the individual, but sometime the parent or spouse, made the journey up to City Hall to harass officials, until finally a house was allocated. Often the narrator asserted their protagonist's independence, through refusing one particular house or insisting on another in defiance of the original intentions of the housing official:

> I used to go every lunch time to the housing office.... And see this pompous little character behind the wicket. 'What, you again? Nothing, we ain't got nothing.' And he, one day, I must have been sort of skint, and not in a very good mood... I had a vile temper in those days, and he was sort of taking the mickey.... So I grabbed him, and I pulled him through this hatch. And I was going to kill him. I would then. And then [laughs] the door opened, next door, and a lady come out. And she said, 'put him down'... [laughs]. So I put this bloke down. And she took me in the room next door, didn't she. And she said, 'I understand your plight, da da da da.' And within ten days they offered us a house.
>
> (Joe Hastings)

Stories such as this highlight the complex relationship between individuals and the state, as personified through officials such as housing officers. While on the one hand, these officials may have been painted as uncaring and tied up in bureaucracy, what is clear however is that in many of the stories recounted to us, encounters took place on a personal level. Whatever a resident thought of the rent man, home adviser or public health inspector, it seems that it was possible to build up a personal relationship via face-to-face encounters. Within such personal contact it might be possible to negotiate room to manoeuvre, to reach a shared understanding or to use it as a means of gaining housing or other services. It might, of course, as in the case of Mrs Fairly, result in ongoing antipathy and official obstructionism.

Following restructuring and a centralization of staff from the 1970s resulting in the cutback in persistent and regular contact with people on the ground, there was a shift from 'faced' to 'faceless' encounters. In the process the onus was shifted onto the tenant to reach the council:

> there were these two open [air] telephones on Larkman Lane... people felt very nervous of the phone, understandably if that was on the edge of the road... where were you going if you didn't have a phone at home? How were you going to do all this complicated negotiation with cars rattling up and down... [Sue] had three little children and... agencies don't understand the barriers people have to get over just to get on a bus with your children and get to some sort of help and how difficult and courageous that is... I'd taken her there [to central Norwich] and then left her [for a short time]... when I got

back she wasn't there and when I went round to see her the next day she said 'I couldn't do it, I couldn't go in. I just couldn't go in. I just looked inside and I could see all these people looking smart and efficient and they had papers, and they had papers in their hands and they knew what all these papers were and I thought, "I don't know any of this, I can't do it," and I just turned around and went home.'

(Penny Langley)

As Penny's observations indicate, individuals' relationships with the council are governed by a range of micro-factors, beginning with how one is (un)able to contact council workers, through to the (in)ability to go to the office and walk through the door. The importance of 'little things' in governing how people experience 'the council' is drawn out in Becky's field notes relating to a visit to the area housing office, which is located on the estates:

When I arrived at the office – grey prefab building, rather tatty looking – noticed the sign in the window – 'if closed please DO NOT BANG ON WINDOWS speak to a receptionist or other staff'. When I got inside the office was a man – late 50s? – speaking to the (young, male) receptionist. He was obviously complaining about the bureaucratic process – said that he votes for the councillors, and the council is there for the people, but he being passed around between people in the office, with no joy. The receptionist said that that was not the point, but he would pass on the man's details; the man specifically asked to be rung when something had happened, and left his number. The receptionist was not rude, but gave me a 'see what I have to deal with' look (thereby identifying me as not being a potential client?).

The unprepossessing environment signalled on the outside of the building was reinforced by the kind of utilitarian interior suggested in the research highlighted by Jones and Novak (1999). While not necessarily 'unwelcoming' and certainly of value in being located within walking distance for tenants, this observation in fact reveals the anonymity of the relationship between the tenant and the council. The emptiness of a faced encounter which was not grounded in an ongoing relationship was reinforced by the fact that the individual with whom the tenant came into contact had no actual power to act on the complaint.

The sign asking visitors not to bang on the windows, in addition to the look given to Becky by the receptionist, signals that the staff working in the office also experienced difficulties with their working situation. If not explicitly feeling threatened, then it is easy to see how frontline staff feel alienated from their clients. Interviewed about how people viewed the council, the housing manager said she felt strongly that people tended to see 'the council' as a faceless bureaucracy, and contact from 'someone from the council' was an undifferentiated and interchangeable experience. The manager observed that this was despite the fact that that even when she had introduced herself, gave someone her card with her contact details on, people would still get in contact with someone else and say simply that they had spoken to 'someone from the council'.

As the interview wound down she spoke about the importance of keeping the area office open, as people liked to have somewhere where they could come and speak to people face to face (even if it was just a receptionist). She acknowledged that a lot of council contact with people was now based on the assumption that people had access to a phone and the Internet. But she noted that while people may have mobile phones they don't necessarily have the credit to make use of them. The spread of technology may have created the illusion of a flexible tenant–council relationship, with each party only a phone call or an email away, but the reality is perhaps no different than pre-mobile days, when many residents were forced to rely on one of the two pay phones on the estates.

Briefly, in this section using selected examples we have shown how face-to-face interactions embodied the state for residents, and saw how, crucially, such encounters opened a space in which individuals might assert their agency. While this form of interaction did not necessarily produce positive outcomes for residents, they nevertheless provided the state with a human face. And as the last part of this section suggests, the decline of faced encounters has been problematic for tenants and the council alike. In the final part of the chapter we move on to discuss how such difficulties fed estate-based community action, and in the context of new discourses of governance, became formalized in the NDC programme.

Community and the workfare state

> There was a lot going on before NELM even come here believe you me...we managed before NELM and we'll manage when they in't 'ere.
>
> (Edith Hughes)

We showed in Chapter 3 how the economic and cultural context of poverty altered significantly over the twentieth century. Such changes mirrored and were reinforced by changing discourses of welfare. Ravetz has observed how, in its 18 years in government, the New Right 'successfully established a new social – and virtually a now moral – order in place of the discredited Welfare State'. This defined disadvantage as a lack of freedom to engage in the market, which had the effect of making it into 'an individual rather than a social or class condition, and consequently one to be addressed by individual effort rather than combined action' (Ravetz, 2001: 196).[27] New Labour did not repudiate, but instead built on this neoliberalist analysis of poverty, which was increasingly discussed in terms of 'social exclusion'. Additionally, both rhetoric and action targeted the (perceived) failings of the state sector, suggesting that the market and individuals, now repositioned as consumers rather than citizens, were best placed to provide services. However, Rose (1999: 168) points out, the free market solution has not been unchallenged, seeing the rise in discourse and governmental creation of 'community' as a 'third space' which both accepts the repositioning of citizens in relation to the state implied by neoliberalism, and is a challenge to it.

The implied 'natural-ness' of the idea of community and its ability to draw on the ideological canons of both the Left and Right allows it to appear 'somehow, external to politics and as a counter-weight to it'. However, in reality community became inextricably bound to ideas of governance, as it is simultaneously 'the object and target for the exercise of political power' (Rose, 1999: 168). In part, this was through challenging the naturalness of local authority service provision for disadvantaged people, with the discourse of community providing a space in which the possibility for new means of delivering services could be considered. Consequently, the mistrust of the function of local authorities continued beyond the period of Conservative government, through New Labour's 'new localism'[28] and community agendas:

> When New Labour started, they were definitely trying to wind down the power and responsibility of local councils...there's definitely an agenda saying 'let's get housing out of councils, let's get education out of councils. Let's get regeneration out of councils.' And to set up special purpose vehicles to do it.
>
> (NELM employee)

The NDC programme thus emerged as part of a wider context of reworking forms of governance. Whatever the wider intentions of this agenda, as Corbridge et al. (2005) suggest, it also created a formal space in which residents might – in the eyes of the state – legitimately assert their voice. Our intention here is not to give an overall assessment of the effectiveness of NELM in delivering its stated targets,[29] but rather to draw out what this initiative reveals about the workings of the state and its interactions with a particular area or 'community' that 'got organised'.

If this is some of the national context, what were the views from the ground on ideas of 'community' and the role of local government? What was clear was the long tradition of estate-based action, and how it was seen as having largely emerged in the context of the absence of state initiative. We recorded people's involvement right across the period in a range of child and youth groups, clubs and activities for the elderly and various church-based activities, which included in the 1960s parishioners raising the money and building a new church on the Marlpit estate. When we asked people about their involvement in action and projects on the estates the stories told were, once again, of the little people standing up to, or revealing, the incompetence of the council: people had been forced to act because of council inaction, and where the council stepped in, it was seen as undermining, and often ruining, community initiatives. Residents spoke with considerable pride of the voluntary efforts they had made in particular to provide community centres – often beginning as a 'hut' on unallocated land on the estate – and activities for the young people of the estates. As Flo Smith commented in relation to the community centre on the Larkman estate:

> Now the Monkey Island, down in Fourways...the locals were running their own community centre and they had something every night for the kids, then the council stepped in, and there ain't a lot going on down there now.

In fact, this attitude were part of a wider sense that the area had been unfairly treated by the council. Mrs Malley spoke for many research participants when she said, 'I think they've abandoned this estate.' A voluntary support worker expanded on this feeling and its implications:

> There was this quite substantial view of this existential injustice that the entire population had. It was almost like they knew they'd been shat on somehow but they couldn't point at it...there was that long history of what they believed to have been neglect...that they, they

saw all of that as being the responsibility and driven by the statutory authorities' attitude to the area.

(Jane Knox)

Jane here touched on an important component of residents' collective identification, how their sense of community was defined in opposition to outsiders. As will become clear as the story of NELM unfolds, this particular take on 'community' had a profound impact on its creation and functioning.

Yet, this powerful feeling of abandonment and alienation is in part contradicted by other evidence. By the mid-1990s, well before the NELM partnership emerged, the council had in fact been actively trying to improve the environment of the estates, its relationship with tenants and the life chances of residents, either through direct council area-based initiatives or through working with partner agencies. The two central organizations were the Community Power forum for council tenants and West Norwich Partnership, both of which placed a great deal of emphasis on the agencies working directly with local people. West Norwich Partnership was a multi-agency grouping which included residents from the estates, and it funded and supported a range of initiatives relating to education, young people's issues and social services.[30] Community Power, was described in official literature as 'what happened when local people get together and do something to change whatever they are (usually) unhappy with'.[31] It was through Community Power that the residents, who later formed the core group bidding for NDC funding, worked together for the first time.

Despite this, what is interesting is how the 'little people' genre of story carried over into narratives about the creation of the NELM community organization. Memories of the creation of NELM revolved around two particular incidents: the discovery that the council had applied for funding for the area without consulting anyone from the area; and a trip down to London where residents were able to find out more about the NDC initiative:

we heard that this money was on offer but that the council had never consulted with … any of the residents and we heard they were having their last meeting. It was mainly with business men and the council, so we went down the City Hall and walked in on the meeting and said as they hadn't succeeded in getting the money we were gonna take it over, which we did. And we got the money.

(Sandra Dyson)

Brenda said to me one day... 'the government's saying there's got to be oh so many millions of pounds going out to... initiatives to regenerate the areas' so I say 'so what? They're gonna turn everything around?' You know, laughing! And so she said 'no', she says 'there's a big meeting up London d'you want a go.' Say 'I can't afford to go to London,' which I couldn't... she said 'oh you ain't got to pay. We're going on a bus they gonna pick us up over Budgens' so I say 'alright then' I say 'I'll come with yer'... I can remember going to this meeting in this big hall up London... then I can remember [the] day, come up there and the minister announced that we got the grant!

(Edith Hughes)

In these accounts residents were at the heart of the action, working on behalf of their 'community', intervening directly, cutting out the (uncaring) local council and going straight to the heart of government, where they were heard and their needs responded to. We have shown just a few of the multiple expressions of mistrust and alienation voiced by residents to us about Norwich council revealing different angles of a dysfunctional relationship between the local authority and (some) estate residents. The council's long-term practice of housing those with multiple difficulties in a small number of streets within the North Earlham/Larkman estate ensured there was a pool of tenants with potentially difficult relationships with the council. The removal of everyday face-to-face encounters with council staff, and the centralization of estate management made it more difficult for some tenants to reach the council, thus substantiating folk belief in a remote and bureaucratic council. And while some sections of the council may have been actively trying to improve matters for estate residents, this did not mean that the whole council was committed to the project. As Carol White, an ex-Community Power worker explained:

Carol: The rest of the council employees weren't too enamoured about this Community Power thing at all. I would ring up other departments saying 'I'm the Community Power worker' and have 'Rer-rer-rer', 'Ooh sorry I spoke'. It was, it wasn't an easy position to be in.

BT: So it was politically difficult for you in terms of your own work?

Carol: Yeah and [sighs]

BT: Even though it was a council initiative?

Carol: Yeah it wasn't signed up to completely by the whole council and or all of it's employees.

By the mid-1990s, estate residents' dissatisfactions with the council consequently chimed with, and reinforced, ideology stemming from central government about the desirability of redirecting the arts of welfare government towards the 'third space' that was 'community'. In this, the inability of the council to coordinate all its personnel to support Community Power and to engage the estate residents in its first attempt to bid for NDC funds reinforced perceptions of it as needing to make way for a new approach.

And yet, as Gardner (2007: 3–4) has observed, the NDC programme revealed a tendency for local residents to 'blame obvious proximal factors for difficulties' while showing a 'lack an appreciation of wider issues and interconnections'. Without wishing to underplay the mistakes of the council in maintaining its housing stock and relationships with tenants, it is clear that in the case of the NDC agenda 'the council' acted as a scapegoat for the more deep-seated problems experienced by the estates. We argue that it is essential to place the relative power of the council in the context of their relative powerlessness in the face of the fundamental shifts in the structure of the British economy since the 1970s, and in wider local authority relationships with central government. The council may have failed to engage fully with its tenants and to provide them with an adequate service, but it was not in itself responsible for the growth in long-term unemployment and absence of the kind of employment opportunities that had sustained estate residents from the 1930s to the 1970s.

And just as the economic climate of Britain fundamentally changed, so too had the governmental climate. For council tenants, central to this change was the 'right to buy' policy promoted in the 1980s. While individual ex-tenants and their families have enjoyed the benefits of the privatization of housing stock, the inability of councils to reinvest the money received from sales into maintaining and creating more local authority housing contributed to the problem of residualization: fewer local authority houses meant that rather than being housing for a broad section of society, councils became increasingly focused on providing homes for the most needy and vulnerable on the housing list. This policy also exacerbated the chronic under-funding of council repairs and maintenance that had been facilitated by the long-term emphasis in Britain (in contrast to much of mainland Europe) on low rents as a crucial factor in state housing provision (Burrows, 1999; Power and Tunstall, 1995; Power, 1999).

For the residents of the NELM estates these structural shifts in the economy and local authority powers had profound consequences. The impact of the right-to-buy policy has largely been felt indirectly as less than 8 per cent of residents of the NELM estates had exercised this right by 1999, compared to a city-wide average of 28 per cent (NELM, 1999: 8). What it meant was that the area continued to hold one of the largest pools of local authority housing in the city, with the tendency towards residualization reinforcing the long-term council policy of housing 'problem families' in the area. We saw in Chapter 3 the impact on the area of growing unemployment on the estates – particularly of young people and of the long-term unemployed – as a result of the gradual closure of the city's factories. Combined with under-investment in the housing stock and the accommodation of multiply disadvantaged households in the estates it is easy to see how the council became a target for the anger of residents who felt they had been 'abandoned'. At the same time, perceived failures on the ground on the part of councils could be interpreted, by a central government keen to prove the inefficiency of local authorities, as evidence of the need for new forms of governance at the local level.

Seen in this light, the NDC scheme can be seen as serving the interests of both central government and, superficially at least, some residents of the NELM estates. For both, the council could act as a convenient scapegoat for past and continuing failures. For both, the idea of 'community' could act as an ideological peg on which to hang their ideas. A central feature of the NDC programme was the way in which it, as a scheme, could bypass existing structures and services and create its own bespoke agenda. While there was an expectation that local authority agencies would be in partnership with the NDC organizations, the programme as a whole was very much about particular localities being singled out by central government, being given not only financial resources, but also direct access to the highest levels of government:

> They were suddenly being listened to, they were being well, Princess Diana came to see them, they've shaken hands with John Prescott.[32] Alright that might not...! [laughter] They had his phone number, they used to 'I'm gonna phone John' [laughs] and this influence, this capability, this opportunity to gain things by virtue of a network of contacts was all new to them.

> (Jane Knox)

In people's memories of the fight for funding and the early years of NELM it is clear that this period was, although requiring very hard work and an enormous amount of commitment on the part of relatively few individuals, fundamentally empowering (Wells, 2003). Their actions stemmed from and reinforced the culture of resourcefulness we discussed in Chapter 3: winning £35.5 million through their own actions and against all the odds, those involved were able to see the money as 'earned' and not as 'welfare'. Shelia Spencer, a lone parent, remembered how she had

Sheila: worked on the original...bid...we designed everything, and we carried it on from there. And that was really exciting time, 'cos you think 'oh and all this money, the things we can do'.

BT: Did it give you quite a sense of personal achievement that you had managed to help get this money?

Sheila: And also the fact that I had come off a nanny state, really. Oh! You could stay quite happily there 'cos you've got a child, you don't need to use any intelligence, you can just have your rent paid every week. And you can do your voluntary jobs and you can get £15 as a cleaner and that was it. And I'd have probably stayed that way.

From residents who had been involved in long-standing projects in the area, which had been staffed by volunteers and funded on an ad hoc basis, the injection of huge sums of money was a concrete endorsement of years of unpaid effort. The community warden scheme, for example, had its roots in an initiative by estate residents anxious to prevent vandalism on the estates' schools. Before NELM it had to put out appeals to cover the £350 it cost to train and equip each volunteer with a radio, torch and waterproof jacket.[33] After NELM won its NDC funding, this scheme was allocated £1.5 million and was able to employ people directly as well as expanding the coverage of their service.

For particular individuals who had worked hard, winning NDC status was a resounding endorsement not only of their experiences of marginalization and deprivation but also of their means of tackling those problems. As Sheila's attitude indicates, this could also signal a profound change in how they saw themselves in relation to the state. We can therefore find resonance with Corbridge et al.'s (2005) argument that changes in governance can be more than simple rhetoric: it is possible for a 'community' agenda to go beyond a shift in language and cover for an emerging agenda of liberalization. It can in fact signal new relations between individuals and the state. In this way residents were able to 'move' the way they were categorized by outsiders, challenging stereotypes of dependency and passivity which had 'fixed' them for so long.

While this may be true, fundamental flaws within the NDC programme ensured that the injection of £35.5 million into the estates was far less effective than envisaged. Central to the NDC programme was defining deprivation in relation to certain places: individualizing poverty within a 'community' rather than seeing it as being located in society more broadly. Such an approach side-stepped deep-seated economic structural changes, focusing attention instead on personal or community failures of aspiration and unwillingness to engage with the workfare economy. While individuals – as individuals – were able to engage with this agenda and use it to construct a route out of poverty, this approach did nothing to unsettle profound and growing classed inequalities. The problematic nature of this approach within NDC areas can be seen in how community organizations worked within this analysis of poverty and created projects tailored to improving individual educational profiles and skill sets. The NELM delivery plan, for example, identified the *root causes* of the area's problems as 'the lack of decent employment *due to poor educational attainment* and *a lack of ambition and horizons*' (NELM, 1999: 1, emphasis added).[34]

Beyond limitations in the analysis of poverty, we can see how bidding for New Deal status was part of the process of being required to 'claim' deprivation (Mosse, 1999). As Gardner (2007) and others (see for example Gotovos, 2005) have observed, there are many people located in defined 'deprived' communities who resent and resist such categorization. In the course of our fieldwork we were actively challenged by some residents who objected to 'deprivation' in the title of our project, even though we tried to explain that we were trying to question this label. Even for those who were involved in the NELM bid such positioning was not unproblematic, despite having had to embrace the process of claiming the area as 'deprived' to win funding:

We're in Cambridge at this conference for regeneration and they had all the ministers up there and this bloke was saying about this community ... and I think, 'God wouldn't live there, how dreadful it must be to live there,' right and then he said, 'Norwich'. Well I nearly fell off me chair Ben, I couldn't believe it! ... I just said 'Excuse me,' you know, 'that place you're describing is where I live, one of four generations,' I said 'and that's my life.' I said 'I thought you were talking about somewhere like Beirut.' I did honestly. I said 'We do have barbecues, you know,' and I said, 'I would strongly object to the language that you're talking about our community.' And when we were having a coffee break this bloke come over ... and he said 'I'm very sorry....

We have to use these words of "deprivation" and, you say these things because you won't get the money.' I said 'Yeah but, you know, that's not nice for us.'

(Audrey Gilbert)

In the competition between areas to show who was the most excluded, the instrumental use of particular identities went beyond emphasizing the deprivation of the area, as the presence of a large settled Traveller population on the estates was deployed as part of NELM's bid:

Jane: Oh it was blatant, you can read it in the press releases and everything and Anne bless her was just she was like Catherine the Great, I mean she was milking this for all it was worth, unbelievable.

BR: Yeah, it's fantastic actually and also you said it was the only one that, you know, 'even Sunderland didn't have Travellers!'

Jane: [laughs] I'm sorry but Sunderland's kind of held up isn't it.

BR: Is it?

BT: Is that the most deprived place?

Jane: Oh well they reckon, you know, 'I'm poorer than you'. [laughs]

(Jane Knox)

Audrey: Politically it's sometimes good to have Travellers in the community 'cos there's reddies in it, but sometimes it isn't politically correct to have Travellers. So if we need money then we will say...

BR: You've got Travellers.

Audrey: Yeah.

(Audrey Gilbert)

NELM did not simply have to claim 'deprivation' and to deploy instrumentally the idea of having an established minority population in order to win funding, it also had to claim 'community'. Participation in the NELM project meant buying into the idea of the three estates as a community unified by geography, needs and solutions. Given the long-term residence of many of the estates' population, this might appear to be relatively unproblematic. However, residence in a particular locality and even knowing people does not necessarily translate into similar needs and solutions, for as we saw in Chapter 2 in reality the area is divided by roads, loyalties, definitions, representations and experiences. We can see here the tension between categorization, identification and agency: those involved in the bid may have been actively 'getting organized', but it was within externally imposed conditions which demanded that the self-identifications of NELM tallied with the preconceived categorizations of the state. This led to those involved in the NELM bid actively categorizing the area, other residents and themselves, something that was an uncomfortable and contested process.

The NELM programme was meant to be 'community led', but despite the huge sum of money given to the organization, there was no reflection on or discussion of exactly what was meant by 'the community'. Jane Knox observed that the individuals who were initially involved in NELM 'were representative of the factions in the community that were active at that time...but those factions were not necessarily representative of the total of the community'. Gardner (2007: 3) has revealed the 'shallow' nature of much involvement in 'community' affairs. Given the very limited involvement of the majority of residents in local action – perhaps reading a newsletter or occasionally attending an event – being active within the estates through running a youth group, lunch club or play scheme by the late 1990s became translated into being a 'community leader', able to represent the needs of the estates. Rose has observed:

> As community becomes a valorised political zone, a new political status has been given to the 'indigenous' authorities of community. For to govern communities, it seems one must first of all link oneself up with those who have, or claim, moral authority in 'the black community' or 'the local community'...in this apparently natural space, the authority of community authorities, precisely because it is governed by no explicit codes and rules of conduct, is often even more difficult to contest than that of experts and professionals.
>
> (Rose, 1999: 189)

And as Gardner (2007: 4) comments, 'dominant voices can drown out those on the margins.' Consequently the story of NELM not only crystallized residents' relationships with the state and new models of welfare, but it also held up to scrutiny their relationships with each other, notably the power inequalities between individuals. Stories relating to the formation of NELM centre again and again on a handful of people who captured the momentum generated by the wider group, and were seemingly able to direct it towards their own ends:

> Vicky would be very good at some meetings in London...looking very smart, and power woman dressing stuff, getting hold of ministers, getting hold of government officials, and putting the Youth

Zone agenda and I was sort of in the back, saying 'Well actually this is about...'... [But Vicky would say] 'My brother was killed by drugs...we want to change this. We are the Lockes, we're gonna change this and this is what we want to do. That's what we're gonna do with this New Deal.' You see. And the rest of us 'Oh no. Oh. Well...'... [There was a] meeting that the Lockes came to with a very well organised poster of Youth Zone and that meeting was dominated by Vicky, completely... so what we've got is loads of the community in the school hall and they were very cross that it had been taken over by the council and they wanted to have their say in this but the person who had most to say was Vicky.

BR: So in, Vicky was able to harness that anger and sort of steer it in a certain direction?

Penny: Yes absolutely.

The ability of a small group to dominate the process was the result of government's unproblematic embracing of a rhetoric of community solutions and the way in which this acted in a toxic combination with existing attitudes towards the council. As we have suggested, part of the culture from which activism within the estates emerged was one in which 'the council' was set in opposition to 'the community':

BT: And have you had much contact with other New Deal areas?

Anne Horsley: Not as much lately as we used to have this, there's very few of them actually community lead. There are some but most of them have involved the council in some way and we don't want that. We want to take it away from the council... which is why it's community lead and it won't change.

Given this context, it is unsurprising that NELM emerged as an organization with a deeply problematic relationship with the council and existing agencies:

[Government] made the mistake of doing... it with a blank sheet of paper: 'right, you decide as a community, this is going to be community lead, community driven'... and the Lockes would say 'this is community driven we don't F-ing need you', and you'd say, 'well actually if you look at the next line...'. 'We're not fucking looking at the next line, it's community lead and community driven get lost.'

(Penny Langley)

The poor relationship between NELM and outside agencies meant that the latter had little or no ability to engage with or mitigate the internal problems of the NDC organization. Through marginalizing existing agencies and individuals with experience, and handing power to 'the community' – when in fact that community had at best only ever been a cobbled together grouping of interests with occasionally converging but often diverging interests, and at worst became the personal empire of a handful of individuals – NELM as an organization was riven through with issues of poor governance:

> [At the first board meeting] there was four or five voices raised up at all times 'f'ing this, f'ing that', threatening people... I think I was terrified of everyone, 'cos you used to sit there and try and get a point across and then there'd be people threatening each other... I've seen people, people being hit, I've seen people being spat on.... When one person left here, they took six hundred pounds of furniture with them. Now everybody including people here knew that's happening and nobody did a thing.... I could go to and knock on people's doors now, say 'come to the MCC [Marlpit Communications Centre] you can have a really good lunch,' you mention NELM, 'Oh, no, don't want anything to do with them, the Lockes run that.' And I say, 'the Lockes do not run that, you might have thought they did in the first place.' But they still have this image of it being ran the way it used to be, with threats. With horrible threats to some people.
>
> (Sheila Spencer)

As Sheila suggests, the problems with governance unsurprisingly spilled over into how funding was directed and issues over outreach. On a day-to-day basis, complaints were levelled at NELM that the beneficiaries of its projects rarely extended beyond the families and acquaintances of NELM staff.

The irony of the story of NELM is that over time it has become taken over by outsiders. First as employees from the council became seconded to NELM, and then through the commissioning process, which required all projects to re-bid for funding leading to money going to projects other than those created by original estate activists. Over time, an increasing number of those who had been involved in the project from the beginning have found their projects cut and/or have become marginalized within the organization – a position reinforced geographically as their offices were relocated away from the main office, on the other side of the busy Dereham Road. As a current NELM employee observed, central government has moved away from its original stress on community-based solutions, and is once again accepting that local authorities may be important vehicles for delivering services:

> Although there is a lot of community involvement in NDC...where does this class power lie, well, it still lies within the middle classes. And it still lies within the structures of the local authority and Whitehall etc. Residents are there, some of them being turned into bureaucrats. Some of them carry on banging their fists against the table, but I don't think there's been a shift in power yet.

For those who have been long involved in NELM what remains is a strong sense, once again, of betrayal:

> we are now what we didn't want to be which is another arm of the government and that's a shame and that is very, very, very upsetting...all our dreams have been taken by other people and that's very sad, very sad, yeah.
>
> (Audrey Gilbert)

Almost at the end of the ten-year programme of funding what can we say about the NDC initiative and its impact on the area it is meant to benefit? Casual encounters and conversations as well as our more in-depth interviews and life histories all indicated a high degree of cynicism for the effectiveness of NELM in all but specific areas. Individuals did have positive experiences of a particular project or an individual within a scheme who had helped them out, but this is a far cry from fundamentally challenging the experience of poverty and exclusion identified as being a major factor in the lives of many who live on the estates:

> I think if that was taken away they wouldn't even know that had been and gone. I'm saying the majority of the, of people who live in this area, it wouldn't make any difference to them whether that was there or not.... I can't see where that really makes a difference to the people in the community. I mean I meet most of the mothers at the school, and I've never ever heard of one of them say anything about it.
>
> (Diane Kemp)

In a very real sense, the history of council estate residents' relationship with the state over the course of the twentieth century has been an ongoing experiment practised by those in power on those with little power. In this chapter we have shown how the relationship between all actors involved in the process of 'translation' of policy has been dynamic, contingent and often fraught with conflict. Within this process it is true that residents have been able to negotiate advantage, though often of a partial and short-term nature, and in the context of specific face-to-face encounters. Overall they have acted from a position of disadvantage, within contexts and categorizations imposed on them by outsiders. While wrapped up in the rhetoric of community and empowerment, the NDC temporarily gave a voice to those who 'got organized', but ultimately they were simply another flawed face of that experiment. In the following chapter we explore in more depth the classed encounters and identifications thrown up in estate residents' personal interactions.

5
Class

In this chapter we focus explicitly on class identifications and how class is experienced subjectively. In contrast to pronouncements of the declining salience of class (Clark et al., 1993; Pakulski and Waters, 1996), it has been shown to be of importance in explaining continuing (even increasing) inequalities in social and economic space, in terms of access to material, cultural and social resources (Bourdieu, 1990; Savage, 2000; Sayer, 2005). Class *identifications* and the effects of being categorized by others as belonging to a particular class have *also* been shown to be of critical relevance in British society (Reay, 1998; Savage et al., 2001; Sayer, 2005; Skeggs, 1997). These are the focus of the present chapter. Just as in Chapters 2 and 6 we argue for the need to understand the fluidity of *spatial* boundaries, here we show how *class* identifications for individuals are not fixed but rather shift over time, and are narrated and change relationally (Somers, 1994).

Thus in this chapter we build on approaches that have conceptualized class as complex, ambivalent and situational, while at the same time being profoundly influenced by material and structural factors (Devine et al., 2005). Like Kirk (2007: 7) we insist on

> the historical mutability of ... class formations and experiences, the centrality of subjective responses and articulations (by class subjects and about class subjectivities), as well as the often neglected importance of the necessary intersection between class and other forms of social identity.

This emphasis draws us in the direction of Thompson's understanding of class as 'a social and cultural formation', which cannot be 'defined abstractly ... but only in terms of relationship with other classes'. This 'dialogic' relation is essential for comprehending class, but it must be capable also of taking in the dimension of time, 'that is, action and reaction, change and conflict' (Thompson, 1978: 85–6).

By exploring the ambivalences surrounding class identifications that emerged through in-depth interviews, and reflecting on our own classed presence in those interviews, we show something of the contingency and relationality of such identifications, moving firmly away from the kind of fixing in place of working class people that Skeggs (2004) argues middle class public policy, media and academic discourses have so often done. Yet beyond this we also show how the importance and meaning of class identifications *change* over people's lives and through time, and how such identifications have in part been produced by processes of categorization, of essentialized ideas about class. This is a result of the historical approach we have taken, and connects with the first sense of moving histories: attempting to unfix and 'move' how histories of class and community are told. Thus our aim here is not to seek to categorize the past and present residents of the estates, but to listen to how class was spoken and/or kept silent in our (classed) interviews with research participants, some of whom were more explicit about class identifications than others.

The relational and narrative constitution of self-identification is central to our discussion here. The value of this approach lies in what it reveals about the continuing production and reproduction of class inequalities:

> Joining narrative to identity reintroduces time, space, and analytical relationality – each of which is excluded from the categorical or essentialist approach to identity... the narrative identity approach embeds the actor within relationships and stories that shift over time and space.... Within these temporal and multilayered narratives identities are formed; hence narrative identity is processual and relational.
>
> (Somers, 1994: 621)

One way in which relational aspects of identification were manifest in the course of fieldwork came through our own interactions with research participants within interview and other (less formal) settings. Sennett and Cobb's classic study in Chicago built in reflections on the class differences between the author-interviewers as upper-middle class and the research participants as working class. The authors asserted that they had to be part of the story they were telling precisely because of these differences, with their presence illuminating the relationships between classes, and how this 'was at once a limitation and a valuable angle of orientation' (1977 [1972]: 40). Here we suggest that in-depth interviews are classed encounters even when the participants being interviewed are of a similar social class to the interviewer(s) as, in these instances, the narrative tools drawn on, the allusions, facial expressions, body language and vocabulary are, just as with cross-class interviews, likely to be revealing of assumptions about the world view, tastes and prejudices of the interviewer. The multiplicity of identifications and oppositions between interviewer and interviewee means of course that class is not necessarily the most salient relation involved. All we are arguing here is that it is one aspect of identification among others which can influence in-depth interviews, though not in any predetermined way (Valentine, 2007).

The meaning of class and the expression and experience of that meaning does not simply shift personally over the course of an individual's life and in the context of particular encounters, but also, as Thompson (1978) suggests, more broadly over time. Consequently 'we need a sense of people's complexity of relationship to the historical situations they inherit' (Steedman, 1986: 19). Historical studies of class in the twentieth century have revealed both the contested nature of class boundaries and how internally differentiated classes could be (Szreter, 1996; Miles, 2003), while Steedman (1986), Reay (1998) and others remind us of the strongly gendered nature of representations of working class lives. Even in the two decades following the Second World War, which are often depicted in popular imagination as the 'golden age' of the full-time male breadwinner, stay-at-home wife and close-knit working class communities (see for example Lockwood, 1966), class experiences could be ambiguous and unsettling. Education, and particularly passing the 11+, might destabilize class identifications – what Summerfield (2000; cited by Cairns, 2008) terms 'discomposure' – as might establishing friendships or (working) relationships with individuals categorized as having or identifying with different class backgrounds.

Willis' (1977) seminal work on working class educational experiences demonstrated the logic behind the rejection of formal education by some of the subjects of his study, and the link between their actions and their gender and class identifications. Similarly, Sennett and Cobb (1977 [1972]) argued that there was no simple transaction whereby those who found white-collar occupations achieved dignity and value. Although the workers they interviewed did not seem to challenge the middle classes' right to judge the working classes, they distinctly devalued white-collar work as non-productive and relatively useless. Consequently

> those who change class, through a white collar job or a higher level of education, feel terribly ambivalent about their success, and the ambivalence they treat as a sign of vulnerability in themselves ... they hold themselves responsible for the anxiety.
>
> (Sennett and Cobb, 1972: 36–7)

Building on such problematising of education and class mobility, more recent research foregrounds the spatial dimension of individuals' ambivalence to schooling and 'getting on'. Corbett (2007: 46), for example, extended Bourdieu's concept of habitus in this way: along with economic capital, he argued, 'individuals may also have symbolic capital that connects them to particular locales' and which is 'useful for profit and identity construction "around here"' (see also discussion in Chapter 2). As well as Corbett's own research in rural seaboard Canada, a US study revealed how Appalachian students often

> consciously exchange[d] the promise of prosperity and alleged comfort offered to those who conform in school for the relative autonomy that comes with irregular employment and the outdoor life of the rural community.
>
> (Brandau and Collins, 1994 cited in Corbett, 2007: 23–4)

Taken together these studies suggest that some individuals give as much, or possibly more, weight to concerns of what might be lost through spatial mobility as to what might be gained through leaving. They also point to the importance of considering the personal, the emotional and the private when seeking to untangle the impact of class identifications on individual life choices.

If education was one way in which class identifications might become blurred or complicated, personal relations across class might also challenge and destabilize apparently bounded categories. In this chapter, therefore, we begin by considering the role of education in categorizing individuals and shaping their self-identifications. In the middle section of the chapter we move on to explore how class was (re)produced and experienced within home/work spaces and personal relations within families. In the final section we consider the interactions and classed experiences of middle class research participants who had moved into or had contact with the area.

Education, identification and ambivalence

In introducing ourselves to the research participants we did not present ourselves explicitly in class terms. When we had to explain ourselves 'from cold' it was the university base of our research that we put forward and our desire to question the stereotype of the area as 'deprived'. We did not say we were middle class researchers seeking to interview working class people or other middle class people. Class was largely unspoken in the set-up. It was however implicit.

Class played a role in producing us as authors of university-based social science/history research and the participants as tellers of their life stories. For both of us, going to university had been an expectation, reinforced by our parents' university backgrounds and the schools we went to. This was not the case for the majority of participants. Going to university as a student was rare, whereas going as a cleaner (for women) or, in the 1960s, as a construction worker (for men) was unexceptional.

In this section we begin by considering the type of education available to children growing up on the three estates, and how in various ways the options were marked by class categorizations. We then move on to show how different individuals experienced and responded to these education systems, and how it affected their self-identifications.

We found in Chapter 4 how it is too simplistic to dismiss the state as unproblematically consigning the children from the three estates to poor-quality education. The progressive Labour council was strongly committed to creating a structure of good-quality new schools for the city, following the most up-to-date educational trends. The school inspectors' reports from the 1940s and 1950s consistently stressed the friendly atmosphere of the schools, the efforts made by teachers to produce a 'secure and friendly' environment, and the 'happy' nature of the pupils.[1] And yet, as we saw, education provision was marked by overcrowding and a lack of facilities, while inspectors' reports reveal how little effort was directed towards pushing pupils academically:

> The children still spend a great deal of time on mechanical and purposeless work which neither contributes to their general development nor aids the acquisition of skills.[2]

The creators of the 1944 Education Act had envisaged parity of esteem between the different types of school, arguing that vocational, technical and academic approaches were equally valid. The reality often had very little in common with the idealized notion of a distinctive and even superior type of education that would be suitable for the needs of the mass of the population. Many schools struggled with inadequate resources and failed to establish themselves alongside more prestigious institutions. National research from the 1950s and 1960s showed that secondary moderns catered primarily for working class pupils and were generally held in far lower esteem than grammar schools: in 1956 the secondary modern inspectorate identified only 140 (out of over 3500) that were 'worth a second glance' (McCulloch, 1998: 101).

And inherent in the secondary modern system was a categorization of the pupils, which meant that teachers assumed children were being prepared for manual and factory work or for home making. Research participants remembered how in their final year of school they were taken round the factories of the city to give them a flavour of the employment options open to them:

> You knew what you got to do. You knew exactly where you got to go. You either got to go in a factory or an office, or probably shop work. And that would be it. 'Cos you couldn't really expect anything else.
>
> (Gina Malley)

In 1964 the headmaster of the Henderson secondary modern school publicly stated that

> some boys were attempting too much in the way of G.C.E. subjects. He suggested that perhaps they should do less. In attempting to assimilate too much on one occasion the boys were liable to 'suffer from indigestion'.[3]

Even after the Gurney and Henderson secondary modern schools were united and became the Bowthorpe comprehensive school in 1970, change was slow. One teacher who had been involved in the shift to the comprehensive system was positive about the changes, believing that the end of the 11+ and catchment areas in the city brought 'immediate benefits'. These included more money, a wider range of subjects and, by 1975, the first pupils going on to higher and further education.[4] These memories, however, have to be set against the recollections of another teacher who joined the staff just after it became comprehensive:

> The teachers who had taught in the old Gurney Henderson schools did have this thing about 'these are children who are deprived, who

come from thick families, they're not likely to be anything other than that' so there was opposition to me taking Merchant of Venice.

(Susan Marshall)

Susan herself was very clear about the classed expectations of her colleagues, which had an impact on the schooling choices she made for her own daughter. When Susan started her job her eldest daughter was coming up for secondary school and Susan and her husband decided that she should apply to City of Norwich School (CNS). In Britain middle class people have been found to be relatively silent in relation to their own class backgrounds, in contrast to the middle classes in the US for whom naming class was not problematical (Devine, 2005). However, Susan told Ben of the schooling decisions she and her husband made for their own children candidly, knowing that he was a middle class parent making secondary school decisions himself. Her narrative was revealing both because of this aspect of relationality (with the interviewer) and also because of another aspect (comparing her decisions about her own children with her understanding of the school she taught in). Regarding her daughter Susan said:

being middle class, and coming from a fairly academic household as well, with her nose in a book the whole time and that would not have gone down well at Bowthorpe at all.... [Whereas at CNS] it was taking for granted a kind of ... milieu, it was a theatre going, concert going, museum going, abroad going culture, ... they were in contact with Europe, with a bigger world. Some of my students, not just sixth but others, had not left Norfolk ever. I remember one boy telling me he'd never been outside Norwich, he didn't go to Yarmouth because he got sick.

Memories of education for those who had attended the Gurney Henderson/Bowthorpe schools were often very vague, with recollections of 'day dreaming' out of the window or being punished for misdemeanours some of the most common experiences. As Harry Wrigley put it: 'when I say fond memories, there's nothing come to mind to be honest, but I always think of my school days as good days.' This is not to argue that these individuals were unmarked by their educational experiences, but rather they took place *within* rather than *across* class categorizations, which treated working class children as 'thick' and as being fit for certain kinds of jobs. John Draper was one of several people we spoke to who described themselves as 'thick', but as we can see here, his lack of academic achievement needs to be placed in a wider context:

BT: Why did you hate school so much?

John: 'Cos I weren't very clever. I couldn't concentrate... even when I was seven at the Larkman School, me and another fellow, we used to dish out the school milk, so I used to have about two hours off in the morning, dishing it out, getting all the empties, putting them in crates. That was for four years I did that. And when I went up the Henderson School, I did the milk in the morning. Then the next thing I'd do the teachers' tea break, ten o'clock, I'd make their tea, wash up, put all the things away, go to class for about half an hour. Then I used to go and help the dinner ladies. I used to lay all the things out, put all the trestles out. Help serve the dinner...

BT: Did you want to do it?

John: Yeah. Better than having lessons.... And I'd have my dinner afterwards. I mean they're all in class then. Then I'd do the teachers' tea again in the afternoon.

Valerie: But I don't know how you got away with it?

John: I wasn't getting away, I was working! I'd do the tea in the afternoon. And wash up... and that was near enough time to come home. But even the bits in between I hated doing it, so I used to truant.

BT: So what did your mum and dad think about that?

John: [indicating being hit] Whack!

BT: Did they want you to do well at school or were they not bothered?

John: I don't know. I can't say bother. I don't suppose they ever thought about it to be honest with you. My dad worked in the boot factory, I would follow suit,...I went in the army at eighteen...I wanted to go into the Royal Norfolk's. So I said to the fellow next to me, 'how do you spell Royal?' 'Can't you spell it?' I said, 'No, I don't have a clue.'

We can see how the authorities – which in John's life meant both the school and his parents – superficially performed the roles expected of them, as his parents expressed disapproval of his truanting, and the school required his physical presence. Yet behind this, the teachers clearly categorized John as someone best fit for being treated as unpaid domestic staff. Equally his parents attributed little value to formal schooling: it was something outside and 'other' – a task that had to be performed before the real work of going out and earning a wage could start – something that Harry Wrigley also articulated:

> I was slow in a lot of things... but I think that's bred into you. Get to school, get to work and be earning some money. 'Cos your family was skint anyway. So if you went out and got a job, you come back and you pay 'em a fiver board money – that'll help towards the bills.

What is also revealed in John's account was his own agency in his education. He challenged his wife Valerie when she said he 'got away with it', pointing out it was 'work' (and by implication, setting it in opposition to school 'work'). In a subsequent interview he reiterated how he had enjoyed doing the milk, particularly the fact that he got a full meal in the school kitchens at the end of it, contrasting this with the empty cupboards at home. Reinforcing Willis, we can see that for John this experience, rather than the schooling itself, prepared him for the world of work in a way that book learning could not.

Not everyone who attended the local schools was as uninterested as Harry and John in formal learning: those who did want to develop academically found themselves working against the dominant culture of both teachers and other pupils. Rather than finding their own class identifications embedded within and reinforced by the categorizations of others, some research participants experienced ambiguity and conflict. Strongly resonant of Willis' 'lad', Joey, who walked 'a very careful tightrope in English between "laffing" with "the lads" and doing the occasional "brilliant" essay' (1977: 32), Mark Fry was torn:

> Mark: you didn't want to be a goody goody did yer, that's the last thing you want, [for the] teachers [to] like you
> BR: Everyone would hate you then if you were
> Mark: [interrupts] Well of course... I did enjoy maths, I did enjoy sciences, I didn't want anyone to know I actually enjoy that, I didn't mind a certain amount of English and I used to enjoy writing. I used to enjoy essays, I love sitting an' writing. I still do it now... I can remember one year when I come top in science and they all start copping the piss and I said 'that's alright I knew the answers', I said 'I see the answer sheet'

Mark's willingness to articulate this tension was in part produced relationally through the interview with Ben, who he understood to value education in its own right.

Although she attended the school after it became comprehensive, Lorna Haley, who later went on to university, looked back at her education and identified the anti-academic atmosphere of the school in explicitly classed terms:

> Certainly up until sixteen, up until sixth form, school for me was a very, not a particularly great place... although I was always in one of the top streams... that's part of the thing of being in a working class school, part of the thing about being there was that you mustn't be too brainy. To be called brainy was very definitely an insult and so you sort of kept your head down, you needed to belong and not have the piss taken out of you. And you didn't want to be one of those, there was the few who, three or four maybe in each class who did their homework and you didn't want to be one of them.

Not all the children from the estates attended the secondary moderns or later the Bowthorpe comprehensive – some of the people we interviewed had passed the 11+ and attended one of the city's grammar schools, or, after 1970, had gone to one of the relatively high-performing ex-grammar schools. Those who made this move found that class categorization affected them, though in different ways. What came through most strongly was the unsettling nature of their experiences: not only were expectations of school and home often very different, but these frequently had a strong material basis:

> *Rita:* I passed the 11+. And I actually went to the Blythe Grammar, which is now Blythe Jex.
>
> *BT:* Did you enjoy that?
>
> *Rita:* No... because we were not very well off, and my mum was always a schemer, they changed the school uniform the year I went there. So that was a plain navy blazer, and a beret. But my mother bought me a second hand blazer, which had all braid on it, which was beginning to fray... I had to wear my black shoes 'cos they couldn't afford to buy me sandals. And also, my mother always worked... [then] she had my brother. And, because she had those two little ones, and she still used to work on the farm, she'd keep me off school.

Two sisters remembered the humiliation they experienced each year when, in front of the class, they had to explain how their father was yet again unemployed; another research participant did not even bother to tell her parents she could go to grammar school as she knew her family would not be able to afford the uniform. Even after the comprehensive system was introduced, sharp differences between schools remained, with (classed) peer relations remaining important too for several participants in our study:

> [My] oldest one went to Bowthorpe. Then that closed. My middle one went to Hewitt.... I thought Bowthorpe was a fantastic school, I can never understand why they closed it but apparently that was bums on seats why they closed it financially. A lot of the best people sent their children to Hewitt School so when you used to go up there on, school nights and that sort of thing they were all sort of what I call 'lar-di-dah' people. There were a lot [of] doctors and solicitors children there at that particular time if they couldn't get in the CNS.
>
> (Margaret Brooke)

> I weren't there that long and I didn't really think that I fitted in there because, I don't know, I was an old Larky, you don't get Larkies going to CNS, it was a bit snobby weren't it.
>
> (Gail Steadman)

The discomforts articulated here demonstrate the importance of setting classed experiences of education in a wider relational context. Our interviews provided spaces to discuss how secondary schools could be and often were the sites for reproduction of class inequality through the playing out of categorizations and stereotypes. This comes through very strongly in the following section where we explore Lorna Haley's educational experiences in more depth.

'Not for the likes of us'

When Lily Haley, who 'always loved to learn', was asked what university would have meant to her when she was growing up, she replied 'even if I knew the word university it certainly wouldn't have been for the likes of us.' And yet, her daughter Lorna went on to study English at university, in no small part due to the encouragement of one of her teachers, Susan Marshall. Lorna's moving history, her journey away from her background through education, spatially reinforced through living away from the estates, is a story of profound and continuing emotional ambivalence and unsettlement.

I remember the first time Susan first suggested the possibility of a university and this to me was incredible ... it had honestly never entered my mind that I could go to a university. It just wasn't in my realm of existence and if I'd mentioned it at home ... they would have gone 'don't be ridiculous', it just wasn't our world.

The fact that it wasn't 'her world' was confirmed when she reached university. She described to us her anger as she became acquainted with middle class culture there:

> *BR:* And when you went to university did you continue to feel very conscious of your class background in these different ways?
> *Lorna:* I think this is when it all sort of kicked off really ... because although I'd always been very, very aware of ... being working class. I hadn't lived in any other sort of world so it was alright but then suddenly ... I had a hard time really adjusting and I was angry.... It's also the time of the miner's strike ... there were these miners' wives coming round and there's all these students collecting money for people. They only had this to live on and I was thinking, 'well I've lived my whole life on that.' ... I had no sympathy at that point for the miners. I did politically but ...
> *BR:* And were these middle class kids coming in collecting money?
> *Lorna:* Oh yes and I remember all sorts of odd conversations. I remember the Socialist Worker students who belonged to that organization who would say you know, 'what do you think a working class house looks like ... would they have a fire place, what would they...?' ... I was just thinking 'Jesus Christ!' It was awful and of course people do make assumptions about when your mum goes to the opera or when you mum does this ... it was very hard I think.
> *BR:* Did you link up with any other kids who felt they were working class in that way?
> *Lorna:* I couldn't find any. I found some I suppose they would have been more lower middle who felt themselves to be quite deprived but again I felt when I listened to their deprivations to me they were luxuries. 'Well we only have one holiday a year', 'well my dad's this', 'my dad only earns fifteen thousand' and I was just thinking 'God!'. It really was a vast gap.

For Lorna, the dislocation she experienced at university did not end when she left, but rather continued to be troubling and unresolved, profoundly affecting the ways in which she related to people within and outside her family. Lorna's discussions with Ben were classed in the sense that she was aware not only that he was a university lecturer, and therefore occupationally middle class, but also that both of them had had daughters in the same year at the same largely middle class state school. She spoke candidly about her present ambivalent identification with regard to the Larkman, overlapping with her uncertain class identification.

> I'm kind of floating around between working and middle and whatever I am now, I don't know but then I have a child with a middle class father who is effectively growing up as a middle class child...in some ways she feels alien to me 'cos you know when you have children...one of the things they give you that I wasn't expecting at all is...your own childhood back. You kind of re-experience, relive things and...but she's reliving things that I never had...It's odd when you see your own child being the sort of child that I would have been really quite intimidated by at school myself...I probably would have hated her.

Her ambivalence is expressed as much within her relations with middle class individuals as it is with close family members. In the presence of another fellow parent from the primary school, Lorna had found herself defending the estates and the people who lived there against an attitude which she found patronizing:

> My daughter was going to spend the day with them. She said 'would you mind, we're doing something, can you drop her off? I'm doing a project thing at Larkman Middle.' 'Oh alright' I said 'Yeah I know where that is derererer.' So I dropped [my daughter] off with her and she said 'yes' – we were in this little shed – 'but of course the children here are not like you and me'. And I was just thinking 'oh for God ...!' And I said 'well actually I was brought up [here]'... I just thought the assumptions people make, it's incredible! And the way she talked about these kids and she would certainly see herself as a very liberal [tuts] she would see herself as unprejudiced [pause]...but incredibly patronising ...

In a similar way she found that middle class people her mother cleaned for were patronizing towards her when she got into university, something she strongly resented:

Lorna: My mum worked as a cleaner.
BR: In private houses?
Lorna: Yeah...so that had another dimension of being patronized, yeah. When I got to go to university it was like they were gonna put flags up and,
BR: Who were going to put flags up?
Lorna: A couple of the women my mum worked for, lovely women
BR: 'Oh how wonderful she's got to university'
Lorna: Yeah, my God it was like a miracle had happened!

Yet when she reflected on her relations with those of her relatives who still lived on the Larkman, Lorna's narrative returned to self-criticism, to 'herself' as patronizing towards 'them', resonating with Sayer's (2005: 175) observation that relations between classes always contain an element of condescension:

Lorna: In a sense now when I see my family, certain members of my family, I'm patronising.
BR: You think you are or they think you are?
Lorna: I am. Not all of them and in some ways I'm not but in some ways I'm just living in a different space to them now...if they were less defensive and uptight about it they'd be great but...they're so entrenched. They've never left the Larkman. It's their legend, it's family legend, any family gathering becomes literally a cluster of these ten brothers and sisters...they just talk about childhood, the old man as they call him, the old man this, the old man that, what it was like, all the other big families on the street and...'oh whatever happened to the....' I think these are all in their fifties and sixties, seventies, one or two of them, and its still their basis. Its still the point they're operating from.

Lorna's discussion about those of her relatives who, as she sees it, still take succour from a shared past, a set of legends about the Larkman, is told as a stuckness in myth, echoing Walkerdine et al.'s (2007) findings on the young men who shunned new kinds of jobs following the closure of Ebbw Vale steelworks in 2000 fearing what they might lose if they moved on.[5] And despite Lorna's criticisms, she remains ambivalent too about her move, envying those of her relatives whose lives have not changed in terms of class:

There's a sense of sometimes I see certain members of my family, I think I don't want their lives but I envy their...comfort. They're still very, they're not... like this when you learned to be self-conscious about who you are or your background or your accent or your class or, then you've lost something then, which is irretrievable, when it's gone.

From Lorna's narrative emerges an ambivalence about class, which is not simply a random set of emotions and attitudes but rather which is strongly relational to the place, time and people she refers to at any particular point. It was told during an interview which was marked by conversations about boundary crossing, the enjoyment of things held in common (same-age children) and the common friend who made the contact. Lorna's account reveals much about the importance of the subjective experience of class. Yet, as Sayer puts it in relation to recent studies of discourses of class,

> these contributions are important not only for understanding the subjective experience of class: the ascriptions of value or lack of value to self and other produce real effects on people in terms of how they are treated, and hence on their life-chances.
>
> (Sayer, 2005: 74–5)

This is not to argue that estate residents in general somehow did not value formal educational achievements. We came across a number of individuals who made great efforts to encourage their children to do well at school, often hoping they would be able to make the most of opportunities which had not been open to them. Rita and Joe Hastings, for example, related how all three of their children were now in professional careers, something they attributed to their support:

Joe: I used to try to tell them a joke a day. Ask them a question a day, so they'd keep the mind fairly sharp, and also buy them something a day, whether that was crisps, sweets or something, just to.... And my kids were all brilliant at maths and tables. 'Cos I'd sit up and say 'nine nines?' in the middle of tea, wouldn't I?
Rita: Yeah [laughter]
Joe: 'six sixes'?... our kids were definitely the brightest kids, weren't they?

It is thus important to move away from a simple analysis that education was something 'done to' the working classes by middle class outsiders. Individual agency might mean, for example, that this could be turned on its head, illustrated here through a story of Marjorie Lovell's work as a cleaner in the halls of residence at the university. Her own school career had been chequered through severe illness. Marjorie related to us a story about one of the students, David, who refused to get up for an important exam:

> I opened the door, he was in bed. So I went 'David, David its Marj.' He got up, you know sat up, so I say... 'Look' I say 'your parents want you to do well here... I would like you to do well, all your friends in the kitchen want you to do well, now' I say 'I want you to get up' and I say 'I want you to get dressed and get changed and get over that exam'. I said 'if you don't', I said, 'I'll go and get the house mother'. He said 'you won't'. I said 'I will David', I said, 'if you're not ready and out there in ten minutes'. So I carried on ten minutes up, went back again, he's in bed so I... the house mother she hauled him up... and do you know afterwards he thanked me.

While Lorna's narrative produces a sense that education necessarily involved boundary crossing and classed discomforts, Hastings' and Marjorie's experiences indicate how this was only one of a range of possible responses. Many of the research participants valued education. However, what often came through during interviews was the way in which individuals had actively sought out training and education in more 'comfortable' contexts. Men were able to use opportunities for learning and vocational training offered by the military, and in fact some research participants gave this as one of the main reasons for joining up. For Tom Crowther, whose schooling had been severely interrupted by the war, it was one central reason for volunteering:

> I knew that once I got in the forces well then it was up to me to grab a first class education which they would have provided... as soon as war would cease then you would be offered opportunities of education and if you didn't grab then with both hands well I mean you were round the twist weren't it?

Mark Fry similarly joined the RAF partly to pursue educational goals in an environment where this would not potentially threaten his identity as a 'lad':

> I kept going, taking jobs on until I was... seventeen and then after I joined the RAF I knew I could get in there and carry on with

my education. And everyone wanted education in the RAF, so you weren't the odd one out. So you could learn in comfort.

No women we spoke to had used the military in this way; however, this did not stop Flo Smith from feeling that her time as a serviceman's wife gave her an education of another sort:

> I did really feel as if I'd had an education, not school-book wise, but world wise, genuine knowledge world wise, travelling. I felt as if I got more of an education that way, than I did school. I hated school.

Informal learning which did not unsettle class identifications also took place more generally in the world of work. In contrast with the troubling experiences of attending grammar school, Rita Hastings, after having to leave school early, found employment in an office of a family firm:

> And the chief clerk, he taught me more than I ever learnt at school. He taught me decimals, and improved my maths no end. And that was such a little office. I did telephone. They sent me to shorthand classes ... and typing. I did some book keeping. I did wages.... And I really did enjoy it there. And he did teach me, he taught me so much.

Unlike her school days, where feeling of shame and marginalization were paramount owing to her family's poverty, Rita's memories here emphasize the pleasure she felt in learning these new skills. And once again, as with Susan Marshall and Lorna Haley, we can see the importance of personal relations operating within a more formal structure.

More recently local activists based in the three estates identified the importance of 'comfortable' learning in encouraging adults with few academic qualifications to attend courses, including in basic literacy. They had found that over and above the practical difficulties of attending courses off the estates, particularly travel costs, residents had expressed fears over the classed nature of education itself. Central to the 'College in the Community' that resulted was an ethos that it was to be embedded not just physically in the estates, but also culturally:

> the community choose [the tutors] because they said they felt intimidated by somebody coming along, someone posh. Found some fantastic tutors. I think the college also learnt a lot from us.
>
> (Audrey Gilbert)

Education was clearly an important aspect in many research participants' lives: while school or university may have proved negative or troubling, this did not mean that it was not valued. Given the long history of how class categorizations were embedded within the educational opportunities available to most estate residents, it is unsurprising that even people with significant academic potential often chose not to move away from their class and locality, but rather to eschew formal education altogether, or to seek it through means other than school.

Encountering 'others', making identity

In the previous section we saw how education was one site in which class categorizations and identifications might be played out. Here we consider cross-class encounters both within stories told to us relating to work and families and in the interview settings themselves.

Just as military life gave opportunities for people from the estates to extend their education, it also provided spaces in which class (often mirrored and reinforced through rank) could be reproduced and challenged. Flo Smith's experiences within army culture gave her the opportunity to develop relationships across rank and class boundaries. In contrast with writers who stress the deeply problematic nature of cross-class interactions (Sayer, 2005), Flo's easy, untroubled and humorous accounts of her relationship with her husband's squadron leader and wife suggest the possibility of a different type of classed interaction.

Flo at no point attempted to hide class differences; indeed they were often central to her humour. First employed directly by the RAF as a cleaner for the squadron leader, she then became employed privately by his family.

> The squadron leader, he was nice, Phil … on the camp we used to go for midnight mass and Holy Communion. Well, I can't take Communion, 'cos I never been christened. So off Phil goes, right, I'm standing behind him, the pew behind. Phil goes off and takes Holy Communion and comes back and he gets his place and he's dead in front of me and I leant forward, and I says to him, 'What some folk will do for a drink.' [laughter] And all of a sudden you could see these shoulders heaving with laughter!… I was very disrespectful… Lieutenant McDowell… No, McDougall, that's it. And I used to go hollering in the office calling him self-raising [laughter] … I was so cheeky I used to get away with it.[6]

Humour can be a cover for discomfort and embarrassment, but this story was related with such relish and enjoyment that it is hard to read such a response into Flo's narrative. This is reinforced by her memories of the squadron leader's wife, in which narrative she deliberately deflected potentially charged and classed situations through absurdity. Although her employer, she remembered the wife, Felicity, as a 'friend', someone with 'no side to her'. In one story, Flo was taken to a 'posh' restaurant for afternoon tea by Felicity:

> I pressed down with this pastry fork, and the pastry shot off [laughter]. I thought, that was me! I was... tears were running down [my face]! And she sat there. And so matter-of-factly, she said, 'My God, I can't take you anywhere, but I can the second time if I apologise for you!'

Flo's narrative throws open how class might be produced in the intimate place that is both home and workplace, and spill over outside that space; and how gender intersects with class to produce outcomes which could not be 'read off' from a simplistic classed analysis. The potential for such relationships to move beyond the superficial was demonstrated in Lily Haley's memories of her time as a cleaner for 'professional people' in private houses in the largely middle class 'golden triangle' area of Norwich. Lily's partner during those years was both alcoholic and violent towards her, which led to her restricting her social circle: 'you never really get too friendly with people because you don't want them to find these skeletons hanging around your house.... I felt very isolated.' Nevertheless, between herself and two of her female employers in particular, close and reciprocal relationships developed:

> *Lily:* it was just a completely different way of life I saw... and two of them I'm still in touch and still see ...
> *BR:* What like cups of tea together, or meals together, or just phone conversations or?
> *Lily:* Well, meals, yeah. Going out.... Cinema. Being invited to their family occasions. And you know, I've watched their children grow up, the same as I have my own... these particular two [women] did know all the gory details about my life. Later, when I got to know them. And they knew all my kids, they knew Lorna.
> *BR:* So in a way they were people you could talk to...
> *Lily:* Yes. You can't talk to everybody, but yes... one of them, when he [Lily's partner] did finally leave, she was the one who listened to

the whole lot for hours and hours and hours and hours and hours. She was fantastic. She virtually got me through it …

BR: And did they also share all that was going on in their lives?

Lily: Oh, yes. [laughs]

BR: So they would sort of use you as a sounding board as well in that way?

Lily: Yes … I suppose it was something that made me realise, whatever people's circumstances, they might have more money, and a different, a better education. But they still have problems. And not necessarily the same as I had, but they still have, you know [inaudible].

In Lily's account, as with Flo, it is not that class was absent or ignored, but rather that commonalities around gender, family and life course provided intersections across class.

However, as much as cross-class relationships within certain work situations might be easier than necessarily expected, class identifications 'within families' could be far from straightforward. Class identifications were often expressed to us in relation to members of the same family who had been socially mobile, or presented themselves as though they thought they had been so. In our study, participants' classification and indeed ridicule of other family members by their attempts at distinction revealed much about the ambivalence of speakers' own class identifications and their own positioning in relation to us as interviewers (Skeggs, 2004). This was itself reflective of the continuing importance of class as identity, of inequality in class relations, and, at the same time, of resistance to being typed and categorized by class others.

Diane Kemp lives in the Marlpit estate with her husband Paul, who, at the time of the interviews in late 2005, was a long-term skilled manual employee for a well-known local company. Diane herself worked as a cleaner in the local community centre, a playground attendant in the nearby primary school and as a carer for her father Bill, who lived in a house round the corner. She also took a leading role in raising her grandchildren. Justine, the youngest of Diane and Paul's four children, lived with her parents. During the oral history interviews with Diane, Justine would occasionally appear in the room and join the discussion, and as a result she was also interviewed on her own. Later we decided to go and interview Bill as well, making this a set of interviews with three generations of the same family.

Bill Fussell was born in the 1920s. He narrated his life history over three long interviews in which he spoke at length of his experience in Asia during and after the Second World War, his work as a council-employed gardener in Norwich and his relations with his family. He talked about his knowledge of gardening (a shared interest with Becky) and his valuing of independence and autonomy, to the extent he talked with satisfaction about one incident when he faced down his manager, locking him in the greenhouse in the council nursery where they both worked.

Bill's reflections on his differences with his brother produce the image of a class other in the family and thus also reveal much about Bill's own class identification. Bill's brother had gone further in formal education than Bill and moved away to a higher paying job. Bill portrayed his brother as snobbish, standoffish and pretentious:

> *Bill:* I was on £4 a week, he was on £40 a week. Think about it, forty to four. Used to come here and tell me what to do.
> *BT:* Did you not get on with him?
> *Bill:* Well, I told him where he could get off.
> *BT:* Did you feel because he'd got an education and moved away he was different to you?
> *Bill:* I got education, I got it all there, he was no better than I was.
> *BT:* Did he think he was better?
> *Bill:* Yeah. Oh, yeah. Now, tell you what sort of brother he was, see his mother, he'd walk the other side of the road rather than walk with her.
> *BT:* Why's that?
> *Bill:* 'Cos she was scruffy.

Bill, a proudly practical person, remembered taking action when his brother's behaviour became unbearable on a visit home:

> Mother had made pea soup. Well of course we loved that. Cold weather. And he turned his nose up. So we opened a window and threw him out. Go and chew the grass!... He['s] got a big head. There's people like that, aren't there, born with it.

For Bill it was his brother's refusal to be ordinary that was offensive and needed action. For 'a member of his own family' to act as though he was superior was just too much to sit and passively spectate. Bill's values here are consonant with those he expresses through his talk of practical work and taste, again in relation to his brother:

I can do anything I can put my hand to anything. Jack of all trades, master of none!... Course he come along, that didn't suit, did it. You had to do them [the curtains] I can't remember what the fashion was, 'cos you know what life's like, 'cos you get your different fashions. 'Cos mine was all solid, he wanted all the frilly ones.

As Bill went on, he explained that the expensive carpet now covering his floor was his late wife's choice. His narration of her taste in relation to his own drew explicitly on the language of class.

> *Bill:* Everything had to be the best. She married the wrong class. Oh, yes, she wouldn't have nothing second hand.
> *BT:* Why's that?
> *Bill:* She didn't want to.... Everything had to be new, it was what she wanted. I could have furnished this house in perfect time, but she wouldn't have 'em. And if that's what she wanted, that's what she got. I'm easy. As long as I got a chair to sit on, I didn't care what sort it was. As I said she married the wrong class, she should have married the upper class. When we moved down here, nobody talked to her, they were afraid of her.... She looked hoity. She was a smart woman... she always looked like she'd just walked out of a blooming tailor's shop. Nothing new, but that was always washed and mended, she'd make everything last.

Bill's description of his wife's approach to clothing revealed that she was prepared to accept second-hand clothes, but also evoked a striving for distinction in relation to neighbours similar to that described by Evans (2006) in her study in contemporary Bermondsey, South London, where some working class women, she argued, would not be seen in clothes that looked worn. In Bill's view the effect of his wife's clothing was that neighbouring women were hesitant to talk to her.

Like Bill, Diane told us that her mother had sought to distinguish herself from others in terms of class. Living in the Marlpit estate, she viewed the residents of the neighbouring Larkman as beneath her, not to be mixed with. This, Diane felt, made her mother a 'snob', something she herself had actively rejected:

> I've got as many friends over there now as I have over here so it don't make no difference to me now, but she would never have that.

Diane was at pains to stress her own down-to-earth, unpretentious nature: 'What you see is what you get, if you don't like it you don't have to talk to me':

> I don't want a show house. My house is to live in as we are.... You can't have a posh home when you've got kids [grandchildren] coming in and out and I wouldn't want one, 'cos that material things do not bother me.

This self-identification, and her class identifications more generally, were expressed most clearly in relation to her children, and their life choices. This came through especially strongly when she spoke about her eldest son Mark, who had gone to university. In reaching university he succeeded in following through the potential that his grandfather Bill had never been able to fulfil; family poverty had meant that Bill went out to work at the earliest possible opportunity, rather than being able to follow teachers' advice and go on to college. This elaboration of an inter-generational educational narrative

> is illustrative of the way narratives of the self are not necessarily just those of individuals but can also be collective and transmitted across generations. They each have journeyed across classed spaces in the process of their education.
>
> (Cairns, 2008, drawing on Chamberlain, 2000)

Although Mark's wife, Rachel, had also grown up in Norwich, this had been in a 'better off' area, and she had had access to money throughout her childhood. Rachel now works as a schoolteacher and Mark has a job involving extensive long-haul travel for a telecommunications company. Diane described how Mark became more of an outsider through his relationship with Rachel during his university years. For Diane, place and class overlap. It is not just how much money and education Rachel had during her childhood but the place she grew up not being the Marlpit estate, or another nearby council estate.

> *Diane:* We're not overchuffed with [her] either really but.... We put up with 'er. We don't see 'er very often so therefore, that is not an issue ... if she lived next door that'd be a completely different thing. But her life has been different to Mark's in some ways.
> *BR:* In what ways would you say?

Diane: Well...I don't know how you'd put it...well she's just thoroughly spoilt really. And then when Mark, he left school, and was waiting to go to uni...he was taking his A-levels tha's right. And 'cos I then had my daughter, Justine then. And she said 'why don't you come and live with us?' [Rachel] said 'There's too much noise there' and Paul's never, ever forgive her for that... And then [Mark] went to...uni, and because Paul work the hours that he works, and the way that we are – we are not people who go out a lot. We don't travel a lot.... We used to go up and see Mark when we could. Well, of course, when he used to come home he used to go there [to Rachel's] and not here. And...I said 'well, it's up to you,' you know.... Mind you we were paying to put him through.... But I think he realises how much, 'cos he always say...he feels like an outsider. So that's him who's lost out rather than us.

Despite her obvious hurt at the way he had behaved, in Diane's view it was Mark who 'lost out' by his apparent upward mobility, and consequent lack of belonging. Diane's class pride ran deep. She expressed pride that she and Paul were contributing money during his university years, and narrated Paul's reaction to Rachel's comment that their home was too noisy for Mark as a slur. It was pride in Mark for what she saw as his achievements, implicitly in relation to Rachel: 'I was proud...more proud for him because...he could only get where he wanted to go by his own means, studying physics.' Later on Diane's pride was expressed explicitly in class terms when she wanted to make clear that it was the estates that she associated with working classness, that 'financially' she had the means to move away if she wanted to. She chose to stay and live there because that is where she felt she belonged:

If you put it...on a basis of what you earn we're not working class. We live here 'cos I wish to live here not because I gotta live here...so I still class myself as working class 'cos I live in a working class area where I've always lived and where I feel comfortable.... I'm proud to be working class. My money's as good as anyone else's.

However, although Diane associated the estates with working classness culturally in relation to herself and to us, she was more ambivalent about Justine's identity, and here she started to refer to differences among working class people:

Even when you get the class system and working class there's a lot of different what I call working class people. If you took her [Justine]...I don't think people would know which class she come from, whereas you can get some others who are right little slappers, and you'd know who they were and what class they come from.

So while criticizing anyone who behaved snobbishly towards the residents of the estates as a whole, Diane was careful to distinguish her own daughter from what were portrayed as rougher aspects of the estates' cultural life. She revealed a strong sense of disassociation here in the sense used by Skeggs (1997) about working class women who distance themselves from practices associated with roughness in order to perform respectability:

> Well, you get working class who... have gone through all the system and they can't read and they can't write. Right so they're basically illiterate.... And then you get people who... are just slobs, live in filth. There's a lot of different sort of people.

Diane's narrative here was entirely relational. In portraying herself as 'respectable' she revealed the relationality of her own self-identification as down-to-earth: to middle class outsiders (including ourselves as researchers) her unpretentious working classness was foregrounded, while in relation to the 'slobs' and 'slappers' her respectability was paramount.

For Justine herself, it was unsettling simultaneously straddling her parents' expectations and the aspirations that her newly middle class brother and his wife expressed for her. In the 1990s, Justine had been headed for Earlham High School like most children from the estates. Rachel recommended she go to Hellesdon School with its catchment in the more distant suburb of Thorpe Marriott, which was the school Rachel herself had attended. Rachel saw Justine's parents as holding her back from achieving her potential:

> [Rachel] thought Mum and Dad didn't encourage us... or push us to go further.... I don't necessarily think it's Mark... because Rachel comes from money, she sees things as totally different. And she saw it as because we're down here, they weren't trying to push us up... she saw it as they were trying to keep us down... and all her family said I was good enough to go and do whatever I wanted.

Eventually, Justine took Rachel's advice and went to Hellesdon School. However, she found the school did not live up to how Rachel had portrayed it, something which unsettled her, causing her to think deeply about her own and her family's identity and that of the Marlpit estate as a whole:

> when you hit puberty and everything's changing, you're trying to find out who you are, what you are, where you are in relation to everyone else... and having those ideas being put in. [It] does make you think, 'well are my family not as good?' Not necessarily my family, but the area: 'are we not as good as everyone else, do we have to get up and go and is this something bad that we should get away from?'

Rachel's, and Mark's, ambitions for her served to unsettle her idea of what was 'normal' and desirable, and caused her to look at the area as much as herself and her family in a different light. While believing her background to be 'normal', Justine was nevertheless aware of the reputation of the estates and the impact that might have:

> Because they see it from the outside... they see and hear about the nasty things – that's their view so they're not bad for thinking that.... But coming from the inside I don't necessarily think it is as bad as all that.... I think if you have it within you, you can do whatever, and people will be supportive and there is loads of help from organisations... that will help you.... I think it's a personal thing rather than a family or a social thing.

For Justine, then, in conversation here with Becky, there was no limit to what estate residents were able to achieve. The crucial factor for her was that you needed to 'have it within you'. In Justine's case, relations with family members who had been socially mobile had been formative, in dynamic and sometimes painful ways, of her own ongoing process of identification. Here we have seen some of the ways in which middle class people categorized working class people in their own family and working class areas. However, as the next section illustrates, there is more than one way of being middle class.

Being middle class

In keeping with our approach of interrogating stereotypes that had grown up around the estates, we sought out and interviewed people who identified themselves as middle class as well as working class. This built on our analysis of the area as more unbounded and diverse than it was represented by outsiders – something that we saw in Chapter 2 was present from the beginning of the history of the estates. In this section, we show how narratives of middle class identification and categorization, both implicit and explicit, were developed relationally, and were contingent on the context being discussed and spoken about at the time, as well as the relations between research participant and researcher. 'Middle class' is revealed as an amorphous category, containing a range of world views and identity practices.

Liz Barnes, a council resident with partner and young children, had lived in Norwich all her life. Of all the research participants, Liz's class position was the one with which Becky most empathized: she was a graduate, with a family, into alternatives to mainstream ways of organizing society, had no money and had not sought professional status. Liz described how in order to get council housing she had to 'go homeless'. This meant she was allocated a place quickly, though not given any choice of accommodation, and ended up moving into a flat in the Marlpit estate three weeks before her son was born.

Liz was surprised at how different living in the estates felt from her experience of the rest of Norwich. She said she was grateful for the one friend she had in the Larkman estate, but that, as we heard in Chapter 2, otherwise the focus of her social life and support network was in the city centre and the golden triangle. She described how she set up a toddler group with her friends, who were 'all a bit alternative and didn't quite fit into ordinary things that were going on.'

It is interesting here that Liz felt the term 'alternative' was not only understood, but that she did not need to explain how it would have felt to be in a local toddler group. Becky, it seems, was identified by her as a fellow middle class person into alternatives. Being 'alternative' in this context was portrayed as being positive because it is distinctive, not 'quite fit[ting] into ordinary things'. In part this was manifested through her willingness to cycle with her child to friends and events around the city, a practice that, despite high bus fares, was relatively unusual for residents of the estates. Liz and her partner Stewart, who was also present for the interview, continued the theme of distancing themselves from other residents in terms of class culture:

Liz: There's a lot of polishing cars goes on on this estate. You don't quite understand what that's about but it goes on for a lot of hours every weekend.

Stewart: There's quite a status thing around cars for a lot of people as well. They fit those alloy wheels next door, all sorts of things
Liz: That sort of stuff, really into that, which is quite intriguing.

As the conversation developed, Liz was able to identify other council residents who had worked in social or care work and not accumulated money:

> I think Hayley and John would be good to talk to on Marlpit in that they're now involved in doing New Deal drama classes ... and they come from somewhere else, more outsiders come in, ended up there a bit like us because ... I think if you've done work that's socially based, isn't big income, if you haven't gone from a big professional career. ... You end up in a council house, broke and I think they're a bit similar.

This category of people mixed up the idea of neat boundaries between classes because they were council tenants and had little money, usually associated with working class, but in educational and occupational terms could be seen as middle class public sector workers, or as 'arty'. However, the middle class solidarity this generated was important to Liz and her partner Stewart in some of the struggles they had had with living in the estates. One of these was over building developments close to their house. In her distress over this issue, Liz found solidarity in the company of other, occupationally middle class people:

> the last six weeks we've been fighting a housing development in the back gardens on Earlham Green Lane. They're trying to put some houses in there and so it's meant that I went to talk with some neighbours further up the road and actually I ended up telling them ... that I'd had a really horrible time down this end and they were very lovely, both of them and that made a real difference. One works for the prison and one is a teacher and they were really supportive, so that was nice.

The middle classness that emerged from the interview with Liz also contained an articulation of, and opposition to, the structural inequalities that were faced by many working class residents. In discussing the location of the chemical plant next to the Marlpit estate, Stewart voiced suspicion of the actions of corporate sector companies in relation to ecology and the health of the population:

> Well they really poisoned the river when it was May and Baker, but sometimes you wonder, on this estate proportionally whether it's something to do with it being a council estate or whether there's other factors, the number of special needs kids that are on the estate, the number of disabilities...whether the factories have any part to play in that.

Like Liz and Stewart, Frances Bailey, who worked in the estates in a voluntary capacity as an activist, belonged to the class fraction that claimed to place little value on material possessions, from a position of significant cultural capital. Unlike them though, Frances had access to relatively high levels of income and wealth. Frances and her then partner, a general practitioner, had moved to Norfolk from London partly because of concerns about the secondary school options available there. Frances described having been disturbed by the residents of the large estate in Kentish Town near to where she had been bringing up her children. She had thought rural Norfolk would be good for her children, but, a cosmopolitan, both she and her partner found the prospect of a rural work base unbearably conservative. Frances had established a common thread of identification with Ben, who had grown up in the same part of London. She was willing to mock the kind of middle class culture she felt she had left behind in North London, but at the same time to champion it as being more accepting of change than the kind of working class culture that she associated with the Larkman:

> it was beginning to understand in a middle class environment change is relatively easy, well some changes are relatively easy, we come with our whole set of different...it was about eating, well like the Islington dinner party so 'Aren't you having tofu tonight' [imitating hyper-posh voice] or whatever it was...although we didn't quite live like that but it was that sort of feeling. And in the Larkman change was incredibly difficult, partly because of the family around you...that would reinforce whatever people had been doing for ages.

As Frances commuted in from the countryside to work on the estates in the 1990s, she got to know local activists well. Like Liz and Stewart (though considerably richer than them), she distinguished her kind of middle classness from the materialistic approach towards household furnishings she found to be common among estate residents:

> *Frances:* We moved into this big old house and we didn't have a viewing and it was all second hand furniture and stuff
> *BR:* Had you ever had new furniture yourself?
> *Frances:* Not really, no, because we didn't have any money in London. I never had new furniture, it was all second hand stuff.... I'd got to know some families [in the estates] very well... I used to be amazed [at] how immaculate, you would go into houses with small children and have coffee tables that were full of little trinkets... they'd quite often be talking about changing colour of walls and a new suite or carpet or curtains... and they said 'What kind of three piece suite are you getting this year?' So I said 'I haven't got a three piece suite'. They said 'Don't be silly of course you have, you must get at least one a year, you're married to a doctor.'

If one takes a Bourdieuvian approach to capital and distinction, what Frances did not point out is that her wealth and cultural capital made such demonstrative consumption redundant. Nevertheless, Frances made no pretence to being anything other than middle class. In reflecting on her role in the estates, Frances described her motivation as 'anger' at the exclusion from public services she found that estate residents were commonly experiencing. She described how she saw herself as a bridge, enabling greater access to services she saw as people's due, but how this had to be in combination with local activists:

> Lisa came in to help as an assistant.... She knew what it was like to hide behind the curtains when the tally man was at the door wanting that week's payment and there was nothing in the kitty for it, so she'd been through that. She also had a credibility with the local community. 'So who was this doctor's wife?' ... if I had the confidence to just kick open any door there was no door shut to me, I could do that bit. But Lisa had the community credibility... maybe it was a classic... middle class thing. You are a doctor's wife.... [But] I was very angry that the services that were supposed to help people were out of the reach of people, because they hadn't been thought through in a way that made them accessible to people... so that's what [I thought] 'I can be the bridge'.

Being an intermediary between people and services was also how Carol White saw herself. Carol, who had grown up in East London, lived in rural Suffolk and Ireland and studied at Newcastle University, had moved to Norwich in 2000 to take up a job with the council and also to live nearer to her daughter. She chose to live on the estate and was closely involved with St Elizabeth's church in Cadge Road. Carol thought that estate residents could identify with her and in doing so reveals assumptions about the people who lived there and her relation to them. Whereas Diane and Bill valued being seen as ordinary, and Liz sought distinction by emphasizing that she associated with people who were not ordinary, for Carol, appearing ordinary was seen as something that would make her better at her job than other community workers:

> I had an unmarried daughter with a child in a council house, I wasn't coming in being desperately different [to] the way some people were ... there were some community workers who had [a] completely different background.

Carol made it explicit that it was her not being identifiable as middle class that helped people to relate to her, and also enabled her to understand that people found it difficult to say 'no' to a professional and were not necessarily going to stick appointments:

> the community activities organiser before me had quite a middle class background and she was very organised. She used to get very frustrated with people who wouldn't be organised whereas I'm probably a bit more laid back [laughs] and [sighs] ... one of the things about people round here I'd cottoned on to very early was that they have a great deal of trouble saying 'no'. So people will say 'Oh yeah we'll do that' and 'see you next Tuesday at three o'clock' and then just not turn up. Because it's easier than saying 'no I don't want to do it', because they don't want to upset you, and professionals in general do find that very difficult.

Just as Frances saw herself as a bridge from one kind of middle class positionality, Carol felt herself able to translate between the way in which residents articulated their positions, and the practices of the council:

> There was a lot of council officers coming out to these evening meetings and talking a totally different language, and I very much felt almost like a translator. Like stopping a meeting saying 'Do you think

you could put that another way please? I don't understand what you're saying' because the locals wouldn't have dreamed of.... I can think of one guy who, his natural way of being was to swear every other word...but I had to work with him and say, 'Oh is this going to be a problem. Do you think they'll stop listening to you if you speak like that?'...We used to practice having agenda meetings and see how long he could go without swearing.

Carol was also active in the local church. The parish priest who had been the incumbent when Carol moved to the area was the Anglican theologian Sam Wells, who has published work on his role in the estates (Wells, 2003). Sam and his wife, a Cambridge academic, were seen by other middle class people, and by Carol, as of another kind of middle classness. As Liz Barnes put it, 'the nice thing about Sam and Jo is they came from a totally different world', or in Frances' words, 'Very middle class, wife...is at Cambridge college and, lovely just lovely woman but he was very middle class.'

A different class fraction again can be identified with the moving into the area of Satnam and Sheela Gill. Both graduates of Punjab University in Chandigarh, they initially moved to Long Beach, California, where Satnam trained in retail and then ran a shop. This gave him enough money to invest in his own business:

I had applied for the big visa here in UK.... And they sent me the letter that 'your visa is approved. You can come here in this country and you can invest'. And that was a time when I had the money and I was looking for something. And I got the letter, looks like that God sent me something.... That was a special visa category I got. The business visa. You can come and invest the money and give some employment to the citizens of this country.... I came, I bought the business, as well as give the employment to other people here.

Like Frances, Carol and Sam, Satnam brought a form of expertise to the area. Unlike them however, he was an entrepreneur explicitly aiming at making money. He took over one of the businesses located in the estates, expanded it and has provided employment for local residents.

In stark contrast to Frances' disavowal of the importance of material possessions, Satnam and Sheela invested considerable money and effort into turning the flat above the shop into a well-appointed, American-style home. In this, the Gills may have more in common with the estate residents of Frances' acquaintance, who put so much effort into their interior décor. Also, like some of the working class research participants, Satnam was clear in valuing practically oriented education not just for others, but for himself. He related of his retail training experience which took place in the US:

> It was a fantastic experience, very wonderful... in the training purpose sometimes you don't learn everything. When you are doing practical things, then you learn a lot of things actually in life.

However, as we discuss in the following chapter, potential intersections between the Gills' lives and those of other estate residents have largely been blocked through their experiences of racism.

In this chapter we have shown how class has been and continues to be important in people's lives, sometimes as a source of pride and belonging, sometimes of shame, discomfort or anger. While it is engrained in material and structural constraints, and reinforced but also remade through education, it is inherently relational. Consequently classed identifications are ambivalent, situational and unpredictable; they also intersect with identifications and categorizations based on gender and 'race'. Through exploring how people's classed identifications changed over time and in relation to different people and situations, we have tried to contribute to 'unfixing' ideas about class, emphasizing the importance, alongside structures of inequality, of contingency, agency and experience. Having concentrated here on some of the complexities surrounding *social* (im)mobility, in the chapter which follows the next brief interlude we consider in more depth the role of *spatial* mobility in people's self-identifications.

Interlude 2: Flo Smith

Becky Taylor

Oral history research might have been specially designed for Flo Smith. Seeing her walk down the street, a tidy woman in her late sixties taking her dog Bella out for a walk, she would not attract a second glance. And yet, time after time, with my legs tucked under me, on a comfy sofa in her immaculate sitting room, I was transported across the world and across time, often carried on waves of laughter.

One lesson Flo taught me was that while everyone has a story to tell, not everyone has the ability to tell it. We met her at the regular community lunch club where Ben and I had gone in order to find some more people to interview. While there were 15 or so people there and we noticed a large degree of willingness to relate anecdotes about the area, there was a general reluctance to be interviewed. Most made excuses, such as 'I recently lost my husband and I spend most of my time with my sister,' or 'I work every morning and afternoon except Tuesdays when I'm here.' Flo, and her friend Marj whom we also interviewed, were the only two willing to put themselves forward. Was this because they felt they had a story to tell, or knew that they had the ability to tell it?

Looking back I now see Flo's response to two random strangers walking in and asking to hear people's life stories as entirely in character. Casting herself as the tomboy, the one who could undermine the pretensions of the unwary with well-placed humour, never one to follow the crowd, Flo's stories showed how she tackled life head-on. I arranged to meet her for a first interview, went back again for a marathon five-hour sitting, and in addition to the over one hundred pages of transcript the interviews generated, I kept reflections and notes of our many other informal chats over coffee. Throughout, Flo's dog Bella might fuss for attention or chocolate biscuits or give up and sleep in her bed. Over time we shared stories of dogs, childbirth, children and Wales, swapped recipes and disagreed over immigration; I listened (tape recorder off) to her detailed stories of feuds and dramas on her street, and (tape recorder on) of her life as a serviceman's wife in Cyprus and Singapore.

Throughout Flo's narrative of her life the themes of hard work and a pragmatic and resourceful approach to life were constant. Her life with an alcoholic first husband, a dominant second husband, her success in bringing up young children in foreign countries as well as surviving cancer and supporting her grown-up children and their families through various crises were all related to me in a matter-of-fact, 'well you just get on with it' tone. More than perhaps any other of the people we interviewed, Flo also used humour as a tool for coping with and relating difficult periods of her life. Her account of failing to get into grammar school, a serious and potentially devastating event, had me exploding with laughter:

> *Flo:* I failed this 11+ and mum come up the school, her and [the head teacher] had a conflab, then he sent for me. And he's so angry with me he took a swipe at my backside with this wooden hand he had, well that flew off! It went skidding down the corridor didn't it.
>
> *BT:* [laughs]
>
> *Flo:* And I laughed! There's this wooden hand with a brown leather glove on, and it went sailing down the corridor. Course I went into hysterics and oh, oh I got another one off him, and I got one off my mum when I got home! Oh, my mum was absolutely furious! So I went to a secondary modern.

At the centre of many of her stories was a tension between belonging and un-belonging: between the estates and its residents as intimately bound with her life, and a feeling of separation, not just from the younger generation (although this was a strong theme) but from the atmosphere of the area more generally, which she described as a Norfolk 'inwardness':

> I've had a hard life and an exciting life, but when I come back here...even when I used to come home on a visit I used to think 'oh God!' you know what I mean, 'oh for Christ sake!'

Although apparently solidly 'Norfolk' herself, with a definite accent (which was the subject of discussion in the interviews and the cause of occasional despair for our transcriber), and living only a few streets away from where she was brought up, her life was patterned by migrations and their fallout. Her mother's Geordie background was something that Flo used to explain her high standards of housework, for example contrasting herself with her daughter-in-law who lived with her for a period and with whom, given the state of my own house, I secretly sympathized. More than this though, it helped her to explain her childhood experiences and general outlook on life, which she felt set her apart from her neighbours:

Flo: Yeah but I don't think like, I know, a Norfolk person.

BT: How do Norfolk people think?

Flo: Erm, I don't know, they're very inwards but I was brought up as a Geordie – can you understand the difference? – practicality, sense and practicality was how we were brought up.

BT: And you don't think Norfolk people have got sense or practicality?

Flo: Why yes and no, it's difficult to explain, 'cos my dad was always on the move, my mum had an overdose of pride and I from nine years old I had to keep house and bring my two brothers up.

Her father, in contrast, was a 'Yank' from Texas, and their settling in Norwich a matter of chance:

Flo: All I know is that my dad came from Galveston in Texas, that's all I know... he went on a tramp steamer and he jumped ship [laughs] and he finished up here... he actually finished up here but he met my mother in London.

BT: So she'd moved down from Newcastle to London for work or?

Flo: Yeah for work. She used to work, oh god... oh... she used to work, she hated cooking, I can never understand this she was a good cook but she hated it with a vengeance. She used to work as a cook for the Duchy of Lancaster for somebody high falutin', and I don't know, I don't know an awful lot about that and that's how they met.

BT: And somehow they moved to Norwich.

Flo: Yeah, he was a traveller for a builder's firm for a while, travelling selling building materials and all sorts of things and drumming up work I suppose for various firms, and she was pregnant with me when they finished up here and she told him she wouldn't go no further: 'That's it, you know what I mean, I'm pregnant I'm staying,' so that's how they actually finished up in the area.

Her father, whom she described affectionately as a 'rogue', for all his faults as a husband and parent, seems to have been successful at bridging the gap between being an outsider and belonging to the estates. In the building trade, he was in fact foreman when the estate was being built, working alongside other men whose families eventually were housed there. In a story which simultaneously revealed her father's success in 'becoming local' and her own more ambiguous 'belonging', she told me how her children had been bullied by the Lawrence children from further down the street. This in part was due to the fact that, having just moved up from their last posting in Oxfordshire following separation from her first husband, the children had what Flo described as 'plummy' accents. That afternoon Flo's parents came round for tea and she told her father what had happened. He immediately went outside and spent the next three hours standing at the gate looking over towards the Lawrences' house. Later, when she asked him why he had done that he said that it was so they knew who her dad was – he had worked with Mr Lawrence in the past and had at some point managed to protect them from the police after an incident. Flo's children were not bothered by the Lawrence family again.

As Flo's stories moved closer to the present, as with other people we interviewed from the same generation, her sense of 'un-belonging' was increasingly articulated in relation to the younger generation of people living on the estates and visible ethnic minority populations. Time and again she expressed her feelings of disjuncture between herself – with her initiative and hard-fought independence – and what she saw as the prevailing culture of the area:

> I lived in a caravan with two kids in the middle of a woods in Hert-fordshire. It was a mile and a half, I was pregnant with Lionel.... I had to walk a mile and a half to the village to take Damon to school, a mile and a half back, a mile and a half again in the afternoon to get him so that was six mile a day I was walking. They wouldn't do that now. They'd be demanding taxis.... Young girl next door she's got, when she came here she had three, on the dole but getting taxis to and from Asda so it's a regular thing and I just don't know how they afford it. I wouldn't dream of it. What, I'm sixty six, nearly sixty seven, I walk to Asda with her [indicating Bella] and me shopping trolley. I go and do some shopping and I walk back again... that's about five or six mile, they just wouldn't do it. They always think of the easy option, not the cheapest way of doing it, what's wrong with shanks' pony... what wrong with it?

For Flo, her materially poor upbringing was an essential part of who she was, part of what gave her the skills to manage what was often an equally hard adult life. Her success in coping with what life had thrown at her has left her with little space to sympathize with what she might think of as the culture of dependency and consumerism among younger generations.

Despite her own travels and the migratory history of her parents, a similar collision between her outlook and what she saw as being new, dominant attitudes was revealed in her way of talking about immigrants. At several points in our meetings she expressed her alienation with 'multiculturalism', weaving in her own life experiences to illustrate her argument:

> *Flo:* When you go to the bigger cities like Birmingham... I just feel as if a white person's a bloody minority. 'Cos there's so many of them there and they're even getting now, they've got their own schools.... And I think they are affecting our lives.
>
> *BT:* In what way?
>
> *Flo:* Well, the way they're taking over. You know what I mean, did you hear all this squit about human rights... if Mrs. Coloured Woman thinks she's being harassed or racially got at, she sues.
>
> *BT:* And do you not think people should have the right to be respected like that?
>
> *Flo:* No, I think if they are being bullied, and I've suffered from bullying at work, for about eight years, and I just stuck it out.

We never did agree on this issue, but then the task of collecting life histories is not about imposing your own views on others, but rather attempting to capture some of the complexity and richness of the lives of others. Each time I left Flo after another meeting I was left with the sense that our conversations had allowed glimpses into the breadth and depth of her life. The expressions of belonging, alienation, disjunctures, migrations and meetings contained in Flo's experiences made up just one thread in her stories, but one that was intimately entwined within so many other parts of her life, and one I can only begin to unravel.

6
Moves

We saw in Chapter 5 that, just as inequalities between classes have continued to shape English society, class *identifications* were situated, relational, often ambivalent, and could shift over time. In this chapter we switch our attention back to the spatial mobility of estate residents old and new. Contemporary representations of working class estates in England often portray their white British residents as an embattled group of 'indigenous' people, confronting mass immigration, and fearing its social and economic effects (see for example Collins, 2004).[1] This was certainly the case with BBC television's *White Season* in the spring of 2008. The series of films, and particularly the material used to promote them, perpetuated the idea of white working class people as a forgotten tribe under threat. In contrast to this, our analysis of moving histories in the present chapter draws attention to earlier as well as more contemporary streams of newcomers in and around the estates, including visible minorities, and to the movement of estate residents to other places, including international destinations. Rather than portraying migration, whether within a nation state or beyond its borders as a one-off event, we draw on the idea of transnational and translocal living to explore the ongoing influence of external connections both for those who stayed behind, and for newcomers to the estate with strong links to previous places of residence.

The challenge to the idea of an 'indigenous' English ethnicity follows Young's demonstration of the centrality of continuous spatial mobility in the making of Englishness, suggesting that Englishness is based on 'a nomadic movement of sameness around the globe, of migrants who refuse to stop, to be rooted elsewhere...' (Young, 2008: 6; see also Winder, 2004). Using as an example the assimilation of the Normans, Young insists that the Norman invasion showed that being English is something that you can 'put on'; it is a perpetual process of becoming, a pursuit of authenticity in which the copy is allowed to be as authentic as any original. Being English was always about being out of place, about displacement from an earlier point of origin – but its dynamics can only be understood by realizing that there was rarely a prior moment of being in place.

(Young, 2008: 19–20)

While most of the literature on transnationalism (see for example Pries, 1999; Thieme, 2008; Vertovec, 1999; Voigt-Graf, 2004) focuses on immigrant and second-generation minorities' continuing cross-border connections with 'home', Jackson et al. argue that the concept has much broader implications and that 'increasing numbers of people participate in transnational space, *irrespective of their own migrant histories or "ethnic" identities*' (2004: 2, emphasis in original). In her treatment of the concept of 'diaspora space', Brah makes a similar point. Such space, she writes, is

inhabited not only by diasporic subjects but equally by those who are constructed and represented as 'indigenous'... the concept of *diaspora space* foregrounds the entanglement of genealogies of dispersion with those of 'staying put'.

(1996: 16; emphasis in original)

This is a grounded view of transnational and diaspora space, akin to Ley's 'transnationalism from below' which highlights how 'flows of people, capital, information and power move across borders and between scales, reconstituting society and space as they are themselves reconstituted' (2004: 156).

As we began to see in Chapter 2, people living in the estates were connected to other places in a large variety of ways. Some residents had moved from other places in Norwich, or England; others had arrived from other countries, including other parts of the UK. In this chapter we use the idea of transnationalism as portraying lives stretched over space 'across nation state borders' and translocalism when similar stretching occurs between places within the UK.[2] Migration is not necessarily a once and for all move. Some research participants had grown up in the estates, had moved away for a period and then returned. Others had not moved far themselves but had close relatives, such as children or siblings, who had moved and stayed away. We use the term 'indigenous' transnationalism to refer to the transnational practices of people who had not moved away but who were related or otherwise connected to people who had done so (see also Fennell, 1997). Connections with other places continued through memories, absences, practices learned elsewhere, through the media, the Internet, through gifts, letters, phone calls and emails, and through ongoing visits and travel. Such manifestations of transnational/translocal life stretching over time as well as space were very often emotionally charged. It is our contention that such flows of things, people and imaginations meant that the estates as places did not possess fixed characteristics, but were always in flux.

In the book as a whole we argue that spatial *im*mobility is as important as mobility in the making of the places of the estates. Moreover, both mobility and immobility are historically situated actions (or non-actions) (Feldman, 2007). These actions have no single motivation, but all occur within historically specific structures of inequality, located within the operations of capitalism and the state at multiple scales. Further, class, gender, ethnicity, nationality and immigration status are each important in constructing the possibilities and compulsions of spatial mobility and immobility.

Both the Second World War and the British colonialism were important shapers of transnational lives in twentieth-century England. As we shall see in relation to the case study estates, the large numbers of American servicemen (GIs), white and black, who lived in bases in the UK, produced relationships, children and in some cases marriage and women's emigration to the US. They also provoked differences of opinion over the proper behaviour of young British women. The GIs' role was different to that of British troops, who had long been based in the colonies as enforcers of colonial rule and continued to live there until (and sometimes after) independence. However, they had in common that both lived on bases, and, as Erik Cohen (1977) has argued in a survey of 'expatriate communities', life on a military base can strongly shape experiences of temporary emigration.

We argue that the often unacknowledged continuities between colonialism in the last decades of the British empire and British participation in the US-led imperialism in Iraq and Afghanistan have shaped both the range of possibilities for spatial mobility, and discourses of 'race', faith, place and immigration in contemporary Britain (see also Garner, 2006: 269). We draw on Said (2003 [1978]) to demonstrate the role of such discourses in imperialist technologies of rule, including those 'turbid taxonomies' (Stoler, 2006: 128) that apply within as well as beyond national boundaries. It is an important part of our argument that the creation and perpetuation of racializing and racist categories are at least as much the work of cultural and political elites as they are of people of any particular social class.

As several historians have shown, migration debates in the UK have long been racialized and have largely concerned immigration rather than emigration (Hampshire, 2005; Joppke, 1999; Paul, 1997). The continuity in official and media discourses belies the changing patterns of spatial mobility over time. Who moves where and why, and how people represent such moves in their own lives is historically specific. Spatial mobility itself has in some sense been normal practice throughout the history of the estates. But the channels of movement in and out have changed. It is perhaps ironic that in the context of strong anti-immigrant sentiment expressed in parts of the media and attributed by them to sections of the British public, in 2006 there were 5.5 million British citizens living 'outside' the UK (Sriskandarajah and Drew, 2006). Recently, academic ethnographers have begun to investigate the cultural practices of contemporary British emigrants and other emigrants from Western Europe (Bott, 2004; Fechter, 2005; Walsh, 2006). We too are concerned with emigration as much as immigration. However, unlike these authors, who have based their studies in 'transnational communities' understood in the more usual sense – migrants living away from their country of birth but still connected to it and to each other – we organize our discussion around what is still, for most current residents we spoke with, their place of origin.

Just as we saw in the previous chapter that our interviews were classed encounters, they were also informed by implicit assumptions around 'race'. Seeing us as white meant that some white research participants freely expressed racist views, where they might otherwise have kept them hidden. While during such occasions Ben did not usually reveal his partner's South Asian heritage, in other cases he actively deployed it, as he recorded of his attempts to interview an Indian businessman resident in the area:

> He was a bit on guard. I said that I would like to have a chat with them – he replied that they had only just moved here – didn't look too happy about that. I elaborated regarding university, said a few words in Punjabi 'menu tori Punjabi andi hai' ['I speak a little Punjabi'] to show that I was not just another white face.

In this chapter we explore three different themes, each of which illumines, in different ways, the transnational space of the estates. The interplay between categorization and identification is an important part of all three. First, we describe the role of the GIs in the lives of the estates in the 1940s and how this has continued to echo in subsequent decades. Alongside this we explore emigration in the colonial military between the 1940s and the 1960s. Both are set in the context (discussed in Chapters 3 and 5) of limited opportunities for education and employment. The second main section explores the workings of 'race', immigration status and individual migration history in the estates, focusing mainly on the period since the 1970s. Following on from the discussion of the production of space in Chapter 2, we see here how, in spite of evidence of hostility to visible minorities, being considered a person who belonged was not necessarily determined by skin colour. In the third section we discuss the relation of estate residents to other places in the UK and Ireland, including the meanings that have become associated with those places through visits to relatives, and periods spent living away from the estates. Here we draw connections in the current decade between a growing sense of street-level Islamophobia and the apparent acceptability of the disparaging of Islam and Muslims in dominant discourses deployed by some leading politicians and national journalists.

Military migrations and transnational space

My father's US Air Force, but I'm true Norwich born.

(Barry Gould)

Even if they had not themselves been in the forces, many research participants' lives and their self-identifications had been shaped in part by the temporary migration of military personnel. In this section we will explore the impact of two streams of military migration on life in the estates: American soldiers – GIs – located on bases close to the estates for the latter stages of the Second World War; and British servicemen and women based in British colonies up to the 1960s.

However significant the presence of American servicemen in the latter stages of the Second World War was militarily, at the local level its impact was felt mainly economically and socially. As we saw in Chapter 3, during the depression of the 1930s there had been few jobs, and families had subsisted on piecing together a livelihood through a range of casual occupations. In the 1940s, during wartime, one important set of livelihood activities related to the GIs living on a base near the city, as they paid for services from people in the estates, including laundry:

I would borrow Stanley's bike. We made a barrel on two wheels which could be towed behind a bicycle and we used to bike out to Weston Longville where I become friendly with the Americans out there, and my mother used to do their washing... not a great deal of money was made there.

(Tom Crowther)[3]

I used to have to [go] with Johnny Simpson 'cos his mother used to do some washing... I forget how we used to go. I think we used to bike. But that was somewhere out in the sticks. But I used to go with him to take this washing back...

(Joe Hastings)

If GIs provided work, they also provided entertainment: children's parties and dances. Rita Hastings remembered a friend who had gone and told her, 'they're funny, they eat fruit with their meat!... they have jam with their ham!' More common were the invitations to young women to dances during wartime. Several participants remembered not being allowed to go by their mothers:

they used to have the buses from the cattle market... to take the girls out to the dances and bring 'em back. Oh I was never allowed that! No my Mum and Dad wouldn't have that.

The older generation were remembered as regarding intimate relations between their daughters and GIs as improper. For some of the young women themselves, the opportunity to go out with GIs was particularly welcome, with the long absence of young British men. Several research participants had sisters, sisters-in-law, other relatives or friends who had relationships with GIs, some becoming pregnant, some marrying them and moving to the US. Research participants with sisters who had travelled to the US as GI brides kept up with their sisters to different degrees. Valerie Draper saw two of her sisters go there to marry. In the case of one of her sisters, she remembered that relations between the two families began badly:

...my sister...she's married to an American, but of course when he was here she was pregnant and not married. Because my Dad, being like they were ['overpaid, oversexed and over here']...used to say 'oh yeah, well, he'll be going back and you won't see him...but he is quite genuine her husband.... He had a job to get [his father] to give his permission to marry my sister. Because Dave was only nineteen.

And in the finish that all worked out all right.... And they're together today.

Valerie's husband John added: 'Best man you could wish to meet.'

Relations with GIs could lead to exchanges of gifts and visits continuing over several decades, and not just when there had been a marriage and children. Pauline Jones remembered that her brother had become friends with an American during the war. Her mother started writing to his sisters:

> When I was born they sent lots and lots of little nighties and things. Then when I was old enough, I used to write to her. And she was called Maggie and her sister was called Pauline, who I was named after.... And from then on I wrote too, and I'd have a parcel come once a year. And they would have things in, girls' clothes. They must have had a daughter or something that was a bit older than me, and they used to come, and I remember getting trousers called pedal pushers...that was when America had more fashionable things than us.... That went on for a lot of years.

Pauline never met the American women who continued to send her gifts throughout their lives, including an annual Christmas card with a one dollar note in it. She was not the only woman who enjoyed access to American fashion. Like many others, Bill Fussell thought that it was this which motivated young women in the area to go out with Americans. He summed it up as being about 'silk stockings', which he said women found much more desirable than the 'nylon ones with the seams' that were available in England.

Flo Smith, who was not allowed out to dances, still met GIs through her father – himself an American immigrant. She particularly remembered that her father invited African Americans to her house and she connected this to a claim (not borne out by other things she said) not to have any 'colour prejudice':

> My Dad...used to bring coloured Americans to our house. We had one – oh he was lovely he was – Eddie, when we lived in Beecheno Road. He was always at our house. At weekends. He was ever such a quiet fella, he was really nice. And he used to read, you know what I mean, he was very well educated, he used to read. Him and my dad used to sit and talk for hours, and my mum used to write to his mum. And funnily enough she come from New York, and my daughter's

just been there, and she weren't impressed. But he was lovely. So I've never, ever been brought up with any colour prejudice.

Flo felt that such was the significance of African American GIs on the estates during this period, that they may have contributed to the categorization of the Larkman as 'Monkey Island':[4]

> Quite a lot of [women from the estates] married Americans and went over to the States...a lot of the women did have American boyfriends.... I don't know for sure, but I think there were so many black Yanks roaming about and...I think that's where [the Larkman] got its reputation from, being called Monkey Island.

Flo was one of ten research participants in their sixties and seventies (eight men and two women) who told detailed stories of their temporary emigration with the British military during the war and in the last years of colonial rule in Aden (Yemen), Burma (Myanmar), Cyprus, India, Malaya (Malaysia), Malta and Singapore. None of the participants described themselves as migrants but each had spent from 18 months to 15 years outside the UK in a range of roles including National Service, volunteering as a regular or as servicemen's wives. Between them participants spanned the army, the air force, the navy and the marines. In Chapter 3 we discussed lives on the estates in the war and the age of austerity (Kynaston, 2007) that followed. In Chapter 5 we learned how provision of formal education was at best patchy; how for a range of reasons children struggled to maximize what chances it offered; and how as a consequence some tried to use the military as a path to education. For others, reasons for joining up varied – including being conscripted – as did the pathways that led to living abroad as a serviceman's wife.

Memories of their time in the forces were personal, specific and focused at the micro-level, with the military/imperial rationale behind their presence almost never mentioned. Not only is this due to the fact that we all necessarily experience history through the personal, but also a result of long-standing military practice which excludes the ranks from wider strategic contexts and decisions. Thus although resistance to colonial presence was fierce in many colonies, and while occasionally 'the enemy' had a place in individuals' narratives, what dominated were accounts of everyday life and how it was *experienced* by the research participants. Often the interviews that the expatriates gave us suggested that this was quite positive. Even those who told us they had hated it – Mark Fry spoke most vividly of being in Malta, 'I hated it with a vengeance... didn't have a cup of tea for three weeks 'cos the water tasted like shit' – also conveyed a sense of the potential, opportunities and differences presented to them through being overseas.

For Fred Hall, who had lived in the Larkman since he was three and did National Service in the marines, there was a collective sense of expanded boundaries. He had enjoyed travelling outside the UK:

> I mean this was at the time when nobody went abroad, you know. So when you joined the navy or marines or anything like that, or even the army... the army had camps all over the world, so you could do that.... That was why a lot of people joined up.... You could sign for twenty-two years.

The contrasts Sidney George experienced between military life in colonized Cyprus and his home in Norwich were revealed in metaphors of size in his memory of coming home:

> And I'll never forget walking through that door... that was like walking into a little box [laughs]... being in the army... everything was, you know.... bigger expanses.

For John Draper the transfer from boot and shoe factory work in Norwich to National Service in colonial Malaya in 1952 had both lifestyle and financial advantages. He remembered enjoying military life:

> I loved it... God, I loved the army. I don't know, even now, why I came out after two years... I liked the order. Up at seven... three meals a day... that weren't in Malaya. You'd eat whenever you like.... And... our cookhouse was in the open air, with just a canvas over the top. And we were in tents.... There was about ten, fifteen tents and that was it. And about once a month, the AKC had come round, that's the films. And they'd put up a screen, wait till it got dark. And then we'd see the films.... The first one I remember seeing was High Noon.... That came out, we saw that, when that was brand new.

When John came out of the army he had saved 'a fair bit of money', including £250 for his wedding.

Given the austerity prevalent at home, part of the transnational living experience was the opportunity it presented for collecting useful objects to send or take back. Bill Fussell was called up in 1944 aged 18 and spent three years in the army, mostly in India and Burma. In spite of his call-up

being in wartime, Bill Fussell remembered having (and taking) the time
to collect things for his mother and later for his wife:

> I mean you get to the transit camp, they let you go into the
> town ... the first thing you find when you go to a shop or a stall they
> barter everything. That's no good – they won't wear it, you got to
> argue with 'em and they'll sit there all day till one of you give in....
> I bought a case size of that ... unit there, about that big. Big solid
> cowhide. You could sit on it. I was quietly filling that up. I bought
> material for the missus to make dresses with, shoes, rings, oh and all
> sorts of things.

John Draper's memories of the high-quality food he had access to in
Malaya contrasted strikingly with the rationing he knew was happening
in the UK:

> We used to have our collected pineapple. Broke it off the stem, and it
> was lovely. The ones you get here are like that, we used to get them
> they were like that.... Bananas, all sorts. We had good grub.... Didn't
> even know what a banana looked like. I may have had them when
> I was right little, you know, but I couldn't remember. All the food,
> yeah.

Given that the positive aspects of living abroad narrated by research
participants were permitted by continuing colonial relations involving
appropriation of economic resources and foreign rule, it should not perhaps be surprising that the military expatriates living on bases in British
colonies often remembered it as being dangerous to go beyond the limits of authorized areas. Indeed, in a wide-ranging review, Erik Cohen
found what expatriate military migrants have in common is that they
are 'planted' rather than 'natural'. They are

> established under the auspices of one major organisation, a company
> or the military; it is completely controlled by its sponsoring organ-
> isation, which provides its institutions and transfers its members in
> and out of the community; it is sometimes a geographically separate
> company town ... or military camp (1977: 25).[5]

None of the temporary emigrants mentioned had initially been motivated by the idea of spending time in the colonies or anywhere else
outside the UK. Moreover, in keeping with the idea of transnational

living, moving away had not necessarily been a one-off departure followed by a one-off return: Flo Smith, for example, had left the estates to become a serviceman's wife:

> Wherever he went, where we could, we followed him as a family... myself and the three children... I was always travelling backwards and forwards.... I spent fifteen years travelling and coming home to my Mum for three months, going off somewhere else again.

As we saw in our extended consideration of Flo's life, this period of time abroad, albeit interspersed with times back on the estates, had a profound impact on her sense of self and the ways in which she viewed other estate residents. For others, the sense of separateness, while present, was less long-lasting – Bill Fussell, while admitting it was 'strange' to be back, after having been in the jungle, also stressed 'I'm pretty adaptable, that don't take me long to settle.' John Draper had more problems fitting back into his old life:

> That was it, that was my life. It was over. [laughs] Yeah, I wish I'd have stayed... I was corporal when I came out.... Couldn't get used to Civi Street. Must have been a year. Don't know how these poor fellows got on, when they were away in the first world war for about five years. Couldn't get accustomed to it. I don't know whether that's to do with being in the jungle when you go on patrol.... And I went back to clicking.[6] And I didn't like that. I [had] loved it before I went in the army, clicking.

We have seen that in the times leading up to their joining the military and departing for postings in British colonies, the research participants remembered class positions at the bottom of British society, which gave them very few options. And as John's memories above show, the military widened their life experiences *and* life chances. Colonialism and the military employment possibilities it entailed (whether chosen or not), therefore, provided opportunities, even for its low-paid foot soldiers, that were otherwise unavailable. As Said put it,

> the scientist, the scholar, the missionary, the trader, or the soldier was in... the Orient because he *could be there*... with very little resistance on the Orient's part.
>
> (2003[1978]: 7, emphasis in original)

In this section we have drawn on memories of research participants to show that spatial mobility and transnational connections were integral features of life from the 1940s to the 1960s. From the mid-1940s, US military personnel on nearby bases, most of them young men, changed what it meant to live in the estates, providing sources of livelihood, entertainment, sexual adventure and marriage, which often meant the emigration of young women. It was also the first time since the estates were built that black people (in this case African American GIs) became part of life there. At the same time, British colonialism required working class people from the UK to enforce occupation and resource extraction overseas. For many of the military personnel and their wives, who had been living in poverty in the UK, this could mean higher levels of food consumption, opportunities to buy clothes and other goods, higher income and educational advance. In the section that follows, we move forward to the 1970s and subsequent decades when more international migrants began to arrive, many of them people of colour, this time to live in houses on the estates or to attend UEA. We explore the categories used by white long-term residents to talk about immigrants of colour (and vice versa), focusing on the differences made by state-determined immigration status (asylum seeker, student, etc.), length of residence and micro-spatial factors to visible minorities' experiences of living in the area.

Newcomers, 'race' and place

The categorization processes used by colonialists are not confined to situations where the territory of one nation-state has been taken over by another. As Stoler has put it:

> imperial formations are not now and rarely have been clearly bordered and bounded polities. We can think of them better as scaled genres of rule that produce and count on different degrees of sovereignty and gradations of rights. They thrive on turbid taxonomies that produce shadow populations and ever-improved coercive measures to protect the common good against those deemed threats to it. Finally, imperial formations give rise both to new zones of exclusion and new sites of – and social groups with – privileged exemption.
>
> (Stoler, 2006: 128)

In this passage, Stoler invokes a timeless imperial governmentality (see also Legg, 2007) reminiscent of current relations between the British state and UK residents the state has identified as Muslims in the context of the US 'war on terror'. As we have seen in Chapters 4 and 5, however, such technologies of rule have also been applied to the working class residents of social housing estates. Indeed, if we are to believe Said, there may have been something in common between Orientalism and how rich white male elites viewed poor people:

> The Oriental was linked ... to elements in Western society (delinquents, the insane, women, the poor) having in common an identity best described as lamentably alien.
>
> (Said, 2003[1978]: 207)

Others too have argued that working class people themselves have been 'racialized' by other classes (see, for example, Charlesworth, 2000; Collins, 2004; Hanley, 2007). Racialized identities thus emerged and were reproduced alongside and in relation to 'class' identities. Yet as Brah has incisively noted, 'once a discourse is established, it begins to have a life of its own, and be selectively utilized by all manner of groups including those whom it excludes' (2007: 137).

Some white British research participants spoke in racist terms variously about people with darker skin colour than themselves, often eliding the presence, status and activities of 'foreigners', 'immigrants', 'Muslims' and 'asylum seekers':

> My grandson who works at Kettles crisps up the Bowthorpe, he says that there's more foreigners now working at Kettles crisps. The government has sent them here, they're paying the firm extra to employ [them]. He said, 'we've got Asians, people from Poland', we're getting so many different people in this county of ours now. And that's all been sent by the government. And, what I say is ... a lot of them come here and they're all on benefits. And the houses situation is difficult, isn't it? There's lots of our young people can't ... get houses and they're all got to be housed.
>
> (Bert Kersley)

Significantly in interviews with us 'place' played a critical role in shaping how categories were articulated and experienced. In contrast to Pearmain's representation of Norwich as 'once famously (*and accurately still*) referred to by the National Front as "the last white city in England" '

(2008: 90, emphasis added),[7] research participants were unanimous in the opinion that there had been an increase in the number of black and minority ethnic people living in the estates in recent decades. There was a common perception among long-term residents that two events in particular had led to this change. The first was the completion of UEA in the 1960s, located directly to the south of the estates. There is the University Village, with halls of residence often allocated to international students, which lies at the western end of West Earlham estate. The second event was the right-to-buy policy that was given a major push forward by the then prime minister Margaret Thatcher in 1984. This policy, which had been on the statute books for three decades but which previously had very little take-up, allowed people renting subsidized housing from the local authority to be able to buy it from them. Once purchased, the house might then be sold after a specified period.

Some participants argued that the increase in visible minorities living in the estates was mainly due to private owners renting out ex-council houses, in most cases not the original purchaser. Margaret Brooke, who held a position with the New Deal organization, focused on the role of a particular landlord:

BR: People would have been used to this area to not seeing many ethnic minorities and now there would be more ethnic minorities. Do you think that's an issue for anybody?

Margaret: That's never been an issue to me. It's certainly never been an issue to my children but there are some very ignorant people in this community who think that's very funny to ... be rude and abusive to people ... we had a landlord who owns about over fifty properties in the community and he's Portuguese and he's not a very nice person. And so he tends to cram people into his properties, doesn't look after the properties, nine times out of ten that's the people who live in the properties who get the rude abuse from the neighbours because the house is dirty or the garden's dirty. He doesn't do nothing about it because all he's worried about is he reddies, and him being Portuguese when we had approached him on it he's gone down the road of racial discrimination so [laughs] you know.

BT: Does he have properties on all three estates?

Margaret: Oh yes.

BT: So they're not concentrated in a particular area?

Margaret: No anything that's up for sale he grabs.

Other participants were less specific about who the landlord or land-lords were, but depicted the tenants as people of colour. They diverged, however, on whether these relatively recently arrived residents were 'asylum seekers' or 'students'. Most participants did not tell us that they regarded the number of people as excessive, as long as they 'kept themselves to themselves', did not cause a disturbance and learned the informal rules of the estate. Harry Collins, for example, had been talking about his role in building the university. He told us how since the university was built:

> we're getting different cultures of people, ie Chinese and whatever moving into houses and we found like there is today... coloured people. I don't think I'm prejudiced but coloured people are buying the ex-council houses up from the Larkman and renting them out to students... one particular house... has about six Chinese people living in it. -

Similarly, for a lifelong resident like John Burnett, the presence of the university accounted for the activity in the private rental market, with people buying up properties 'as quick as that'. For one teenager Dean, who had been born on the estates, recently arrived residents were 'students', a term he elided with the pejorative 'Paki':[8]

> *BT:* What do you think about people moving into the area?
> *Dean:* There's more Pakis and everything.
> *BT:* Are there?
> *Dean:* Students everywhere, ain't they.

Among the teenagers we interviewed, there was a sense of feeling looked down upon by the 'students', of being despised, akin to a sense of being racialized themselves as working class estate residents. Dean felt he got 'dirty looks' from the 'students': 'They look at us and go, "oh, yeah, chavs." ' Charnelle was explicit that she felt that 'students' were racist towards the white youth who had grown up in the area:

> *BT:* What do you think about there being a lot of black people coming into the area?
> *Kelly:* Annoyed.
> *Charnelle:* I don't mind it. It's just if we go over there we get shot. That's what annoys me. If we go over their country.
> *BT:* Like which country?

Kelly: I don't know. Some country you get shot, don't you? 'Cos you're white.

BT: Do you?

Charnelle: Yeah. And they come over here and say that we're racist, and they be racist to us.

BT: Has anyone ever been racist to you?

Kelly: Not that I know of. 'Cos they speak in their language, don't they? You can't really tell.

The presence of visible minorities in the estates was interpreted by other white participants as being due to the housing of refugees and asylum seekers there. According to Margaret Brooke, the 'Portuguese landlord' was housing the asylum seekers for a year in order to receive rent from the organization who were being contracted by the government to rehouse refugees. For some, like Liz Barnes, a white British woman who had moved to the estate as an adult, this could be positive. She spoke about a Somali family, 'a refugee family I think ... they weren't trouble, it wasn't rowdy, it wasn't like, they weren't threatening, they just met up and played football and had a lovely time together'. Other research participants were simply hostile, perceiving that 'asylum seekers and refugees' received benefits from the government that they did not have access to and that this was unfair:

> The only thing I can really say what ... do[es] annoy me, more that worry me, as when all these people come over and they just get everything handed to them on a plate.... God forbid they should have a child what is hungry, I believe in feeding the children and that but they come over they get a car, they get a house, they get this, they get that. I've been trying to get a little off my rent and I can't get it and my husband's flogging his guts out for twenty seven years and that's what really [pisses – mouthed almost silently] me off. And I don't think I'm alone when I talk like that ... and all they do is sit on their backsides all day long, that's how I look at it.[9]
>
> (Maureen Grant)

Margaret Brooke felt that the business of housing asylum seekers and refugees was channelling money straight from government to private landlords: 'he can buy a house for a hundred thousand pounds and get a thousand pounds a month rent.' There was a common perception among several white long-term residents that this process of buying and selling council houses and renting them out whether to 'students' or 'asylum seekers' meant that newcomers were getting things they did not deserve: 'I personally don't agree with that because...them houses...they were built for council tenants' (Harry Collins).

There were in fact very few asylum seekers and refugees living in the estates in 2005 according to Fay Duncan, whose voluntary sector organization coordinated support to asylum seekers and refugees throughout Norwich. Fay explained that the council's policy on dispersal had been to find people private rented housing evenly across different parts of the city: 'They didn't want sort of ghetto areas.' Consequently, there were only a handful of refugee families living in or near the estates that Fay was able to introduce us to. These research participants had found that irrespective of whether or not one was actually an asylum seeker or a refugee, being thought of in either category by long-term residents could easily lead to exclusion or outright hostility.

Abdul Masoud, a Palestinian architect who was employed as a car park attendant at the time of interview, explained how he had experienced what seemed to him to be a widespread dislike of asylum-seekers and refugees within and beyond the estates. Speaking of his immediate neighbours in the house that his family had been allocated when they were asylum seekers, he told us:

> They believed that we are here to take their money, to take their tax...they refused to let us speak to them that we are not as they think.... For us from Palestine, I have no other solution but to leave my country.

He described the drip-by-drip low-level harassment he received from these neighbours, revealing a conflict over micro-spaces. One day there was an accident in the neighbour's front garden. Someone had parked at the top of the hill and left the handbrake off:

> So the jeep it just went straight into their...garden. And into the living room. And they were outside the house. So, for me, I've done like we do in our country. I went outside, stayed with the people, let no one in the house. I called the police. And when they get back, they couldn't get access to the house, because of the car. So they had to use my house, to go out, to go through the garden, in through the kitchen. And I helped them as much as I could. But even so, they didn't, after one week, they still [behaved towards us as they had before]. They didn't accept asylum seekers, that's it.

Subsequently, Abdul's family received refugee status and were able to move house to West Earlham. In his relations with his new neighbours, he was more streetwise, taking an instrumental approach to avoid being identified as a refugee: 'As long as they don't know you are [or were] asylum seeker they are good.' The same was true at work. He noticed this when his colleagues read the newspaper, and explained that he kept his immigration status hidden:

> You know sometimes in the newspaper they talk about asylum seekers or about refugee or something like this, and most of my colleagues... they are not happy with asylum seekers. They start talking about them.... They don't know that I have been asylum seeker, or that I am refugee now. Because I have all my documents but I am working [just like them].

Living in the West Earlham estate, he takes cover in the proximity of the university, and in the tendency he has identified in white residents in that area to see people of colour as students:

> *Abdul:* Some people who are far away from the university, they always have troubles. Even if they are students. But here, because we are close to university, we are like one of the students of the city. Like if we are walking, or go to shop in West Earlham, in a big shopping centre, some people think, yeah, they may be from the... University Village.... So they don't exactly know that we... are an asylum seeker...
> *BR:* And you think that makes the key difference?
> *Abdul:* Yeah. A very big difference. I've never met anyone happy with asylum seekers in this country. Except people who are working with say Red Cross, or Peace of Races, or something like this.

Unlike a family of refugees from Iraqi Kurdistan we spoke to in the estates, who found that the lack of public transport and its expense made it very difficult to travel into the city centre, Abdul had been well-to-do in Palestine and was more mobile. He could drive away from West Earlham to visit friends in another part of Norwich. Yet here too, he told us, he continued to experience hostility:

> sometimes when I've gone in the car, they always, if they're on bicycles or walking, 'Get the fuck out of this country.' Or

something like this... they tried many times to take off the mark of the Mercedes.

Abdul's story reveals ongoing struggles over space and place in and around the estates and the importance of categorization and identification in those struggles. It also illustrates the downward occupational trajectory often associated with asylum seeking, and, in the advantages he perceives in living nearer to the university, the importance of the micro-geography of the estates. Yet, at the same time, the story suggests that labelling these three estates in particular as racist would be unjust. Prejudice against and hostility towards asylum seekers extended to other areas too. Indeed, another research participant of colour, a retired school teacher with south Asian heritage, had not only noticed racism in the city get worse over time, but also related her family's experience of its 'middle' class manifestations. For Khushi Chatterjee, teaching at the local comprehensive in the estates in the 1970s and 1980s:

> the issue of colour began to get worse and worse... as the school ran down.... I think for [the kids] it was this non-white person, maybe it was also because sometimes I would wear saris. Sometimes I would wear trousers... by the time it started becoming an issue, the fact that I was different... and black was the main thing.... Maybe had I been wearing... very trendy... western, modern clothes it might have been different.

Importantly, Khushi's own children experienced 'race' in the family's more middle class area and at the school that had an intake of predominantly middle class children. She described how, while one of her children 'looks white', the other was darker-skinned. The latter daughter had experienced being called 'chocolate face' in the street. At school it was

> the usual middle class thing which hides it in all kinds of ways....
> When [my daughter] went to... City of Norwich School, one of the things that really... made me very very angry was that the head master... had given her [a] name [using word-play on her actual name] to rhyme with toilet. I was so angry.... And there was one occasion when in the middle of the lesson... [she] was called out for a cello lesson.... She came back and finished the test and still got the top marks. So at that point one of the other girls said 'She's cheating, can't possibly [have come top]'.

Similarly, Sandra Dyson's grandson, whose father was Egyptian, attended a school in the largely middle class 'golden triangle' area. Sandra described to us how she remembered him having been called a 'four-eyed Paki bastard' by some of his classmates. While children of colour could experience racism within a middle class setting, Barry Gould, son of an African American GI and a white British mother, talked about feeling very safe on the North Earlham and Larkman estates. True, as a teenager growing up in the nearby South Park Avenue estate, Barry had been very scared of visiting them. But he thought the danger lay more in the identity of his home locality rather than in his skin colour, as he remembered himself as part of a wider group which

> didn't go over the Larkman because we knew that it would probably kill us.... We used to venture over here very rarely, once in a while just come over just to scare ourselves really. These were scary people these were... [laughs]

The big silence in Barry's account of his own life is 'race'. Barry said he did not recall overt or even more subtle hostility to him on the grounds of his skin colour being darker than those of the other teenagers in the estates, although he was given the racialized nickname Chalky.[10] He felt accepted, known and knowing of the area, 'true Norwich born'. Being of the locality, feeling part of the place, played a defining role in Barry's experience of teenage social life, and in his adulthood. Later in life he spent several years living with his white girlfriend in her house in the Larkman estate. What makes this sense of being *in* place even more convincing is that Barry talked of facing overt racist hostility elsewhere, specifically when he went to Kings Lynn to train as a nurse:

> I took more racial abuse in one day in Kings Lynn than I've had in all the time I've lived on [these estates]. One particular day in Kings Lynn...I felt lucky to get back to my flat without being attacked.... That was the most scary time I'd actually had.... three different events in one night.

Further evidence that, for people of colour, being identified as local to the place of the estates could be crucial to the experience of living there came from research participants, including Barry himself, who related stories of a small number of particular incidents of extreme hostility.

Lily Haley: And we did actually have a family opposite, a few years ago. And I think they were virtually driven out. Poor souls. Kids were awful.

BR: What sort of thing happened?

Lily: Well, the usual 'Paki' thing. It was, I'm sure...the parents, you know, allowing their children to do it. Thinking it's fine to do that.

The idea that the estates were dangerous places, particularly for racialized newcomers, has echoes with the narrated experiences of military emigrants if they ever strayed into 'out of bounds' areas. However, this idea was put into comparative perspective by some of the newcomers themselves, both people of colour and white people, who were leading transnational lives. The narratives of these residents did not confine themselves to the issues of 'race', racism or xenophobia, but also concerned different degrees of poverty and dispossession, the outcome of differently unequal structural contexts. One newcomer, Frank Levett, a white South African, was forthright that the estates were not as dangerous as they were made out to be:

When our friends come from South Africa, I take them on a drive through here. And I say to them, this is one of the six most poorest areas you'll ever find in England, and they can't believe it. Their jaws hit the ground, they say, 'come on, these are decent houses'. You know, they've all got satellite dishes. In South Africa, if you can afford satellite TV, you've really made it.

The contrast was also evident in other ways. Frank was keen not to perpetuate images of South Africa as inevitably dangerous for whites either, but also emphasized that people were much more desperate and that he felt in South Africa he always had to 'look over his shoulder' there:

I lived there for thirty eight years. I was never mugged once.... But unfortunately, it's right now reaping the harvest that it sowed.... In South Africa, if you lose your job, you are in serious trouble. There is no welfare; there is no dole; there is no nothing. There is no government benefit, there is nothing at all. You lose your job: tough.

Just as white racism was not the property of a particular social class, so, for residents of the estates, apparently belonging to a visible minority did not *necessarily* lead to jibes or any kind of hostility from the white majority. As we have seen, 'race' could be mediated by the proximity of the university and by immigration status (not being categorized as an asylum seeker or refugee). Importantly, carrying the marks of belonging to the locality in terms of accent and bearing, having a face that had been recognized by long-term residents since childhood, and knowing and following the unwritten rules of living there, could also change how a person of colour was interacted with by other residents. As Mark Fry put it: 'I don't recognise her as black, I recognise her as my mate Rose.' This bears out the importance of place-based identity and belonging. In the final section we return to the theme of lives stretched out across time and space (within the UK and beyond) that we explored at the start of the chapter, focusing here on transnational life as infused with emotion through visits, absences and departures, and the connection between the narrations of coming and going from the estates by some long-term white residents and national discourses of Islamophobia.

Emotion in transnational and translocal lives

Absences and visits

As we saw in relation to the GI brides and their relatives, some of the white long-term residents, *who had never moved out of the estates*, maintained transnational lives through connections with people who *had* moved away. Even for people who had been relatively immobile, the flows of goods, ideas, information and people across space have helped to shape the meaning of living in the estates. For those who did move to live outside Britain, common destinations other than the US included Ireland and Australia, with several participants mentioning relatives or acquaintances who had moved to Australia in the 1960s under the 'ten pound Pom' scheme (Hammerton and Thomson, 2005). Over time, the range of countries white British emigrants have headed to has expanded, and in conversations with research participants recent destinations included Spain, Thailand, the Philippines, Vietnam and the Gambia. In this section we discuss the effect on long-term residents of seeing close relatives leave for other countries, particularly Australia, and its mirror image: the effect of migration on newcomers who have moved away from familiar people and places. In both cases, oral history interviews revealed some of the emotions involved in maintaining relationships (or not) over time. We also draw on the memories of people who continue to maintain strong connections to other places in Britain or in Ireland, either through having lived there themselves, or through ongoing visits to relatives who moved away.

Long-distance migration is often infused with emotion. Sisters Greta Fawcett and Jean Holmes told Becky about their younger sister Theresa, who left Norwich for Australia on the 'ten pound Pom' scheme in her early twenties. She apparently hated it there for the first six months, but, like working class immigrants in other contexts, instant return was not possible because of the financial resources required. The turning point came when Theresa met her husband-to-be and she ended up staying. She still lived there at the time of the interview in February 2006. Greta remembered the moment of parting vividly:

> I'd arranged, before I knew... what day she was going, to go to London with a friend. And Mum went to London with Theresa to see [her] off at the airport. And we met up with them, and I thought, oh dear, she looks so, she was only little, she was the smallest one of us, and I thought, you know, she doesn't look old enough.

For Eva Garland, her son Michael's departure for Australia was particularly painful. He and his wife had been living with her and they had a son:

> I was absolutely distraught when they took him. I was more bothered about the grandson than I was them two going, but I mean they made their lives.

For Bill Fussell, whose younger brother emigrated after the war, his feelings of loss were reconciled through his account of how his brother had succeeded in challenging and circumventing class boundaries through becoming a successful mechanical engineer in Canada. Like Bill, his brother Stanley stood up to his boss in the Parks' Department of the council:

> *Bill:* Something they got arguing about.... He didn't do no more, he got the bucket, and tipped the whitewash all over [his boss and resigned].... So, that time of day they were looking for people to emigrate to Canada and Australia and places like that ...
> *BT:* And did he ever want to come back to England?
> *Bill:* No. He won't come back here, no.
> *BT:* Why's that?

Bill: Well, he didn't think that was good enough. 'Cos he was badly treated, wasn't he? At work. And he was like me, got a will of his own, he knew what he wanted to do.

The frequency of visits varied from family to family. Bill, although maintaining telephone contact, only visited his brother once in Canada, while Eva has been to Australia seven or eight times, as she felt it was the only way to see the grandchildren. In Margaret Brooke's case, contact with her sister was minimal after she left with her new husband, also an estate resident, in 1964. Her sister never visited England and Margaret, who had been 7 when she left, never went to Australia:

> I speak to her at Christmas round Mum's and she always writes to my Mum and, and there, my Mum always get like photos every year of the grandchildren and that sort of thing but she's never ever come home.

The turbulence of emotions – hope, unsettlement, struggle, homesickness – relating to migration is encapsulated in Edward Dale's recounting of how he and his wife finally decided to stay in Australia:

> I have always wanted to travel overseas so when they were advertising for bricklayers in Australia I talked it over with my wife, she was very reluctant at first as she was very close to her mother. So when she said she would give it a try, I filled in the forms and sent them away.... We landed in Fremantle in 1958 then on to Perth. It was a bit of a shock, as at that time there was very little work for bricklayers [if we had gone on to Melbourne there was plenty of work] but eventually I found work with my own efforts but I had to leave my wife and children for two or three weeks at a time for work, but I made sure that they never wanted for anything... but I knew that my wife was homesick for her family, so I said we would save up and go back to England. I knew after a month in England that I could never settle back there, plus the children missed Australia and was always asking, 'when are we going home?'...So, we both worked hard to save the money to come back. One of my wife's brothers decided that he and his family would give it a try. So once more after saving up for our fares we sailed back to Australia, and I can honestly say that we have had no regrets.[11]

As Edward's account suggest, visits and returns could be as painful and unsettling as absences. Lily Haley told us that she was just getting over the return of her son Simon to Australia after his recent visit home. The visit had been extended because Simon's wife had had an accident and had been treated in hospital for a facial injury.

> But I think that extension then made it very difficult when we all had to part again. That was awful.... He's been gone back about three weeks now.

While Lily is adamant that, having never flown in her life, going to Australia is unthinkable, Simon's presence there is the main reason she uses the Internet. She uses it to send and receive photographs.

Recent arrival Satnam Gill is by contrast a regular flyer. As we saw in Chapter 5, having grown up and been to university in India, he moved to the US for three years and still maintains relations in both countries, through visits, phone calls and electronic communications. However, invoking similar emotions to longer-term residents missing relatives abroad, but from the point of view of one who had moved, he described his homesickness when he was away from India, and how happy he had been to return home there from the US:

> It felt like finally...you came back to your home again [laughter]. I mean when you are like there for long, long time you know, twenty years, twenty five years...you're always homesick...wherever you are.... Because you've got all your old friends, your circle, your relatives ...

Living in the estates since 2004 and managing a business there, Satnam described a sense of isolation that he felt was produced by not being white in the Norwich estates, and which contrasted with his experience of running a business in a largely working class African American area in California:

> *Satnam:* I've seen that Americans are a little more, you know, coop-
> erative people.... Over here, nobody stands there with you.... [In
> the US] any time any incident happens, everybody stands with you.
> 'Don't worry, we are here for you. You can call the police. We'll be
> witness to you.'

BR: What do you think the reason was that those African Americans that you were with in Long Beach, that they stood with you more? What made that happen?

Satnam: I don't want to lie and I don't want to hide. But those people were also black. Those were a different colour [than white] actually, we are also a different colour. So sometimes, what they think and I'll think, we think, it's the same.... Colour doesn't matter to me. But it's just, you know, colour looks like to the white people. It matters to them.... But again, you know, it's only five per cent or ten per cent, that's all. I mean ninety per cent people fine with us. Don't have any problems.

Satnam and his wife Sheela's daily lives are lived both transnationally and locally. Their children attend a local school, they employ long-term estate residents as shop assistants and they meet residents as customers. At the same time, Satnam's parents come from India to spend long periods with them, helping out in the shop and with the children, and Satnam himself continues to travel to India and the US. TV in their living room is often tuned in either to a Bollywood channel or a South Asian religious one.[12] Revealing the often instrumental approach to identification and transnational living that individuals can adopt, when Sheela was pregnant with their third child, she travelled from the UK to the US to give birth so that he, like his older siblings, would have US citizenship. Recently arrived residents like Satnam Gill and Frank Levett, a white south African, are contributing to remaking the place both discursively and through the ways they lead their lives.

White residents with memories of living in other places in Britain and Ireland, and people who continued to visit relatives in other places, also had lives that stretched across space. Their moves, and other forms of communication, like those of newcomers, shaped ideas about identification, community and belonging at both local and national scales. Carol White, a community worker who had grown up in London, had been living in rural Suffolk when she decided to take her daughters to Donegal, mainly because she felt they would get a better education there. She also enjoyed what she saw as a greater 'sense of community' than in England:

it's good fifty, sixty years behind here so there was still that sense of community there that here has [been] lost.... I actually found it comforting 'cos it was what I was looking for, rather than that kind of like anonymity that...you can have in other places. But...there was the downside of it that if you blew your nose everyone knew you had a cold.

It was Carol's experience of conflict in Northern Ireland that positively influenced how she related to the estates when she arrived to live there in 2000 to be near her daughter, and to take up a post in the council:

I was living with my daughter in Knowland Grove, I would walk to work...and the number of people saying 'You don't walk round here at night do you?' 'Yeah, why not?'...I've got lost in the Bogside once. There are some really seriously nasty people round there, to be British and lost...walking around Northern Ireland with guns all over the place...

In contrast to Carol, Eileen Donald had migrated from Ireland to England. Describing her move as having been driven by extreme poverty and a violent father, she said she identified closely with the book *Angela's Ashes*. She found it was too upsetting to watch the film though, as it was too close to her own experience. Her visits home were tempered by emotion as well. She felt unable to go for the funeral when her father died:

I wouldn't go home. My sister arranged everything. And I just wouldn't go, because I just couldn't forgive him. See my sister left home a lot longer and I was only a kid ...

We have already seen how Eva Garland's experience of transnational living when her son moved to Australia was emotional from the start. The connection between spatial mobility and emotion in her life was also evident in the description of her continual longing for home while she herself lived away from Norwich in another English provincial city: Leicester. Eva had moved there in 1955 and lived there for 20 years because her husband got a job in a shoe factory:

I was always homesick [in Leicester]. I mean I enjoyed being [there] but I always longed for Norwich. If I was ill or anything, or bogged down, I would come home, have a week and then go back.... When I was down in the dumps I used to sneak back...home...in the end, we saved enough and had a little caravan at Hemsby. When I say we saved enough, I think we only paid about sixty-something for it. [laughs]

It was not only Eva who came and went. One of her daughters had stayed on in Norwich with Eva's mother, and she would come regularly to visit her in Leicester. When Eva did eventually return to live in Norwich it was to the Lakenham estate rather than North Earlham as she was able to exchange her Leicester council house with somebody there. For other residents, the emotion they experienced when talking about absent relatives related to the fact that they refused to come and visit the estates, now seeing the area as 'beneath them'. Flo, with typical humour (although overlying a degree of anger), told us about her eldest brother Fred:

> *Flo:* Christ... for him to come and visit... about once every three years! That's like coming into Glasgow Gorbals as far as he's concerned.... Fred's a snob and his wife.
> *BT:* What does he, is that particular to this area, he thinks it's ...
> *Flo:* Oh he thinks it's dreadful, 'oh I don't know how you could possibly live here sis. I don't know how you could possibly stay here' [putting on posh accent]
> *BT:* Does he talk different to you?
> *Flo:* Yes very 'frightfully, frightfully' 'cos he mixes with a better class of people [with posh accent].

Here we can see how Fred's social and spatial distancing of himself from the estates has been embodied through adopting a different accent, and through his 'othering' and categorizing the area.[13] Such categorization of the area by people who were once 'insiders' but no longer see themselves as belonging illustrate how people's lives become stretched socially as well as spatially through migration. And with the rest of this section it also shows how, for individuals and families, emotion and migration become entangled to create moving histories.

Transnationalism, translocalism and Islamophobia

As we have suggested, transnationalism and translocalism are not simply experienced by those who move away, rather it also exists – materially and conceptually – in spaces thought of as home by 'indigenous' residents. Although she has never lived abroad, Eva's life has become part of a wider transnational space, partly through her other daughter who remained in Leicestershire and is a Christian lay preacher. In talking about her, Eva revealed how she herself felt threatened by Islam, which she regarded as strong in Leicester and nationally and internationally resurgent:

> What's worrying me… [and] I shall be glad when I'm gone and that is the honest truth, is the Christians and the Muslims, they're my main worry. Because [Muslims] are completely taking over. And my daughter and her husband, they have been inducted as lay preachers. And her religion is everything to her. Well, it is to me too. And I wouldn't like anything to happen to them.

Similar concerns were also raised to us by people who had travelled and lived abroad. While her expatriate life had been spent largely in compounds separated from colonized people, Sandra Dyson placed the onus on immigrants to the UK to do the integrating: 'getting more foreigners… it doesn't bother me… as long as they integrate… some do, some don't… they won't talk to you half the time.' In contrast to her approval of what she saw as Jews' tendency to stick together, Sandra raised questions in particular about the willingness of 'Muslims' to integrate. She told a story she had heard (it was not clear whether this was from a media source or a personal contact) that a Muslim family in London had insisted on having female fitters for their new windows: 'I thought it was ridiculous. But that's the way they are. That's their religion….' Referring to Muslims in general, she later told us:

> Nothing against them. As long as they don't go to extremes like some of them have. But if they're going to live in this country, I'm sorry, they should live under our rules, not theirs. If they want to be Muslims and behave the way they did in their own country then go back to it.
>
> … I mean, where have they built a mosque – right in the middle of Regent's Park! Could you go into their country and build a Protestant Church in the middle of one of their parks? No. They wouldn't allow it. So what's the matter with this government? It's a Protestant country. It's a Christian country…. That's my attitude. Please or offend, I don't care.

Nowadays Flo Smith, who spent long periods in the same colonial locations as Sandra, travels regularly to Birmingham to visit her one of her daughters. Like Sandra, she felt differently about Jews and Muslims. She also strongly objects to the location of mosques:

We've always had Jews here. And we've had, over the years, a build up of a lot of Chinese. But they've never bothered you, they've gone in with you. Can you understand what I mean? But these Muslims, I just can't explain how I feel. You go Peterborough. You're on the train to go to Birmingham, you're going to, there's...blasted great, within yards of each other, two mosques with these big green domes, and to me they don't blend in...with our churches, they stand out like sore thumbs. And I think, why do they bring everything of theirs with them and it seems like a takeover bid. I just don't like it Becky, I'm sorry. But I've got no prejudice against them, but I just don't like the way they're taking over.

The fear of and antagonism towards Muslims and their apparent agenda of 'taking over' in contemporary England was shared by Tom Crowther, who had both served in the colonial military and spent two years in Northern Ireland in the 1950s. He elided the category 'Muslim' with that of 'Arab' and made an explicit link to the emigration of (implicitly white and non-Muslim) Britons:

I see this eventually as the Muslims taking over England. I really do because they breed like rats and rabbits and...they've already established themselves in mosques here, there and everywhere and...eventually I mean a great number of Britons are going to emigrate away from this island and consequently it will be an Arab state. I really do feel that most strongly.

Yet, almost paradoxically, the dynamics of integration were explicitly considered from the perspective of a new migrant when Flo Smith reflected on the possibility of moving from Norwich to be near one of her daughters in Wales. Although she said she felt comfortable in that part of Wales 'because there's so many English live down in that part now', and there had been 'only' one incident of anti-English behaviour (being ignored in a shop) that had upset her 'in all the years I've been going there', she thought again and added:

But I think once you shut your door, you'd be very isolated. You'd have to join in the Women's Institute, you know what I mean. You'd have to join all that sort of thing, to get yourself integrated, can you understand what I mean? But the best way...to get in is to have a dog.

Thus in thinking about *her own* possible migration, Flo articulated the advantages there would be in being in an area with a good number of fellow English people. However, she did not apply this very human criterion to Muslims, nor indeed to black and minority ethnic people more generally:

> *Flo:* I don't know nothing about the Muslim religion. I ain't that bothered. But why should we have to conform everything for them, for their human rights? Why should we turn our lives round to fit them in all the time?
>
> *BT:* But, do you feel that you have? I mean, has it affected you, having lots of Muslims in this country?
>
> *Flo:* No, it hasn't affected me as much as [I] don't have anything to do with them, but, when you go to the bigger cities like Birmingham, like to my daughter's... I just feel as if a white person's a bloody minority. 'Cos there's so many of them there and they're even getting now, where they've got their own schools.... And I think they are affecting our lives.
>
> *BT:* In what way?
>
> *Flo:* Well, the way they're taking over.

This shows the importance of understanding lives as they are stretched across space and time. It also suggests the importance of media discourses in dialectical processes of identification and categorization. Said has shown that essentialized, fearful and hostile ideas about Islam have a history of several centuries deeply embedded in European literature. 'Muslim' and 'Arab' remained unified categories, opposed to the category of 'the West'. Said argues that the discourse of what he refers to as Islamic Orientalism has been used as a means of control: 'Like Walter Scott's Saracens, the European representation of the Muslim, Ottoman, or Arab was always a way of controlling the redoubtable Orient' (2003 [1978]: 60).

In contemporary times, there is strong evidence that what has become known as Islamophobia is particularly prevalent in the UK, and that this has been perpetuated in mainstream media:

> Britons are now more suspicious of Muslims than are Americans or citizens of any other major western European country, including France. According to an international Harris poll last month...38% think the presence of Muslims in the country is a threat to national security...and 46% believe that Muslims have too much political

power in Britain.... The fact that a large minority of Britons have some of the most Islamophobic attitudes in the western world has passed without comment. Instead we have been treated to a renewed barrage of lurid and hostile stories about Muslims which can only have further inflamed anti-Muslim opinion and the community's own sense of being under permanent siege.[14]

Writing after the 9/11 attacks in the US, Said connected the apparent acceptability of anti-Muslim sentiment with new forms of imperialism. This could be seen as a symptom of the kind of 'turbid taxonomies' referred to by Stoler: 'The web of racism, cultural stereotypes, political imperialism, dehumanising ideology holding in the Arab or the Muslim is very strong indeed' (Said, 2003[1978]: 27). Said was angered by writers, mostly members of the same elite university class circles in which he moved, who promoted such discourses. He was particularly scathing about Bernard Lewis:

> [Lewis'] ideas are... fairly current among his little acolytes and imitators, whose job seems to be to alert Western consumers to the threat of an enraged, congenitally undemocratic and violent Islamic world.
>
> (Said, 2003[1978]: 342–3)

Although their books were published later, influential journalists Michael Gove (*The Times*) and Nick Cohen (*The Observer*) may be the kind of writers Said had in mind in his reference to Lewis' followers.[15] Neither of these authors analyses the nature of British colonialism or imperialism, including contemporary British foreign policy. Crucially, although the two books state that they are opposed to Islamism rather than to Muslims per se, they take no account of the potential effect of their writing on the experience of being seen as 'Muslim' in contemporary Britain. Indeed sections of their text can be read more generally as anti-Muslim:

> Islamic nations were crippled, relative to the West, by their institutional liability to adapt politically. The faith that had imbued traditionalist Muslims with conquering fervour also narrowed minds to such an extent that they were closed to innovation.
>
> (Gove, 2006: 16–17)

The contempt for universal standards of judgement suit the liberalism of the late twentieth century which placed an inordinate emphasis on respecting cultural difference and opposing integration even if the culture in question was anti-liberal and integration would bring new freedoms and prosperity.

(Cohen, 2007: 115)

We have drawn attention to the role of political and media elites in creating and perpetuating negative meanings of the category of Muslim because we do not believe that Islamophobia stems inherently from working class white people – it is a cross-class ideology, and it is beyond the scope of our book to establish how much writers such as Gove, Cohen and more widely read media outlets, such as *The Sun* and *The Daily Mail*, influence the self-identification and categorization of their readers. However, such writings, composed from seats of metropolitan comfort, do chime with the views of some white research participants, including some who lived part of their lives in the colonial military and who now travel regularly to spend time with relatives in British cities with large black and minority ethnic populations. It is significant that, when talking to us, participants frequently collapsed categories of 'race' and faith into each other. There was a clear juxtaposition between the silence on, and thus taken-for-grantedness of, colonial occupation under the British empire in the past, that we commented on earlier, and views on immigrants to Britain (those of colour that is), and on settled members of visible minorities, in the era of the new imperialism (see also Rogaly and Taylor, forthcoming).

More generally in this chapter we have tried to break down categorical boundaries by placing the stories of emigrants and immigrants alongside each other to analyse commonalities and differences between historically specific processes of spatial mobility. We have drawn attention to the importance of transnational and translocal ties for many people's individual and collective identification processes, even people who have not themselves moved very far across space. The evidence suggests that a range of emotions may be associated with spatial mobility and transnational/translocal living. A longing for 'home' was strongly articulated by some research participants who had moved away from the estates and later returned, and by a newcomer thinking of the 'home' he had left. Participants also gave emotionally charged accounts of their relation to people in other racialized groups, and the effect of this on their sense of belonging at various scales.

Finally, 'indigenous' transnationalism and translocalism are influenced by larger national discourses regarding 'race' and citizenship. Yet by grounding these observations in a detailed case study we have also shown that categories produced by such discourses are permeable, that self-identification can be as much about place as 'race' or immigration status, and that people sometimes actively seek to move the ways in which they have been categorized.

Afterword

In some ways it feels strange to be completing a book on identity, at a time when (late September 2008) political leaders in the US, the UK and elsewhere talk of whole economies on the brink of financial and economic meltdown. Yet we have covered a period that stretches back to the Great Depression of the 1930s, heard older people remember the poverty and struggles of those times, and seen the significant, though shifting, role of self-identification then and in subsequent decades. We have also shown, through archival sources, the important consequences of the diverse, contested and changing categorizations used by state officials and others regarding the residents of social housing estates. While we've been writing the book, some journalists in particular seem to have upped the ante in the use of 'white working class' as a fixed, apparently 'indigenous', cultural category, and in the process have themselves contributed to anti-immigration and racist sentiment, while ignoring expressions of white middle class racism and xenophobia (Rogaly and Taylor, 2009). High society has simultaneously adopted the racializing language of 'chav'.[1]

In writing about 'indigenous' transnationalism in this book, we hope we have given pause for thought to those who would divide people engaged in similar material struggles. When the commonality of migration itself and of transnational living become more widely acknowledged (see also Hickman et al., 2008), there is a chance of moving away from singling out particular groups for chastisement. We hope we have contributed to an alternative discourse that advocates solidarity among people experiencing marginalization and growing inequality (Cruddas, 2008; Obama, 2008; Stubbs, 2008).

Our perspectives have continued to shift since we started working together on this research in 2003, influenced throughout by changes in our own lives; and by involvement with the research participants during the process of intensive oral history interviewing, ethnographic presence, and writing. Becky gave birth to her daughter, Rosa, in 2007, while applying for planning permission for her land cooperative, and seeking to make her livelihood more secure. Since then, and during the writing process, she has persevered in spite of lack of, at times almost no, sleep. She was actively supported by her family and friends, which included some of the estate residents we have come to know. Ben moved away to Brighton to take up a new job, and, with his children, renewed his acquaintance with Arsenal Football Club (now transformed with a space age stadium, and many black players and middle class fans). He went back to India to visit the place where he and his family had lived during his previous research. As we were finishing the book, his father had a major operation to try to contain the increasingly painful effects of his Parkinson's disease.

We kept going back to the estates, which could be an emotional process. In addition to two research participants, Tom Crowther and Joe Hastings, who died during the course of the research, we were told on one visit about the death of one more, John Burnett. Through this continuing contact we learned of the anger of some of those who had been involved in the New Deal for Communities project since its inception, at their continuing marginalization from the organization they helped create. We also heard of the deep pain experienced by one family regularly taunted with the term 'Paki'.

Two research participants read the whole draft manuscript and gave us feedback: One said it had made her tearful in places, and at one point she had winced, but overall she felt it affirmed her experiences. The other suggested that we should have said something more on gender and education. She wrote to us that it was not just that residents in the estates as a whole had been stereotyped as 'thick', but that as recently as the 1970s, girls had been held back by the notion that they could not be good at maths or sciences and were expected to aim for marriage and children – in the rare cases of girls who stayed on into the sixth form, they 'had to work most weekends to pay for their keep; there was little time for reading and even homework because boy friends were so demanding'. Yet she also wrote that there were signs of change in the 1980s, referring to women she knew who had gone back to education years later, 'and done really well'. College in the Community, a 1990s initiative we referred to in Chapter 4, may have been another such sign.

However, the same research participant sent us a recent newspaper cutting which revealed how deeply educational provision continued to fail estate residents. We had found that while, for several participants, pride in practical skills were paramount, obstacles within state-provided education were structured in such a way as to reproduce separate education for working class and middle class people, leading to profound discomfort and discomposure. Yet, the cutting revealed, most ironically given its location on the edge of the UEA campus, that only 6 per cent of 16-year-olds at the local secondary school gained five or more GCSEs (including Maths and English) in 2007, against a national average of 46 per cent.[2] Moving histories are thus continuing, unevenly: to paraphrase Lily Haley, like it or not, 'we are all classed'.

Notes

1 Introduction: Moving Histories

1. Like the names of all the research participants referred to in this book, Lorna Haley is a pseudonym.
2. To clerk is to sell on goods that have been stolen or acquired illicitly.
3. Milne (2008). While defined as a 'young working class person who dresses in sports clothing', the word is strongly derogatory and has connotations with anti-social behaviour, and with limited cultural capital and social aspirations (see Hayward and Yar, 2006).
4. Reflecting this, in March 2008, a high profile BBC television series about white 'working class' Britons was simply entitled *White Season*, as though it was self-evident that this meant white working class season.
5. This risk works both ways. Graham Day warns us that sociologists involved in community studies often 'treated communities as solid, unified entities because this is what they had been told they were by influential informants' (2006: 163; see also O'Byrne, 1997: 15). Pahl's review of working class studies in the 1950s and 1960s carefully shows how stereotypes of this kind became influential well into the 1970s, ignoring gender differences (1984: 4–5).
6. The area between the university and the city centre had been given its nickname by estate agents seeking to cash in on rising house prices in the 1990s.
7. For a critique of the use of the category working class to mean white British working class, see Cruddas (2008). Similarly, from a gender perspective, Day (2006: 66) notes how fictionalized representations of the working classes in post-war Britain almost exclusively base their accounts on male experiences.
8. Just five participants were under 20. A minority of people were interviewed in pairs (siblings, couples, friends). There were 90 sittings in all, with 13 people interviewed twice and 3 people interviewed on three occasions. Each interview varied in length, up to 3 hours, and the vast majority involved open-ended conversation to draw out people's own oral histories. All but a small handful were taped and just over two-thirds were transcribed. Participation was based on written informed consent, anonymity and confidentiality were assured, and participants were told they could end their involvement at any time. Further consent was obtained for photographs, for permission to quote from transcripts and, for 25 participants, for the deposit of transcripts in the UK Data Archive.
9. Three volumes of historical work produced by Bonnie Carpenter, Fred Hewitt and other members of the group have been deposited in Norwich Heritage Centre and at the Archive Centre, County Hall, Norwich. These are *Brief History of the Larkman Family*, *The Early Years of Mill View* and the *History of the Marlpit and Surrounding Area*.
10. We might also suggest that academic sites of opinion formation can also be, differently, marginal.

2   Place

1. Thanks to J Milo Taylor for bringing this work to our attention.
2. Norfolk Record Office, Norwich (hereafter NRO): Norwich Housing Committee (hearafter NHC) minutes, 16 October 1939.
3. NRO: N/AR 1/17, *Eastern Evening News* (hereafter *EEN*), 1977.
4. 'The good old days?', *EEN*, 10 November 1994.
5. Mabel Clarkson was Norwich's first female sheriff and Labour sheriff (1928–29), and was mayor for 1930–31. She chaired the Education and Health Committees.
6. NRO: N/TC 54/67, Rotary Club of Norwich: Report of the Community Service Committee on the appeal of the Lord Mayor for the cooperation of the Club in clearing the city of its slums, 12 November 1930.
7. The National Archives, Kew (hereafter TNA): HLG49/1079, emphasis in original.
8. NRO: Norwich Housing and Flood Prevention Committee, 2 February 1927.
9. Letter to the editor from AW and VE Self, *EEN*, 22 November 1994.
10. NRO: N/TC 53/5, Statement B.
11. NRO: Norwich Housing (Sub) Tenancies Committee, 2 February 1927.
12. NRO: Norwich Housing (Sub) Tenancies Committee minutes 1927–33.
13. NRO: Norwich Housing (Sub) Tenancies Committee, 21 January and 17 June 1931.
14. NRO: Norwich Housing (Sub) Tenancies Committee minutes, 4 February 1931.
15. NRO: NHC, 31 July 1935 and 23 May 1945.
16. NRO: NHC 1 April 1931, memo from the Deputy Town Clerk to the Housing Committee.
17. NRO: NHC minutes, 3 January 1940.
18. NRO: N/TC15/24-37, Unsatisfactory households sub-committee, 1943–63.
19. For the impact of ruralism (as an ideology) on house building during this period, see Heathorn (2000).
20. NRO: Norwich Housing and Flood Prevention Committee, 4 May 1927.
21. NRO: NHC minutes, 2 June 1943.
22. This has continued to be an issue throughout the life of the estates. See, for example, NRO: NHC minutes, 10 November 1971, and Norfolk Heritage Centre, N.364.43, West Norwich Partnership Steering Group minutes, 1997.
23. As documented in Hanley (2007).
24. For local comment on this see Norwich Heritage Centre, N.711.4: City of Norwich plan, 85; and Casson (1956: 5). More generally see Ravetz (2001).
25. See for example Burnett (1993: 237), Giles (1995: 63), Hanley (2007) and McKenna (1991: 177).
26. Rose and Josephine did not divulge their second names, although we explained that all transcripts would be anonymized.
27. NRO: NHC minutes, 7 November 1956.
28. As was common elsewhere in the country (Ravetz, 2001).
29. Monkey Island is referred to here as part of the Larkman estate. The origin of this term is disputed (see a brief discussion of this in Chapter 6 and a longer explanation in Rogaly and Taylor, 2007).

3   Poverty

1. As Beresford et al.'s (1999) research with a range of groups of people with direct experience of poverty reveals, the term 'poverty' was contested by participants, with some seeing it as deeply stigmatizing. Others however felt it was important to be clear and unashamed of the word, observing that if you don't 'call it poverty then it's going to be invisible' (1999: 65, 68).
2. The literature relating to these ideas are vast. A clear analysis of the different conceptualizations of social exclusion/inclusion can be found in Levitas (1998), while Lister (2004) provides an exemplary overview of poverty generally as well as its relationship with social exclusion.
3. TNA: MH66/783, 'Norwich county borough', memo by JE Green, 13 April 1932.
4. TNA: MH66/781, Dr James Pearse, Survey of Norwich County Borough Council, July 1932, 56.
5. Ibid., 30–1. The percentage of unemployed in the town on 1 January 1932 stood at 15.9 per cent.
6. Ibid., 2.
7. NRO: N/TC15/26, report to sub-committee, 21 July 1947.
8. NRO: N/TC15/29, health visitor's report, 3 July 1950, home adviser's report, 27 November 1950.
9. NRO: N/TC15/28, report to sub-committee, 16 May 1949.
10. We deal with 'getting organized' in the final section of Chapter 4 and consider migration as response to poverty in Chapter 6.
11. NRO: N/TC15/35, health visitor's report, 17 March 1960.
12. Newmarket Road is in a leafy middle class part of Norwich, and has located on it a private school for girls.
13. NRO: N/TC15/36, home adviser's notes, 28 March 1960.
14. For difficulties experienced by migrant families with young children in combining childcare with paid work see Wall and Sao Jose (2004).

4   State

1. 'First Norwich Nursery opened', *Eastern Daily Press* (hereafter *EDP*), 12 May 1939.
2. Conversely, see Savage (1987) for an account of how a strong trade union presence could shape Labour Party and local authority provision of social and health care.
3. Dorothy Jewson was from a prominent Liberal family in the city and was elected in to the council in 1927, having been a Labour Parliamentary candidate from 1923.
4. TNA: ED 21/58445, letter from EW Woodhead, Director of Education to BoE, 25 April 1938.
5. 'First Norwich Nursery opened', *EDP*, 12 May 1939.
6. TNA: ED 69/208, BoE minute, 21 February 1940. See also ED 21/58431, BoE minute, 2 July 1942, letter to BoE, 14 July 1944.
7. TNA: ED 21/58431, correspondence between Norwich and BoE, 20 March and 11 November 1936.

8. TNA: ED21/58445, BoE minute paper, 15 February 1937 to 5 May 1937 and ED 21/ 58431, NEC minute, 10 December 1937.
9. TNA: ED 21/ 58431, BoE, interview memorandum, 15 April 1937.
10. On its creation in 1919 the Ministry of Health took over from the Local Government Board general responsibility for central government's dealing with local authorities. It retained this role until the creation of the Ministry of Housing and Local Government in 1951.
11. TNA: ED 69/208, letter from BoE to Norwich LEA, 11 March 1938. See also TNA ED 21/58445, BoE interview memorandum, 15 December 1937.
12. TNA: ED 21/58445, BoE minute, 29 November 1939.
13. TNA: ED 21/58445, BoE to the Norwich Education Authority, 16 February 1940.
14. TNA: ED 21/58445, letter from Woodhead to BoE, 10 February 1941.
15. TNA: ED 21/58445, BoE minute, 21 November 1939.
16. TNA: ED 21/58445, BoE minute, 29 November 1939.
17. NRO: N/TC15/29, health visitor's report, 13 July 1951.
18. For an extended discussion of this in the Norwich context see Taylor and Rogaly (2007); more generally see Welshman (2006) and McNichol (1999).
19. NRO: N/TC15/29, health visitor's report, 17 September 1951.
20. NRO: N/TC15/33, health visitor's notes, 17 January 1957.
21. NRO: N/TC15/36, notes of the home adviser and health visitor, 28 March 1960.
22. NRO: N/TC15/33, home adviser's notes, 10 January 1957.
23. NRO: N/TC15/27, health visitor's notes, 20 September 1948.
24. NRO: N/TC15/27, report to the sub-committee, 20 September 1948.
25. NRO: NHC, 16 June 1954.
26. NRO: NHC, 14 February 1968.
27. For an example of this understanding of poverty see for example Murray (1990).
28. For a discussion of new localism in relation to foundation hospitals see White (2006).
29. For an analysis of the NDC programme generally see Lawless (2005).
30. Norwich: Norfolk Heritage Centre, N.364.43, gives a flavour of the monthly activities of the project development coordinator.
31. Ibid. It also shows the range of initiatives supported by Community Power, from tackling vandalism on the estates to supporting young people to learn to ride motorbikes safely.
32. The then Deputy Prime Minister.
33. 'Schools to step up crime fight', *EEN*, 10 April 1996.
34. For New Labour's analysis of the problem of the 'poverty of aspirations' in relation to 'culture', see Jowell (2004). Thanks to Chris Land for drawing the parallels to our attention.

5 Class

1. NRO: N/ED 4/3, Larkman Lane Infant HMI's report, 21–22 November 1950; N/ED 4/4, Larkman Lane Junior HMI's report, 28–30 November 1950.
2. NRO: N/ED 4/4, Larkman Lane Junior HMI's report, 28–30 November 1950.

3. 'Public opinion not always right', *EEN*, 27 November 1964.
4. Testimonial of a teacher in authors' possession.
5. See also the discussion of nostalgia in Savage et al. (2005: 115).
6. McDougall is a household brand of flour.

6 Moves

1. Following Brah (1996), we hold that although people may have been categorized by themselves or others as descendants of original inhabitants, longer-term patterns of spatial mobility meant this could only be a social construction. Hence we keep the term 'indigenous' in inverted commas throughout.
2. We agree with the implications of Thieme (2008) that there can often be dynamics akin to transnational ties when close kin move apart within national borders, and this is the sense in which we use translocalism here. Translocalism has been used differently by Sinatti to refer to the identity practices of international migrants (2008).
3. Weston Longville is situated approximately 8 miles from the estates.
4. An interpretation disputed by other research participants (see Rogaly and Taylor, 2007).
5. Thanks to Anne-Meike Fechter for bringing Cohen's work to our attention.
6. 'Clicking' involved cutting out leather patterns for the shoe uppers with a sharp knife.
7. In her excellent report 'Not in Norfolk' (1994), Derbyshire explained the problems with the idea of Norwich as a 'white' city, and with the attendant notion that Norfolk/Norwich did not have racism because there were so few people of colour living there.
8. Ahmed describes the term as a 'racist epithet... that conceals other silent concepts within it such as outsider, dirty, immigrant and such' (Ahmed, 2004, cited by Munt, 2007: 12).
9. Contrary to the implications of Maureen's complaint here, any government support is subject to strict rules and allows for only minimal subsistence. Equally, asylum seekers in the UK are not permitted to enter employment and refugees face major obstacles in the labour market (Collyer and de Guerre, 2008).
10. Like the black gang member in the film on 1980s gang life, *This is England* (2007).
11. The Dales still live in Australia, and sent this account to us via email.
12. Television was an important means of transnational living. Another example occurred during our interview with a family of Iraqi Kurds – Saddam Hussain's trial was kept on live on Al-Jazeera's Arabic service.
13. Although Flo here expresses this through her own categorization of 'the Gorbals', an inner-city area of Glasgow.
14. S. Milne, *The Guardian*, 20 September 2007.
15. Gove certainly cites Lewis with approval: 'As the noted scholar of the Middle East Professor Bernard Lewis has explained, the decline of the Islamic world relative to the West provoked agonized soul searching within Muslim minds' (2006: 16).

Afterword

1. See   http://www.dailymail.co.uk/femail/article-1053175/Chelsy-chav-Prince-Harrys-girlfriend-pictured-wearing-baseball-cap-tracksuit-tasteless-jewellery.html, accessed 26 September 2008.

2. *EDP*, 23 August 2007.

Bibliography

Abel-Smith, B., & Townsend, P. (1965) The poor and the poorest. *Occasional Papers on Social Administration*, no. 17.

Ahmed, S. (2004) *The cultural politics of emotion* New York: Routledge.

Alexander, C., Edwards, R., & Temple, B. (2007). Contesting cultural communities: Language, ethnicity and citizenship in Britain. *Journal of Ethnic and Migration Studies*, 33(5), 783–800.

Alleyne, B. (2002) An idea of community and its discontents. *Ethnic and Racial Studies*, 25(94), 607–627.

Anderson, B. (1983) *Imagined communities: Reflections on the origin and spread of nationalism* London: Verso.

Aronowitz, S. (1992). *The politics of identity: Class, culture and social movements* New York: Routledge.

Barnes, M., Heady, C., Middleton, S., Millar, J., Papadopoulos, F., & Tsakloglou, P. (2002). *Poverty and social exclusion in Europe* Cheltenham/Northampton, MA: Edward Elgar.

Bauman, Z. (1998). *Work, consumerism and the new poor* Buckingham and Philadelphia, PA: Oxford University Press.

Bauman, Z. (2004a). *Wasted lives. Modernity and its outcasts* Cambridge and Malden, MA: Polity Press.

Bauman, Z. (2004b). *Identity: Conversations with Benedetto Vecchi* Cambridge and Malden, MA: Polity Press.

Beck, U. (1992). *World risk society* Cambridge: Polity Press.

Beck, U. (2000). *The brave new world of work* Cambridge: Polity Press. Trans. P. Camiller.

Beresford, P., Green, D., Lister, R., & Woodard, K. (1999). *Poverty first hand: Poor people speak for themselves* London: Child Poverty Action Group.

Bott, E. (2004). Working a working-class Utopia: Marking young Britons in Tenerife on the new map of European migration. *Journal of Contemporary European Studies*, 12(1), 57–70.

Bourdieu, P. (1990). *The logic of practice* Cambridge: Polity Press.

Bourke, J. (1993). *Working class cultures in Britain, 1890–1960* London: Routledge.

Brah, A. (1996). *Cartographies of diaspora: Contesting identities* London: Routledge.

Brah, A. (2007). Non-binarized identities of similarity and difference. In M. Wetherell, M. Lafleche, & R. Berkeley (eds), *Identity, ethnic diversity and community cohesion* London, Thousand Oaks, CA, New Delhi and Singapore: Sage.

Brooke, S. (2001). Gender and working class identity in Britain during the 1950s. *Journal of Social History*, 34(4), 773–795.

Burchell, G., Gordon, C., & Miller, P. (1991). *The Foucault effect: Studies in governmentality* Hemel Hempstead: Harvester Wheatsheaf.

Burnett, J. (1993). *A social history of housing, 1815–1985* London: Routledge.

Burrell, K., & Panayi, P. (2006). Immigration, history and memory in Britain. In K. Burrell & P. Panayi (eds), *Histories and memories. Migrants and their history in Britain* London, New York: Tauris Academic Studies.

Burrows, R. (1999). Residential mobility and residualisation in social housing in England. *Journal of Social Policy*, 28(1), 27–52.

Byrne, B. (2006). *White lives: The interplay of 'race', class and gender in everyday life* London and New York: Routledge.

Cairns, T. (2008). Class, gender and education in the twentieth century: An exploration of education life histories of correspondents to the Mass Observation Archive. Unpublished DPhil, University of Sussex.

Camina, M. (1980). *Bowthorpe – The implementation of a dream. A case study in the frustrations of local government* Norwich: Centre for East Anglian Studies, University of East Anglia.

Casson, S. H. (1956). *Journey through Subtopia* Norwich: BBC Home Service.

Castells, M. (1997). *The power of identity* Oxford and Malden, MA: Blackwell.

Castree, N., Coe, N. M., Ward, K., & Samers, M. (2004). *Spaces of work: Global capitalism and the geographies of labour* London, Thousand Oaks, CA, and New Delhi: Sage.

Chamberlain, M. (1989). *Growing up in Lambeth* London: Virago.

Chamberlain, M. (2000).The global self: Narratives of Caribbean migrant women. In T. Cosslett, C. Lury & P. Summerfield (eds), *Feminism and autobiography: Texts, theories, methods* Routledge: London.

Chamberlayne, P., & Rustin, M. (1999). *From biography to social policy* London: Centre for Biography in Social Policy.

Charlesworth, S. (2000). *A phenomenology of working-class experience* Cambridge: Cambridge University Press.

Clark, C. (2004). Work and employment. In C. Rawcliffe & R. Wilson (eds), *Norwich since 1550* London and New York: Hambledon and London.

Clark, T., Lipset, S., & Rempel, M. (1993). The declining political significance of social class. *International Sociology*, 8(3), 293–316.

Coates, K., & Silburn, R. (1983). *Poverty: The forgotten Englishmen* Nottingham: Spokesman.

Cohen, E. (1977). Expatriate communities. *Current Sociology*, 24(3), 5–90.

Cohen, R., Coxall, J., Craig, G., & Sadiq-Sangster, A. (1992). *Hardship Britain: Being poor in the 1990s* London: Child Poverty Action Group.

Cohen, A. (1985). *The symbolic construction of community* London: Tavistock.

Cohen, N. (2007). *What's left? How liberals lost their way* London: Fourth Estate.

Collins, M. (2004). *The likes of us: A biography of the white working class* London: Granta Books.

Collyer, M., & de Guerre, K. (2008). *'On that day I am born...' The experience of refugees resettled to Brighton & Hove under the Gateway Protection Programme October 2006 to October 2007* Brighton: Sussex Centre for Migration Research and Brighton and Hove City Council. http://www.sussex.ac.uk/migration/documents/080225_gppreport-web.pdf

Corbett, M. (2007). *Learning to leave: The irony of schooling in a coastal community* Black Point, NS: Fernwood Publishing.

Corbridge, S., Williams, G., Srivastava, M., & Veron, R. (2005). *Seeing the state: Governance and governability in India* Cambridge: Cambridge University Press.

Crompton, R., & Scott, J. (2005). Class analysis: Beyond the cultural turn. In F. Devine, M. Savage, J. Scott, & R. Crompton (eds), *Rethinking class: Culture, identities and lifestyle* Basingstoke: Palgrave Macmillan.

Cruddas, J. (2008). A new politics of class. *Soundings: A Journal of Politics and Culture*, 38, 141–155.

Datta, K, McIlwaine, C., Evans, Y., Herbert, J., May, J., & Wills, J. (2007). From coping strategies to tactics: London's low-pay economy and migrant labour. *British Journal of Industrial Relations*, 45(2), 404–432.

Damer, S. (1989). *From Moorepark to 'Wine Alley': The rise and fall of a Glasgow housing scheme* Edinburgh: Edinburgh University Press.

Day, G. (2006). *Community and everyday life* London and New York: Routledge.

Delanty, G. (2003). *Community* London: Routledge.

Dench, G., Gavron, K., & Young, M. (2006). *The new East End: Kinship, race and conflict* London: Profile Book.

Derbyshire, H. (1994). *Not in Norfolk. Tackling the invisibility of racism* Norwich: Norfolk and Norwich Racial Equality Council.

Devine, F. (2005). Middle-class identities in the United States. In F. Devine, M. Savage, J. Scott, & R. Crompton (eds), *Rethinking class* Basingstoke: Palgrave Macmillan.

Devine, F. & Savage, M. (2005). The cultural turn, sociology and class analysis. In F. Devine, M. Savage, J. Scott, & R. Crompton (eds), *Rethinking class* Basingstoke: Palgrave Macmillan.

Devine, F., Savage, M., Scott, J., & Crompton R. (eds) (2005), *Rethinking class* Basingstoke: Palgrave Macmillan

Dewilde, C. (2003). A life-course perspective on social exclusion and poverty. *British Journal of Sociology*, 54, 109–128.

Dinneen, S. (1994). *The future of the Norwich area economy* Norwich: Norwich City Council Economic Development.

Docherty, S.M. (1989). *Project Link: Project of inter-agency collaboration of the caring services and three schools in Norwich* Norwich: Norwich City Council.

Doyle, B. (2004). Politics, 1835–1945. In C. Rawcliffe & R. Wilson (eds), *Norwich since 1550* London and New York: Hambledon and London.

Dupree, M. (2000). The provision of social services. In M. Daunton (ed.), *The Cambridge urban history of Britain, iii, 1840–1950* Cambridge: Cambridge University Press.

Eade, J. (1997). Introduction. In J. Eade (ed.), *Living in the global city: Globalisation as a local process* London and New York: Routledge.

Elias, N., & Scotson, J. (1965). *The established and the outsiders* London: Frank Cass.

Etzioni, A. (1995). *The spirit of community* London: Fontana Press.

Evans, G. (2006). *Educational failure and working class white children in Britain* Basingstoke: Palgrave.

Fechter, A.-M. (2005). The 'other' stares back: Experiencing whiteness in Jakarta. *Ethnography*, 6(1), 87–103.

Feldman, D. (2007). Global movements, internal migration and the importance of institutions. *International Review of Social History*, 52(1), 105–109.

Fennell, G. (1997). Local lives – distant ties: Researching community and global conditions. In J. Eade (ed.), *Living the global city: Globalisation as local process* London: Routledge.

Fenton, S., & Dermott, E. (2006). Fragmented careers? Winners and losers in young adult labour markets. *Work, Employment and Society*, 20(2), 205–221.

Ferguson, J., & Gupta, A. (2005). Spatializing states: Toward an ethnography of neoliberal governmentality. In J.X. Inda (ed.), *Anthropologies of modernity: Foucault, governmentality and life politics* Oxford: Blackwell.

Fontaine, L., & Schlumbohm, J. (eds) (2000). *Household strategies for survival 1600–2000: Fission, faction and cooperation* Cambridge: Cambridge University Press.

Frankenberg, R. (1966). *Communities in Britain: Social life in town and country* Harmondsworth: Penguin.

Fuller, C., & Harriss, J. (2001). For an anthropology of the modern Indian state. In C. Fuller & V. Benei (eds), *The everyday state and society in modern India* Delhi: Oxford University Press.

Gardner, G. (2007). Recognising the limits to community based regeneration. What is the added value of the community-based partnership approach? Lessons from the New Deal for Communities programme and beyond. Brunei Gallery, School of Oriental and African Studies, 16 July.

Garner, S. (2006). The uses of whiteness: What sociologists working on Europe can draw from US research on whiteness. *Sociology*, 40(2), 257–275.

Gazeley, I (2003). *Poverty in Britain, 1900–1965* Basingstoke: Palgrave Macmillan.

Giddens, A. (1990). *The consequences of modernity* Cambridge: Polity Press.

Giles, J. (1995). *Women, identity and private life in Britain, 1900–1950* Houndsmill, Basingstoke and London: Macmillan.

Gilroy, P. (2004). *After empire* London: Routledge.

Goode, J., Callender, C., & Lister, R. (1998). *Purse or wallet? Gender inequalities among families on benefits* London: Policy Studies Institute.

Goodson, I. (2006). The rise of the life narrative. *Teacher Education Quarterly*, Fall, 7–21.

Gordon, D., Adelman, L., Ashworth, K., Bradshaw, J., Levitas, R., Middleton, S., Pantazis, C., Patsios, D., Payne, S., Townsend, P., & Williams, J. (2000). *Poverty and social exclusion in Britain* York: Joseph Rowntree Foundation.

Gorz, A. (1982). *Farewell to the working class: An essay on post-industrial socialism* London: Pluto Press.

Gotovos, A. (2005). Minority discourse, social state and the imposition of identity: Side effects of the ideology of multiculturalism on Gypsy identities in Europe: Policy and research, October, University of Ionnina, Greece.

Gove, M. (2006). *Celsius 7/7* London: Weidenfeld and Nicolson.

Hammerton, A. J., & Thomson, A. (2005). *Ten pound Poms: Australia's invisible migrants* Manchester: Manchester University Press.

Hampshire, J. (2005). *Citizenship and belonging: Immigration and the politics of demographic governance in post-war Britain* Basingstoke: Palgrave.

Hanley, L. (2007). *Estates: An intimate history* London: Granta.

Harriss-White, B. (2003) *India working: Essays on economy and society* Cambridge: Cambridge University Press.

Harvey, D. (1989). *The condition of postmodernity. An inquiry into the origin of cultural change* Oxford: Blackwell.

Harvey, D. (1993). From space to place and back again: Reflections on the condition of postmodernity. In J. Bird, B. Curtis, T. Putnam, G. Robertson, & L. Tickner (eds), *Mapping the futures: Local cultures, global change* London: Routledge.

Harvey, D. (1996) Cities or Urbanization. *City*, 1(2), 38–61.

Harvey, D. (2006). *The limits to capital (new edition)* London and New York: Verso.

Hayward, K., & Yar, M. (2006). The 'chav' phenomenon: Consumption, media and the construction of a new underclass. *Crime, Media, Culture*, 2(1), 6–28.

Heathorn, S. (2000). An English paradise to regain? Ebenezer Howard, the Town and Country Planning Association and English ruralism'. *Rural History*, 11(1), 113–128.

Hickman, M. (2007). Multiculturalism in one country? *Economy and Society*, 36(2), 318–324.

Hickman, M., H. Crowley, & Mai, N. (2008) *Immigration and social cohesion in the UK: The rhythms and realities of everyday life* York: Joseph Rowntree Foundation.

Hill, M. J. (1969). The exercise of discretion in the National Assistance Board. *Public Administration*, 47, 75–90.

Hobcraft, J. (2003). *Continuity and change: Pathways to young adult disadvantage, CASE paper 66* London: CASE.

Horsey, M., & Muthesius, S. (1986). *Provincial mixed development. The design and construction of Norwich Council housing under David Percival, 1955–1973* Norwich: University of East Anglia.

Huxley, M. (2007). Geographies of governmentality. In J. Crampton & S. Elden (eds), *Space, knowledge and power: Foucault and geography* Aldershot: Ashgate.

Jackson, P., Crang, P., & Dwyer, C. (2004). Introduction: The spaces of transnationality. In P. Jackson, P. Crang, & C. Dwyer (eds), *Transnational spaces* London: Routledge.

Jackson, P. (2005). Identities. In P. Cloke, P. Crang, & M. Goodwin (eds), *Introducing human geography* London: Hodder Arnold.

Jenkins, R. (1996). *Social identity* London: Routledge.

Jenkins, R. (2000). Categorization: Identity, social process and epistemology. *Current Sociology*, 48(3), 7–25.

Jones, C., & Novak, T. (1999). *Poverty, welfare and the disciplinary state* London: Routledge.

Joppke, C. (1999). *Immigration and the nation state: The United States, Germany and Great Britain* Oxford: Oxford University Press.

Jowell, T. (2004). *Government and the value of culture* London: Department of Culture, Media and Sport.

Keith, M., & Pile, S. (1993). *Place and the politics of identity* London: Routledge.

Kempson, E. (1996). *Life on a low income* York: Joseph Rowntree Foundation.

Kerr, M. (1958). *The people of ship street* London and New York: Routledge and Kegan Paul.

King, S., & Tomkins, A. (2003). *The poor in England, 1700–1850: An economy of makeshifts* Manchester: Manchester University Press.

Kirk, J. (2007). *Class, culture and social change* Basingstoke: Palgrave MacMillan.

Knowles, C. (1999). Cultural perspectives and welfare regimes. The contributions of Foucault and Lefebvre. In P. Chamberlayne, J. Cooper, R. Freeman, & M. Rustin (eds), *Welfare and culture in Europe: Towards a new paradigm in social policy* London and Philadelphia: Jessica Kingsley Publishers.

Kynaston, D. (2007). *Austerity Britain, 1945–51* London: Bloomsbury.

Larkman Project Group (c.1984) *The Larkman Project Group* Norwich: University of East Anglia.

Lash, S., & Urry, J. (1994). *Economies of signs and space* London: Sage.

Lawler, S. (1999). Getting out and getting away: Women's narratives of class mobility. *Feminist Review*, 63, 3–24.

Lawless, P. (2005) *Research Report 17: New Deal for Communities, 2001–2005: An interim evaluation* London: ODPM.

Lefebvre, H. (2002). The production of space. In M. Dear & S. Flusty (eds), *The spaces of postmodernity: Readings in human geography* Oxford and Malden, MA: Blackwell.

Legg, S. (2007). Beyond the European province: Foucault and postcolonialism. In J.W. Crampton & S. Elden (eds), *Space, knowledge and power: Foucault and geography* Aldershot: Ashgate.

Leisering, L., & Leibfried., S. (1999). *Time and poverty in Western welfare states: United Germany in perspective* Cambridge: Cambridge University Press.

Levitas, R. (1998). *The inclusive society?* Basingstoke: Macmillan.

Ley, D. (2004). Transnational spaces and everyday lives. *Transactions of the Institute of British Geographers*, 29, 151–164.

Lister, R. (1997). Women, social security and citizenship. In C. Ungerson & M. Kember (eds), *Women and social policy. A reader* Basingstoke and London: Macmillan.

Lister, R. (2004). *Poverty* Cambridge: Polity Press.

Lockwood, D. (1966). Sources of variation in working class images of society. *Sociological Review*, 14, 249–267.

Lowe, R. (1986). *Adjusting to democracy: The role of the Ministry of Labour in British politics, 1916–39* Oxford: Clarendon.

Lowe, R., & Rollings, N. (2000). Modernising Britain, 1957–64: A classic case of centralisation and fragmentation? In R. A. W. Rhodes (ed.), *Transforming British government, Vol. I: Changing institutions* London: Macmillan.

McCall, L. (2005). The complexity of intersectionality. *Signs: Journal of Women in Culture and Society*, 30, 1771–1802.

McCrone, D. (1994). Getting by and making out in Kirkaldy. In M. Anderson, F. Bechhofer, & J. Gershuny (eds), *The social and political economy of the household* Oxford: Oxford University Press.

McCulloch, G. (1998). *Failing the ordinary child? The theory and practice of working class secondary education* Buckingham and Philadelphia: Open University Press.

McDowell, L. (2003). *Redundant masculinities? Employment change and white working-class youth* Oxford: Blackwell.

McDowell, L. (2007). Respect, deference, respectability and place: What is the problem with/for working class boys? *Geoforum*, 38, 276–286.

McDowell, L. (2008). Thinking through class and gender in the context of working class studies. *Antipode*, 40(1), 20–24.

McGhee, D. (2003). Moving to 'our' common ground – a critical examination of community cohesion discourse in twenty-first century Britain. *The Sociological Review*, 51(3), 376–404.

McKenna, M. (1991). The suburbanisation of the working-class population of Liverpool between the wars. *Social History*, 16(2), 173–189.

McNichol, J. (1999). From 'problem family' to 'underclass', 1945–95. In H. Fawcett & R. Lowe (eds), *Welfare policy in Britain: The road from 1945* Basingstoke: Macmillan.

Mackintosh, J. M. (1953). *Trends of opinion about Public Health, 1901–51* London and New York: Oxford University Press.

Mass Observation (1943). *An enquiry into people's homes. A report prepared by Mass Observation for the Advertising Service Guild* London: John Murray.

Massey, D. (1995). The conceptualisation of place. In D. Massey & P. Jess (eds), *A place in the world?* Oxford: Oxford University Press.

Massey, D. (2005). *For space* London: Sage.

Mayne, A. (1993). *The imagined slum. Newspaper representation in three cities, 1870–1914* Leicester, London and New York: Leicester University Press.

Miles, A. (2003). Social structure, 1900–1939. In C. Wrigley (ed.), *A companion to early twentieth-century Britain* Oxford, Melbourne and Malden, MA: Blackwell.

Milgrom, R. (2008). Lucien Kroll: Design, difference, everyday life. In K. Goonewardena, S. Kipfer, R. Milgrom, & C. Schmid (eds), *Space, difference, everyday life* New York and London: Routledge.

Milne, S. (2008). Either Labour represents its core voters or others will. *The Guardian*, March 13th.

Mitchell, D. (2008). Which side are you on? From Haymarket to now. *ACME*, 59–68.

Modan, G.G. (2007). *Turf wars: Discourse, diversity and the politics of place* Malden, MA, Oxford and Carlton, VIC: Blackwell.

Mosse, D. (1999). Responding to subordination: Identity and change among south Indian untouchable castes. In A. Rew & J. R. Campbell (eds), *Identity and affect. Experiences of identity in a globalising world* London and Sterling, VA: Pluto Press.

Munt, S.R. (2007). *Queer attachments: The cultural politics of shame* Aldershot: Ashgate.

Murray, C. (1990). *The emerging British underclass* London: Institute of Economic Affairs.

NELM (1999). *New deal for communities, breaking the circle: North Earlham, Larkman and Marlpit partnership, Norwich, delivery plan 2000–2010* Norwich: NELM.

Newman, O. (1973). *Defensible space. People and design in the violent city* London: Architectural Press.

Nora, P. (1996). General introduction: Between memory and history. In P. Nora (ed.), *Realms of memory: Rethinking the French past, Vol. I: Conflicts and divisions* New York: Columbia University Press.

Obama, B. (2008). A more perfect union. Speech at Constitution Centre, Philadelphia, Pennsylvania, 18 March.

O'Byrne, D. (1997). Working-class culture: Local community and global relations. In J. Eade (ed.), *Living the global city: Globalisation as local process* London: Routledge.

Pahl, R. E. (1984). *Divisions of labour* Oxford and New York: Basil Blackwell.

Pahl, R. E. (1988). Disaggregated capitalism – editor's introduction. In R. E. Pahl (ed.), *On work. Historical, comparative and theoretical approaches* Oxford and New York: Basil Blackwell.

Pahl, J. (1989). *Money and marriage* Basingstoke: Macmillan.

Pakulski, J., & Waters, M. (1996). *The death of class* London: Sage.

Painter, J. (2007). Stateness in action. *Geoforum*, 38, 605–607.

Pantazis, C., & Gordon, D. (1997). Poverty, debt and benefits. In D. Gordon & C. Pantazis (eds), *Breadline Britain in the 1990s* Aldershot: Ashgate.

Parekh, B. (2007). Reasoned identities: A committed relationship. In M. Wetherell, M. Lafleche, & R. Berkeley (eds), *Identity, ethnic diversity and community cohesion* London, Thousand Oaks, CA, New Delhi and Singapore: Sage.

Parr, H. (1996). Mental health, ethnography and the body: Implications for geographical research. Paper presented to Conference of Feminist Methodologies, Nottingham.

Passerini, L. (1987). *Fascism in popular memory* Cambridge: Cambridge University Press.

Passerini, L. (2002). Work ideology and consensus under Italian facism. In R. Perks & A. Thomson (eds), *The oral history reader* London and New York: Routledge.

Paul, K. (1997). *Whitewashing Britain: Race and citizenship in the post war era* Ithaca and London: Cornell University Press.

Pearmain, A. (2008). England and the 'national-popular'. *Soundings,* 38, 89–103.

Peden, G. C. (2000). *The Treasury and British public policy, 1906–1959* Oxford: Oxford University Press.

Pile, S. and Keith, M. (eds) (1997). *Geographies of resistance* London: Routledge.

Portelli, A. (1997). *The battle of Valle Giulia. Oral history and the art of dialogue* Madison, WI: University of Wisconsin Press.

Power, A. (1999). *Estates on the edge. The social consequences of mass housing in Europe* Houndsmill, Basingstoke and London: Macmillan.

Power, A., & Tunstall, R. (1995). *Swimming against the tide: Polarisation or progress on twenty unpopular housing estates, 1980–1995* York: Joseph Rowntree Foundation.

Pries, L. (1999). *Migration and transnational social spaces* Aldershot: Ashgate.

Ravetz, A. (2001). *Council housing and culture. The history of a social experiment* London: Routledge.

Reay, D. (1998). *Class work: Mothers' involvement in children's schooling* London: UCL Press.

Reay, D. (2005). Doing the dirty work of social class? Mothers' work in support of their children's schooling. In M. Glucksmann, L. Pettinger, & J. West (eds), *A new sociology of work* Oxford: Blackwell.

Roberts, E. (1995). *Women and families: An oral history, 1940–1970* Oxford and Cambridge, MA: Blackwell.

Rogaly, B., Fisher, T., & Mayo, E. (1999). *Poverty, social exclusion and micro-finance in Britain* Oxford: Oxfam.

Rogaly, B., & Taylor, B. (2007). Welcome to 'Monkey Island': Identity and community in three Norwich estates. In M. Wetherell, M. Lafleche, & R. Berkeley (eds), *Identity, ethnic diversity and community cohesion* Los Angeles, London, New Delhi and Singapore: Sage.

Rogaly, B., & Taylor, B. (2009). Moving representations of the 'indigenous white working class'. In K. Sveinsson (ed.) *Who cares about the white working class?* London: Runnymede Trust.

Rogaly, B., & Taylor, B. (forthcoming). 'They called them communists then... what d'you call 'em now... Insurgents?' Narratives of British military expatriates in the context of the new imperialism. *Journal of Ethnic and Migration Studies.*

Rose, G. (1997). Situating knowledges: Positionality, reflexivities and other tactics. *Progress in Human Geography,* 21, 305–320.

Rose, N. (1999). *Powers of freedom: Reframing political thought* Cambridge: Cambridge University Press.

Rosser, C., & Harris, C. (1965). *The family and social change: A study of family and kinship in a South Wales town* London: Routledge and Kegan Paul.

Said, E. (2003 [1978]). *Orientalism* Harmonsworth: Penguin.

Samuel, R., & Thompson, P. (eds) (1990). *The myths we live by* London: Routledge.

Savage, G. (1989). *The social construction of expertise: The English civil service and its influence, 1919–39* Pittsburgh, PA: University of Pittsburgh Press.

Savage, M. (1987). *The dynamics of working class politics. The labour movement in Preston, 1880–1940* Cambridge: Cambridge University Press.

Savage, M. (1996). Space, networks and class formation. In N. Kirk (ed.), *Social class and marxism* Aldershot: Scholar Press.

Savage, M. (2000). *Class analysis and social transformation* Buckingham: Open University Press.

Savage, M., Bagnall, G., & Longhurst, B. (2001). Ordinary, ambivalent and defensive: Class identities in the Northwest of England. *Sociology*, 35, 875–892.

Savage, M., Bagnall, G., & Longhurst, B. (2005). Local habitus and working-class culture. In F. Devine, M. Savage, J. Scott, & R. Crompton (eds), *Rethinking class: Culture, identities and lifestyle* Basingstoke: Palgrave Macmillan.

Sayer, A. (2005). *The moral significance of class* Cambridge: Cambridge University Press.

Schafer, R. M. (1977). *The tuning of the world* New York: Knopf.

Scott, J. (1998). *Seeing like a state. How certain schemes to improve the human condition have failed* New Haven, CT and London: Yale University Press.

Scott, J. (2005). Afterword to 'Moral economies, state spaces, and categorical violence'. *American Anthropologist*, 107(3), 395–402.

Sennett, R. (1998). *The corrosion of character: The personal consequences of work in the new capitalism* New York: W. W. Norton.

Sennett, R., & Cobb, J. (1977 [1972]). *The hidden injuries of class* Cambridge: Cambridge University Press.

Shotter, J. (1984). *Social accountability and selfhood* Oxford and New York: Basil Blackwell.

Sibley, D. (1981). *Outsiders in urban societies* Oxford: Basil Blackwell.

Sibley, D. (1995a). *Geographies of exclusion. Society and difference in the West* London: Routledge.

Sibley, D. (1995b). Families and domestic routines: Constructing the boundaries of childhood. In S. Pile & N. Thrift (eds), *Mapping the subject* London: Routledge.

Silk, J. (1999). Guest editorial: The dynamics of community, place and identity. *Environment and Planning A*, 31, 5–17.

Sinatti, G. (2008). Diasporic cosmopolitans and conservative translocalism: Narratives of nation among Senegalese migrants in Italy. *Studies in Ethnicity and Nationalism*, 6, 30–50.

Skeggs, B. (1997). *Formations of class and gender: Becoming respectable* London: Sage.

Skeggs, B. (2004). *Class, self, culture* London and New York: Routledge.

Somers, M. (1994). The narrative constitution of identity: A relational and network approach. *Theory and Society*, 23, 605–649.

Spencer, S. (2005). *Gender, work and education in Britain in the 1950s* Houndsmill, Basingstoke: Palgrave Macmillan

Sriskandarajah, D., & Drew, C. (2006). *Brits abroad: Mapping the scale and nature of British emigration* London: Institute for Public Policy Research.

Steedman, C. (1986). *Landscape for a good woman* London: Virago.

Stoler, A. L. (2006). On degrees of imperial sovereignty. *Public Culture*, 18, 125–146.

Strangleman, T. (2008). Sociology, social class and new working class studies. *Antipode*, 40(1), 15–19.

Stubbs, S. (2008). In place of drums and samosas. *The Guardian*, 14 May.

Summerfield, P. (2000). Dis/composing the subject: Intersubjectivities in oral history. In T. Cosslett, C. Lury, & P. Summerfield (eds), *Feminism and autobiography: Texts, theories, methods* London: Routledge.

Szreter, S. (1996). *Fertility, class and gender in Britain, 1860–1940* Cambridge: Cambridge University Press.

Tanner, D. (2000). Labour and its membership. In D. Tanner, P. Thane, & Tiratsoo, N. (eds), *Labour's first century* Cambridge: Cambridge University Press.

Taylor, B., & Rogaly, B. (2007). 'Mrs Fairly is a dirty, lazy type': Unsatisfactory households and the problem of problem families in Norwich, 1942–1963. *Twentieth Century British History*, 18(4), 429–452.

Taylor, B., Stewart, J., & Powell, M. (2007). Central and local government and the provision of municipal medicine, 1919–1939. *English Historical Review*, 122(496), 397–426.

Taylor, B., Stewart, J., & Powell, M. (2008). The role of Labour in the provision of municipal health care in Britain, 1919–39: A study of Barnsley and Newport. Unpublished paper.

Taylor, B. (2008). *A minority and the state: Travellers in Britain in the twentieth century* Manchester: Manchester University Press.

Taylor, P., & Bain, P. (2008). United by a common language? Trade union responses in the UK and India to call centre offshoring. *Antipode*, 40(1), 131–154.

Tebbutt, M. (1992). Women's talk? Gossip and 'women's words' in working class communities, 1880–1939. In A. Davies, & S. Fielding (eds), *Workers' worlds. Cultures and communities in Manchester and Salford, 1880–1939* Manchester: Manchester University Press.

Thane, P. (2000). Labour and welfare. In D. Tanner, P. Thane, & N. Tiratsoo (eds), *Labour's first century* Cambridge: Cambridge University Press.

Thane, P. (ed.) (2007). *Equalities in Great Britain, 1945–2006* London: CCBH.

Thieme, S. (2008). Sustaining livelihoods in multi-local settings: Possible theoretical linkages between transnational migration and livelihood studies. *Mobilities*, 3(1), 51–71.

Thompson, E. P. (1978). *The poverty of theory and other ideas* London: Merlin Press.

Thompson, P. (2000). *The voice of the past* Oxford: Oxford University Press.

Thrift, N. (2000). It's the little things. In K. Dodds & D. Atkinson (eds), *Geopolitical traditions: A century of geopolitical thought* London: Routledge.

Titmuss, R. (1962). *Income distribution and social change* London: Allen & Unwin.

Tolman, R. M., & Raphael, J. (2000). A review of research on welfare and domestic violence. *Journal of Social Issues*, 56, 655–682.

Todd, S. (2004). Poverty and aspiration: Young women's entry to employment in inter-war England. *Twentieth Century British History*, 15, 119–142.

Townroe, P. (2004). Norwich since 1945. In C. Rawcliffe & R. Wilson (eds), *Norwich since 1550* London and New York: Hambledon & London.

Townsend, P. (1979). *Poverty in the United Kingdom* Harmondsworth: Penguin.

Townsend, P. (1993). *The international analysis of poverty* Hemel Hempstead: Harvester Wheatsheaf.

Townsend, P., & Gordon, D. (2002). *World poverty* Bristol: Policy Press.

Truax, B. (1978). *The handbook of acoustic ecology* Vancouver: ARC Publications.

Valentine, G. (1990). Women's fear and the design of public space. *Built Environment*, 16(4), 288–303.

Valentine, G. (2002). People like us: Negotiating sameness and difference in the research process. In P. Moss (ed.), *Feminist geography in practice: Research and methods* Oxford and Malden, MA: Blackwell.

Valentine, G. (2007). Theorizing and researching intersectionality: A challenge for feminist geography. *Professional Geographer*, 59, 10–21.

Vertovec, S. (1999). Conceiving and researching transnationalism. *Ethnic and Racial Studies*, 22(2), 447–462.

Voigt-Graf, C. (2004). Towards a geography of transnational spaces: Indian transnational communities in Australia. *Global Networks*, 4(1), 25–49.

Vogler, C. (1994). Money in the household. In M. Anderson, F. Bechhofer, & J. Gershuny (eds), *The social and political economy of the household* Oxford: Oxford University Press.

Waitt, G., Hewitt, T., & Kraly, E. (2006). De-centring metropolitan youth identities: Boundaries, difference and sense of place. In D. Bell & M. Jayne (eds), *Small cities: Urban experiences beyond the metropolis* New York and London: Routledge.

Wall, K., & São José, J. (2004). Managing work and care: A difficult challenge for immigrant families. *Social Policy and Administration*, 38(6), 591–621.

Walker, C. (1993). *Managing poverty: The limits of social assistance* London and New York: Routledge.

Walkerdine, V., Lucey, H., & Melody, J. (2001). *Growing up girl: Psychosocial explorations of gender and class* New York: New York University Press.

Walkerdine, V., Jimenez, L., & Fairbrother, P. (2007). Regenerating identities: Subjectivity in transition in a South Wales workforce' paper presented to the panel on Memory, *British Sociological Association annual conference*, April, University of East London.

Walsh, K. (2006). Dad says I'm tied to a shooting star! Grounding (research on) British expatriate belonging. *Area* 38(3), 268–278.

Weis, L. (2004). *Class reunion: The remaking of the American white working class* London and New York: Routledge.

Wells, S. (2003). *Community-led regeneration and the local church* Cambridge: Grove Books Ltd.

Welshman, J. (2006). *Underclass: A history of the excluded, 1880–2000* London and New York: Hambledon Continuum.

White, J. (1986). *The worst street in London: Campbell Bunk, Islington, between the wars* London: Routledge & Kegan Paul.

White, J. (2003). *Rothschild's buildings: Life in an east end tenement block, 1887–1920* London: Pimlico.

White, J. (2005). From Herbert Morrison to command and control: The decline of local democracy and its effect on public services. *History Workshop Journal*, 59(1), 73–82.

Whitemore, F. (1986). The Labour Party, municipal politics and municipal elections in Norwich, 1903–33, *Norwich in the nineteenth and twentieth century*. September, Norwich, University of East Anglia.

Williams, F., Popay, J., & Oakley, A. (1999). Changing paradigms of welfare. In F. Williams, J. Popay, & A. Oakley (eds), *Welfare research: A critical review* London: UCL Press.

Willis, P.E. (1977). *Learning to labour. How working class kids get working class jobs* Westmead, Farnborough: Saxon House.

Willis, P. (2000). *The ethnographic imagination* Malden, MA: Polity Press.

Winder, R. (2004). *Bloody foreigners: The story of immigration to Britain* London: Little Brown.

Wrightson, K. (2000). An introduction to acoustic ecology. *Soundscapes: The Journal of Acoustic Ecology*, 1(1), 10–13.

Young, M., & Willmott, P. (1957). *Family and kinship in east London* London: Routledge and Kegan Paul.

Young, R.J.C. (2008). *The idea of English ethnicity* Oxford: Blackwell.

Zorbaugh, H.W. (1929). *The Gold Coast and the slum* Chicago: University of Chicago Press.

Author and Place Index

234   *Author and Place Index*

Subject Index

Note: Page numbers in **bold** type indicate maps or photographs, page numbers in *italic* type indicate tables